RUN WHILE THE SUN IS HOT

W. HAROLD FULLER

Author, *African Adventures* (Moody Press)
Editor, *African Challenge* (1952—1965)
Editor, *Africa Now*

Book design, maps: Charles J. Guth

W. HAROLD FULLER

RUN WHILE THE SUN IS HOT

Contents

1. Incredible Safari

We were bouncing along a trail in southern Ethiopia. Ato Mahari, the local bank manager, was driving us back to the mission bungalow after a trek to a "lost island" in the middle of Lake Abaye.

"What will be the name of your book?" asked Ato Mahari.

"That's a good question," I said. "I'd like to use an African proverb which would describe the work of the gospel in the context of Africa today. Any suggestions?"

Our Ethiopian friend didn't answer right away. We passed a flock of Maribou storks, which strutted off into the tangled brush like huffy colonels disturbed during a club luncheon.

Wild pigs found shelter from the noon heat under flat-topped gum trees.

"We have an Amharic proverb," he said at last, shifting his Land-Rover into four-wheel drive to crawl over the boulders of a dry river bed. "It says, '*Run while the sun is hot.*' I think it describes the way the whole church needs to work."

It wasn't the kind of proverb I had been looking for, but the more I thought about it, the more I realized Ato Mahari was right.

"Don't you have an English proverb, 'Make hay while the sun shines'?" he continued. "That's what our Amharic proverb means. In Ethiopia we say you have to get moving along the trail while the sun is high if you want to reach your destination; otherwise the darkness will overtake you, and you may lose everything in the dangers of the night."

I was nearing the end of research travels totalling 12,000 zig-zagging miles across the widest part of Africa. All I had seen in this incredible continent convinced me that Ato Mahari's proverb applied to the work of missions in more than one sense.

As I saw pagans donning Islamic robes and beads, as I saw crescent-capped minarets rising in traditionally Christian territory, I knew the church of Jesus Christ had to work quickly.

As I ducked under the low door of a grass hut and saw the fetishes around the emaciated neck of a dying grandfather, I wished the messenger of light had run sooner to his village.

As I heard a Communist trade union leader say he hoped his nation would collapse so it could be rebuilt by Marxism, as I saw Red Chinese magazines on city sidewalks, I knew we had to run well with the gospel.

The way the Lord Jesus expressed it was "I must work . . . while it is day; the night cometh, when no man can work."

But apart from the time element, the proverb pictured for me the conditions under which the gospel runners have to work. The sun *is* hot today in Africa.

It is hot for the evangelist who is in prison for preaching the gospel.

It is hot for the doctor struggling to save the life of a 13-year-old girl in childbirth.

It is hot for the electronics engineer feverishly trying to trace a "gremlin" in a transmitter just before the Congo broadcast is due to start.

It is hot for the Dinka believer who told me his whole family had been wiped out by marauding soldiers.

It is hot for the teacher who finds a student strike on his hands.

It is hot for the pastor and missionary wrestling in prayer for the soul of a demon-possessed pagan.

Not the heat of the tropical sun—but the heat of tensions, shortages, revolutions, emergencies, attacks from unseen powers. Devoted men and women from many lands are battling in that intense heat to win victories—triumphant victories. The kind of victories which bring a shout to your lips, and at the same time a lump to your throat.

But the stories of the lost island and of those people I met running while the sun is hot, must wait their turn in this eye-witness account of what I saw under the sun in Africa.

On this safari I traveled by every kind of vehicle, from a two-cylinder French Citroen to a six-cylinder German Mercedes Benz. I traveled by motorcycle, Land-Rover, mule, horse, camel, dugout canoe, three-seat Piper plane, 110-seat jet. I ate snake steak, camel burger, and watermelon, and drank iced Coke as well as hot coffee trimmed with rancid butter and salt. I slept at varying altitudes from sea level to 8,000 feet, in humidity from 10 to 100 percent. Although eight revolutions took place during my research, the only time I was detained was when police arrested me for taking a photo of a peaceful city street.

My safari began on the western bulge of Africa, when the jet's tires bit the tarmac at Robertsfield International Airport, Liberia. As I stepped from the air-conditioned plane I knew I was in a different world. The humid air closed in on me like a hot, wet burlap sack. Behind the rambling one-story terminus was a backdrop of lush palms and lofty ironwoods.

Outside the whitewashed building four ebony-faced men spread out a grass mat, kicked off their sandals, and bowed till their blue fezzes touched the ground. Their white robes stuck out stiffly as they prayed to Allah before boarding the onward flight. Inside the terminus other passengers waited—a lady in floor-length cloth embroidered with golden peacocks, a pink and purple headtie, and the latest spike-heeled pumps; a businessman whose immaculate white suit set off his swarthy skin. A Liberian policeman with a pistol at his waist looked on as we passed the Health, Immigration, and Customs desks.

"Welcome to Liberia," a voice boomed from the other side of the barrier. It belonged to Ray de la Haye of the Sudan Interior Mission's radio station ELWA.

"I thought this was Monrovia," I said. "But I didn't see any city as we flew in—only an endless stretch of green forest."

"You're fifty miles from the capital," Ray told me. "This was the nearest flat spot that wasn't swamp, so they put the airport out here."

The road in to Monrovia took us through the backbone of Liberia's economy—the Firestone rubber plantation. It is the world's largest, with 87,000 acres under cultivation. The 12 million spindly trees are laid out in corrugated ridges over the undulating hills.

Closer to the city we passed more typical Liberian communities: a group of thatched huts, a decrepit two-story house painted in three shades of green and four of red, with a purple door. By a roadside stall stood a teenage girl covered all over with white paste, in preparation for an initiation ceremony.

The 100,000 residents of Monrovia crowd on a neck of land surrounded by swamps and sea. Dominating the skyline is the modern architecture of the Presidential Mansion and other government buildings. Below them nestles a conglomeration of houses and shanties. Down the streets big men drive American cars. A taxi passed us bearing the motto, "Just Trying."

There was a friendly, easy-going air about the city. Barefoot boys and girls crowded around an American movie poster. Three children rang handbells and waved undergarments in the air to attract customers to their mother's lingerie stall on the main street. A perspiring woman dressed in a bright blue headtie, a loose blouse, and an ankle-length wrap-around skirt covered with brilliant designs tried to enter the *exit* door of a supermarket; a kindly shopper showed her the right door.

In front of an ice cream shop a woman sat on a stool roasting plaintains over a charcoal fire. A companion plaited a friend's hair in a star design, binding the braids with black cotton thread. Girls with trays balanced on their heads sold peeled oranges to pedestrians, who sucked them to slake their thirst. The street vibrated to the throb of a calypso record extolling Liberia.

In a tiny tailor shop measuring eight feet by eight feet, six men were working. Their equipment consisted of three treadle sewing machines, a table, one iron, and a mirror hanging from a string nailed to the low ceiling. Clients' measurements were chalked all over the dark blue walls. The manager told me he could sew me a "too fine" suit for $35 in one week.

To Western eyes, Liberia looks like Africa, but to the rest of Africa it may seem like America. Apart from the inland tribes many of the nation's 2,000,000 people use American slang, and they buy American products with American dollar bills.

Liberia has had a precarious history. Desiring a haven for freed slaves, a group of benevolent Americans bartered with local chiefs to form Liberia in 1822, next door to Sierra Leone, a similar colony begun by the British in 1787. The state has 350 miles of coastline, and extends an average of 120 miles inland. It became independent in 1847 and was Africa's only republic until 1953.

President William V. S. Tubman, whose father was a gospel preacher, has given hope to the Republic with progressive economic measures and serious attempts to abolish the discriminating distinction between "American-Liberians" and the 23 indigenous tribes. Public functions are grand affairs at which guests often wear top hats and tails.

I stood on a street corner watching this warm-hearted, happy-go-lucky stream of humanity flow by. So this was urban Africa! This was all part of a continent which was . . . I searched for a suitable adjective. Fantastic. Incredible. Phenomenal. While one nation worries about traffic jams and city congestions, another country appeals for hunters to kill off herds of elephants devastating the land. There are 20,000 in the Zambezi valley alone. The world's newest universities rise alongside the most ancient stone-age cultures. In shopping centers you can buy frozen foods, and around the corner a magic potion of ground-up monkey skulls.

One out of every 10 of the world's population lives in Africa (nearly 300 million). It has one-fifth of the world's land mass —11,600,000 square miles—and could easily swallow India, USA, and all of Europe without getting indigestion. On the map, Africa stretches all the way between the same longitude as Iceland eastward to Persia. North to south, it extends from the same latitude as Washington southward to Buenos Aires, or from Tokyo, Japan, to Sydney, Australia. A flight from London to Moscow would cover only a little more than half of Africa, north-south or west-east.

It is a continent of surprises as well as extremes, with snow on the equator and ice in the Sahara. It has a mountain higher than the Alps (Kilimanjaro is 19,565 feet) and a desert 400 feet *below* sea level, in Libya. On Cameroon's coast the annual rainfall exceeds 400 inches—over 33 feet of water!—while its northern neighbor, Chad, has places where rain never falls. The Congo has the world's shortest tribe; Pygmies average four and one-half feet. Its neighbor Rwanda has the tallest; many Watutsi are seven feet tall.

But the Africa I was seeing on the street corner was not what the average movie or novel portrays. This was modern Africa on the move. There were no savages beating drums; there were no fetishes hanging from vines. The old Africa seemed a long way off. Or was it? Ray de la Haye pointed to a Volkswagen van rolling down the street.

"There goes our ELWA mobile newsroom," he said. "Our men have been covering the international football match between Liberia and Sierra Leone this afternoon. Reporting like that builds up our radio audience—and they stay tuned to hear the gospel."

Later I heard the staff describing the game. "Liberia won 2–0. Great players. Funny thing, though. As we were setting up our equipment, we looked up, and there was the Sierra Leone team climbing over the stadium's 10-foot wall. Don't know why they didn't come through the gates. One way of getting attention!"

That evening I read the reason in the *Daily Listener*, which has the motto: "With God and a Determined Mind All Things Are Possible". Under a bold headline, "No Juju in Football," the paper pointed out that the visiting team had jumped over the wall to avoid fetish allegedly placed at the gates to keep them from winning. "This is not the first time this foolishness has happened. We have heard rumors about juju, fetish, medicine men. Witchcraft in football is rubbish."

Perhaps I would find that the modern and ancient worlds weren't so far apart after all.

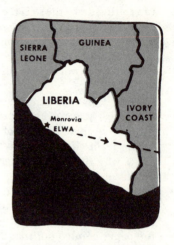

2. "The Man Who Beats the Drum..."

Yard-high letters spelled E L W A on the highway signboard eight miles from Monrovia. Turning on to a side road, Ray de la Haye pointed out a grove of cottonwoods towering above the palm trees ahead.

"Those were a landmark on the coast for slave ships," he explained. "We once thought of getting that property for ELWA, but it is 'Devil Bush'—a sacred fetish grove no uninitiated person may enter."

Beyond the grove another small "forest" appeared—the metal masts of ELWA's antennae field, supporting a cobweb of cables pulsating with unseen power. A dozen buildings squatted around their base: studios, offices, workshops, transmitters, and classrooms. In the distance was the ELWA hospital. A 90-year-old Texan Negro, whose father had been taken as a slave from the Liberian coast, gave $15,000 of her life savings to build one wing.

We drove down to the water's edge, where modest bungalows overlooked a mile-long stretch of glistening sand. While Ray's wife served a welcome lemon drink on their patio, we looked out over the Atlantic, framed by coconut palms. A wall of blue-green water rose from the heaving sea and advanced majestically toward us. A white line ripped across its edge, and the breaker crashed down on a jagged reef with the sound of thunder, rolling on to the beach in salty foam.

Ray told me the miraculous beginnings of the radio station. In 1944 the SIM approached President Tubman about broadcasting from Liberia. Ethiopia, the only other African state which would then allow independent stations to operate, was also under consideration. But the way did not seem clear, and no arrangements were finalized.

Meanwhile, three young men studying at Wheaton College in America's Midwest prayed that God would help them preach the gospel by radio in West Africa. God brought the SIM and them together; technical engineers and program producers joined the team. After three years of muddy slogging through Liberia's 260-inch annual rainfall,* they announced ELWA's call letters over the airwaves on January 18, 1954.

From the first, ELWA enjoyed remarkable rapport with the Liberian government. The Senate gave the station the best stretch on Liberia's coast—reefs keep back the sharks and break the undertow. Not only cabinet ministers but also President Tubman have taken a personal interest in the station. Returning from one overseas trip, the President told General Manager Dick Reed that the first radio sound he picked up from Africa was ELWA. He is a regular listener.

"Your religious and educational programs, newscasts, and rich variety of public services these past 10 years have made

* Annual average in New York is 43 inches, in London 23 and one-half inches.

ELWA's contribution to Liberia invaluable," the President told ELWA's staff on the station's tenth anniversary. "Today we can boast of the blessings derived from a service known as 'Eternal Love Winning Africa'—ELWA!'"

In recognition of ELWA's service, he decorated Ray de la Haye with one of Liberia's highest investitures: Grand Commander of the Humane Order of African Redemption. Significantly the Order's medal shows an African man and woman kneeling before a cross, broken chains at their feet.

I wandered through the sprawling studio and office building, and thought I had dropped into an organized Tower of Babel. Snatches of Kru and Swahili and Hausa and Twi came from different control rooms. In an auditioning cubicle, Suhail Zarifa, a converted Arab from the Gaza Strip, checked an Arabic tape. Max Weber, French Department Director, was going over a French script. Someone else was auditioning an English tape. "Aunt Clara," a personable Liberian widow who gave up a high government post to join ELWA's staff, was recording her "Kiddies' Korner" program with a group of lively white and black children around her.

And these were only a few of the 49 languages which ELWA uses. Before ELWA had an Arabic speaker on staff, a well-intentioned operator once played an Arabic tape backwards for half an hour before he realized it didn't sound right. The ELWA transcription library contains 20,000 tape recordings. New programs are constantly coming in from the 25 recording centers working with ELWA in different lands. Station Manager Bill Thompson had just returned from a trip to Beirut, Lebanon, nerve centre of ELWA's latest advance. Christian Arabs prepare tapes there, to be beamed from Monrovia out to Islamic countries in North Africa and the Middle East.

"The Voice of the Koran in Egypt now hurls the message of Mohammed over desert and jungle," I read in a report by SIM General Director Raymond J. Davis. "Broadcasting in eight major languages of Africa all available listening hours of the day, they have the strongest signal on the dial. We believe the increasing number of transistor radio owners among the 100 million Muslims of North Africa and the Middle East deserve to hear the gospel. We dare to ask God to enable us to do this."

This brought up the subject of expansion plans. ELWA would like to install a 100 kilowatt transmitter, double the power of any it now has, and a 450 kw diesel generator, with a second 100 kw transmitter eventually. A new antennae field is also needed. With these the station could penetrate the radio barrage being set up around Africa not only by Islam but by Red China and Russia. Kuwait in Arabia is installing two 750 kw transmitters to cover the world with Islam's voice.

"We don't know how God will provide the large amount needed for all this," say the staff. "But He has told us to ask of Him in faith."

I stepped into Control Room One and found a Liberian operating the complicated control board. When the studio clock pointed to the hour, he stopped a tape playing traditional music and started reading a script in Krahn.

Studio clocks have two sets of hands—a silver-colored pair indicate international GMT time; a black pair give local Liberian time, which is 45 minutes different. A Liberian visitor from up-country gazed in perplexity at the two sets of hands, then grinned: "I see, the white hands show the white man's time, and the black hands show the black man's time." At noon I heard an announcer greet his listeners on each side of the time zone, "Good morning and good afternoon."

Fifty-five nationals work at the station in the different departments. With their 47 missionary colleagues they obey the merciless commands of the studio clocks—writing news, reading scripts, operating control boards, editing tapes, typing letters, tending transmitters, repairing equipment.

Those missionary technicians can do anything, it seemed to me, and they often have to, in a land where they can't phone an electronics manufacturer for spare parts. Two of the small transmitters had been built by missionary staff before they came to Africa. One engineer made a synchronization system which automatically lines up all the studio clocks every five minutes. Even the process camera in the station's small print shop was built by a technician out of odd refrigerator and camera parts, for one-fifth of its commercial price. A discarded automatic telephone system brought from America provides station-wide communication.

One of the missionary technicians showed me around the transmitter building. "There's a lot of power in this place," he said, picking up a fluorescent light tube. As he pointed it toward a set of antenna switches, the tube lit up as if it had been connected to electric wires. The building was hot from the myriad electronic tubes in the six transmitters—tubes ranging in height from one inch to two feet; the latter cost $1,600 each but last for 20,000 transmitting hours. Between them, the transmitters have aired as much as 460 hours of programs per week.

"Ever have any trouble just as you're ready to go on the air?" I asked.

"It can happen! Then the operator starts phoning the control room or the duty engineer, and there's a lot of activity until the problem is licked. One night lights started flashing on the control board. A cable had fallen on the 50 kw antenna —we have a lot of trouble with salt spray from the ocean and the humidity, which set up an electrolysis action between the aluminum girders and steel bolts. There was no broadcast to the Congo that night until our antennae engineer and his crew made repairs."

It had been light outside when I entered the transmitter building. Now half an hour later it was pitch dark—night descends like a window blind in the tropics. I stepped outside and walked into the antennae field, looking up at the 22 gaunt towers supporting the nine antennae. Red beacons blazed on the tallest one, 250 feet in the air. The rising moon caught the ragged edge of a gathering storm. In the distance the generators droned and beyond them the ocean breakers rumbled.

I could hear no sound coming from those giant towers, yet I was standing at the center of tremendous power beaming the Word of God across the continent. I could visualize people listening at that very moment—in lands as far apart as Morocco and Madagascar, Angola and Arabia. As the earth rotated, there also would be listeners who could hear ELWA in Brazil to the west and India to the east, and even on the Fiji Islands, right on the opposite side of the globe.

In the Counseling Department I had seen the continuous stream of letters from listeners—an average of 70 a day. Once two letters arrived from two soldiers in Congo—one a loyalist, the other a rebel. Said one: "The message of Jesus Christ is the only answer to our problems." Said the other: "The Word I hear over ELWA can bring our people together."

The counseling staff carefully follow up all letters, answering their spiritual problems and sending three mailings of literature over a 12-month period. The past year brought a response of 25,982 letters (besides 88,000 "listener's request" letters) with 500 indicating a decision to trust in Christ as Saviour. Altogether 52,717 listeners are enrolled in ELWA's Radio Bible School, which offers 20 home study courses.

"We have a Liberian proverb," said Edwin Kayea, assistant to the Station Manager. " 'The man who beats the drum doesn't know how far the sound goes.' Day after day we beat the drum, sending out the Word of God. All those letters tell us the sound is getting across, but even then only in heaven will we know how many have come to Christ. I wish I could take you to my own village to show you how God is using radio."

That wish came true. Kayea and I took off from the local airport in a tiny plane not much larger than one of Monrovia's mosquitoes. It belonged to the Worldwide Evangelization Crusade, the mission working among Kayea's Gio people. We left Monrovia's suburban houses and modern buildings behind, and flew over villages of round thatched huts, looking like clusters of mushrooms. A chocolate-brown river snaked among the green rubber plantations.

It was a well-watered land stretching in low undulating wooded hills from the sea to the Nimba mountains 250 miles inland—everything that tropical Africa is supposed to look like. But there were also reminders of the new age of technology: a bright orange diesel flashed along a railroad track, pulling a train of iron ore mined in the Nimba range—the world's highest grade ore, so rich that lower grade ore has to be added before smelting furnaces can handle it.

Nearly two hours after take-off our WEC pilot pointed the Piper's nose down toward what looked like a gash in the jungle. "This is the airstrip at my village," Kayea shouted in my ear. I thought the plane's wings were going to tangle in the vines hanging from the palm trees as we slid in on the grass strip.

The place was called Bahn, and the WEC missionaries at the station beside the airstrip invited us into their white-washed bungalow for a cup of coffee. "ELWA is a blessing to us all," they said, "and we're so glad that Ed Kayea, one of our own Christians, is able to serve the Lord there." I found this to be typical of the attitude of other evangelical missions throughout Africa. ELWA aids their gospel ministry, and is thankful to be a servant of the Church of Jesus Christ.

"Now you must meet my grandfather," Kayea said. "He's the paramount chief for this whole area."

In the middle of the rambling town of whitewashed, mud-walled houses, we came to the chief's one-story palace. As Kayea approached, men and women ran from the surrounding houses to embrace him, clapping their hands and dancing.

Chief Tuazama, probably 100 years old, was propped up in a red upholstered armchair, dressed in a gray corduroy robe and blue skull cap, but no shoes. A few of his Muslim aides and 200 wives lounged around him on the sagging porch. Kayea bent low, took both his hands in his, and snapped his fingers.

I had to catch on to this finger-snapping business. Liberians know right away if a person is a stranger to their country, because most other Africans and white people don't know how to snap fingers properly. After shaking hands, you slide your thumb and middle finger off the other man's thumb and finger, snapping sharply when you reach the end. It really pained a Liberian if I didn't do it right—somehow our friendship wasn't "sweet" and he'd stand there flicking his extended hand in frustration until I took hold of it again and performed properly.

Kayea's father—chief of another clan—had allowed his boy to "learn book" at a WEC school, but was angry when Kayea left the Islamic religion to follow Christ, changing his name from Mohammed to Edwin. The old grandfather disowned him at first, but through the years both father and grandfather have softened, and now they listen intently—not without some pride—to Kayea's voice preaching the gospel over "the talking box."

As we later climbed into the plane to take off for the town of Garpley, six Gio elders pressed into my hand four rumpled US dollar bills and a 50-cent piece—two weeks' wages in that area. "We are sorry you can't stay to eat with us," they said through an interpreter. "Take this to help pay for your trip." The money was too precious for that; we put it back into broadcasting the gospel in Gio.

At Garpley the people had heard we were coming, over Kayea's Gio broadcast the night before. The WEC schoolchildren in bright red and blue uniforms lined up at the edge of the airstrip to sing us a welcome song. Elders from surrounding villages had trekked in through the night—some 12 miles. At a gathering in the church I heard some of the results of the work of those "who beat the drum" back at Radio ELWA.

"In the olden days," said a man whose hair was flecked with gray, "the chiefs beat drums to tell us there was an important announcement. We would run to the market square to hear the news. But now we have a wonderful thing—clearer than the drums. We can even lie on our beds and hear the Word of God explained clearly!"

A Christian who had been backslidden 30 years testified how he came back to Christ through listening to messages over the radio. A pastor told how gospel broadcasts prepare the way in the villages, making the people ready to listen when he visits them. A farmer said ELWA has made him more concerned about spiritual things, because he hears God's Word taught every day, not just on Sunday.

"I thought I could hide from God, until I heard His Word over the radio," testified a woman. "That made me realize He can see me anywhere, just as radio can be heard anywhere and anytime."

"I learned how to give regularly to God by tithing," said another.

"ELWA programs teach me how to train my children scripturally," said a father of 11 children.

"Our people used to be careless about what they ate," explained a dispenser. "Over the radio we have received instruction. We thank God for this help."

As Ed Kayea said, "The man who beats the drum doesn't know how far the sound goes." We flew back to the coast with thankful hearts—and a thank-offering from the Christians: sixty pounds of rice and four clucking hens.

Back at ELWA, the staff insisted, "You *must* go on a crocodile hunt before you leave Liberia." I was interested until they added that we had to go at night and might not get back until three or four in the morning. I couldn't back out, though; Dale Graber, one of the radio engineers, already had the station's battered 12-foot rowboat on a trailer hooked up to his Land-Rover. Four of us headed off for the river. A half-moon outlined the banks of tangled foliage.

We pushed the boat into the water, bolted on an outboard motor, and shoved off. In the beam of a spotlight hooked up to a car battery, the narrow river opened up before us. It was a story-book jungle, dark and impenetrable. Star-shaped water lilies cast their fragrance on the humid air, the blossoms forming a white margin between the foliage above and its perfect reflection in the inky water. Aerial roots and vines hung from overhanging branches.

As we cut the motor and drifted downstream, I began to realize that the primeval forest was very much alive, even at midnight. An owl hooted and a bullfrog croaked a resonant chorus with his mate. Huge bats swooped between the palm fronds. A black tree branch, with leaves like elephant ears, swayed as a python slithered along it. A disturbed heron lifted silently from its perch and flew deeper into the jungle. From the dark recesses echoed the crack of a dead branch as some larger creature stalked his midnight lunch.

"Don't know where the crocs are tonight," said Dale, opening the throttle. "Last month we saw 20 on the river—shot two and took them back for our staff to eat. Tastes like pork. Guess the water's too high tonight; the tide has backed it up. Crocs like to lie on the mud when the water is lower."

Silvery darts glinted in the spotlight as fish leaped ahead of our bow. Then suddenly two red spots glowed in the beam, like bicycle reflectors floating on the water.

"That's a crocodile!" cried Dale, killing the motor and seizing the spear gun. "Paddle softly."

We slid noiselessly toward the sinister red eyes. An evil snout pointed toward us for a moment, then slid under the surface.

Dale fired the harpoon at the spot where the reptile disappeared. The spear slapped into something and stuck fast.

Cautiously peering into the water, we found that the three-pronged head was buried in a submerged log on which the crocodile had been lying. It took a tussle to extract the spear— no doubt watched with amusement by Mr. Crocodile from a safe distance.

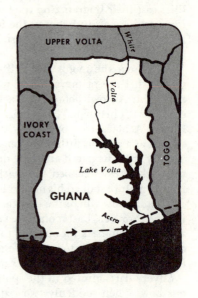

3. Christopher Columbus and Kwame Nkrumah

One of the SIM's trim little red-and-white Piper Comanches was waiting at Monrovia's local airport to fly me 800 miles eastward along the coast to Accra, Ghana. Pilot Bob Ediger showed me his route map after we were airborne. I noticed large areas marked, "Relief Data Incomplete."

"That's just a polite way of saying nobody knows what's in there," Bob explained. "There are no charted landmarks for a pilot to check his course. And if a plane ever had to crash land in that jungle, it might never be spotted. It'll take us longer to fly around by the coast, but it'll be safer. We don't take chances. Then, when we've done everything we can, the Lord looks after the rest."

Then this crew-cut pilot started musing about how slowly we learn to trust the Lord . . . and wasn't it too bad teenagers don't find out sooner that God has a route map for them . . . think of the potential their lives would have. . . . So this is what today's "specialists" are like, I thought—concerned about spiritual things while doing a first-class professional job.

We skimmed low over an endless strip of sand washed by dazzling foam. Fishermen mending their nets under the coconut palms waved at us. Their dugout canoes were drawn up on the sand, except for an occasional one battling through the breakers to land a catch of crawfish and barracuda. Women and children ran out of thatched shacks to see what was disturbing the serenity of their primeval world.

Then the world suddenly changed as we landed at Abidjan, Ivory Coast, to refuel. All over this city of 300,000, modern buildings were going up. Unlike neighboring Guinea, Ivory Coast did not sever ties with France; 24,000 Frenchmen live in the country—more than before independence. The nation has become a showpiece of what European technology and African ambition can do in partnership. It is here that the SIM plans to move its French magazine, *Champion*, as part of the Evangelical Publications Center being established by missions working in *Afrique francophone*—the states which use French as an official language; total population 100 million.

Back in the air we sped over a coastline which had taken days of dangerous sailing in the frail barques of adventurous Carthaginian traders 2,000 years ago, or European slave galleons 200 years ago. Christopher Columbus visited this coast 20 years before he discovered America. We flew over El Mina Castle, a white fortress on an outcropping of black granite on Ghana's coast, built by the Portuguese in 1482 to protect their trade with a nearby gold mine. Some of Ghana's ancient forts changed hands with successive waves of Danish, Dutch, and English adventurers.

The European traders knew nothing about the impenetrable rain forests, except that out of them came diamonds, ivory, gold, palm oil, and slaves. So when they drew pencil lines around the trading forts marked on their maps, they named the areas Ivory Coast, Gold Coast, Oil Coast, and Slave Coast. And they called the whole area "The White Man's Grave."

Independence and anti-malaria pills have come to West Africa, but the influences of the colonial era hang on. In Ivory Coast, motorists drive on the right, as in France. In Ghana, they keep to the left, as in Britain. If you drive across the border, you have to change your driving reflexes or you'll be in trouble.

In Liberia you put "gas" in your car. In Ivory Coast you put in "essence." In Ghana it is "petrol." Over in Ethiopia it is "benzine," and "ghaz" in Somalia. You won't go very far if you use the wrong term, because "petrol" in French means "kerosene," not "gas".

Gold Coast changed its name to Ghana (after an ancient inland black empire) when it became independent in 1957. As we flew over its coast we began to see more hills, less swampland, and many more communities. In most towns a church steeple rose above the rusting corrugated metal roofs. Ghana has seven million people, and is the most effervescent African country I have been in. I could sense its bubbling enthusiasm the moment we landed on Accra's international jet strip, our Comanche looking like a fly on a ping pong table. The gigantic air terminus is indicative of a nation reconstructing itself on modern lines.

John Bergen, in charge of the SIM's literature distribution in Ghana, met us at the airport and whisked us around the city. Accra is the only city where I saw three lanes of traffic on a one-way street—each lane staying in its place. Police wearing white "London Bobby" helmets direct traffic. And people actually line up in orderly queues to wait for the city buses. On the streets are women in gay print frocks and men in shirts and slacks—or with Ghana's famous *kente* cloth tied toga-like over one shoulder, leaving the other bare. The brilliant cloth may have combinations of orange, green, red, yellow, or blue hand-woven little rectangles, and may cost $400 per outfit.

The last time I visited Accra, I was warned to be careful what I said in taxis—my conversation might be reported to the secret police. Kwame Nkrumah was in power then. Nkrumah actually did a lot to unify and develop his country, but his egotism and hyper-nationalism changed him from a national idol into a hated dictator.

Coupling Marxism with nationalism and personal pride, he banned all opposition parties, threw close friends into prison after they had served his purposes, and declared himself life-time President of a one-party state. Ghanaians are tradition-ally religious, but Nkrumah began indoctrinating their chil-dren at the age of four with an atheistic catechism: "Nkrumah is our messiah; Nkrumah never dies."

John told me about the military coup that changed all that. The army took the opportunity of Kwame Nkrumah's visit to Peking to end his dictatorship. As news of the coup spread, crowds of jubilant Ghanaians filled the street. They danced, they sang, they carried placards denouncing "Nkrumaism," and toppled his nine-foot statue outside Parliament House.

In Accra's big Kingsway department store I bought a book, *Nkrumah's Subversion in Africa*, just published by the National Liberation Council. It documents Nkrumah's plans to overthrow other governments, showing photos of Red Chinese army officers training guerrillas, plans of secret indoc-trination camps, and incriminating letters.

In the store I saw radios and other items from Communist countries being sold at reduced prices, now that it was possible to import goods from Western countries. The Young Pioneers head office, built by Red China, is now used for storing grain and dried milk supplied by America. Black Star Square, one of Nkruma's extravagant projects which nearly bankrupted the country, no longer echoes to Marxist slogans. Instead, a

sign on a government building reads: "No more Nkrumaism."
Outside the airport another sign announces: "Ghana welcomes private investment."

The six SIM missionaries in Ghana were giving thanks that
the ban on selling Christian literature in Accra schools was
lifted. Although the SIM's work in Ghana is chiefly literature
distribution, the Mission has made an impact on the nation out
of all proportion to the small investment of only three missionary families. The magazine *African Challenge* is the main
literature distributed, but Moody paperbacks and other gospel
books sell well too. In the colonial era, the British had established Religious Knowledge as part of the education syllabus.
African Challenge, with its combination of educational and
Bible features, is a "natural" for sales in schools. Some teachers
include it in tuition fees as an aid to their students' learning.

As Nkrumah gained power, he tried to change Religious
Knowledge to Moral Instruction, which turned out to be
socialist indoctrination. *Challenge* popularity was a thorn in
his flesh, and eventually the Government banned its sale in
the capital's schools. But the more stringent the dictatorship
became, the more the people looked to the Word of God for
solace.

Because the SIM was willing to ship in copies of the *Challenge* without demanding that payment be exported, it was
able to get import licences for Christian literature when most
importers could get licences for Communist bloc goods only.
Christian literature sales increased. When Kingsway Stores
couldn't import secular literature, they filled their shelves with
the *Challenge*, Moody books, and Scripture Union publications.

Then the Minister of Education promised free textbooks
and asked all schools to submit lists of requirements. Requests
for half a million Bibles came in! It is to Nkrumah's credit
(or perhaps his political acumen) that the government honored
its word and placed the order with the Bible Societies.

Now the *Challenge* ban was off, and I went with Bergen to

distribute the latest issue of the paper. John is as effervescent as any Ghanaian, and the people respond to his rollicking laugh. We left 500 copies of the magazine at the first three schools. At the last one, three boys were blowing the last post on battered bugles; it was closing time. The children stood up and sang, "Lead Kindly Light" and recited the Lord's Prayer. A year ago it would have been a Young Pioneer's song—by order.

"We're grateful for the *Challenge*," said the headmaster, dressed in white shirt and shorts. "Nkrumah stopped us getting it for a while. We don't know how it was possible for Nkrumah to deceive us all. He came in with many fine promises; we didn't know it was atheistic. Now we thank God for delivering us."

Later in the day we took 4,000 copies of the *Challenge* down to the truck and bus depot to send them off to "Bud", another of the *Challenge* distributors. A gang of louts stood around trying to bully passengers into joining their masters' lorries. A rusty mini-bus roared in amid a flurry of shouts and arm-waving. Out jumped the driver, one eye closed—an insect had blown in it. One of the louts removed the insect by holding the man's eyelids apart and sticking his tongue into the eye socket. On the bus was painted the motto: "Ah Yes God is Good." Such mottoes are common. The name of a nearby mechanic's workshop was "God Will Provide Diesel Shop." A taxi had on its rear window, "Jesus Saves."

These mottoes do not indicate that the driver or owner is a true believer, Bergen explained. Along the coast Christianity is embraced by many as a progressive way of life; too often it is only a veneer covering pagan practices. The mottoes are usually inscribed as talismans, to protect the vehicle from dangers on the road.

One driver who really meant it when he put "Jesus Saves" on his taxi was Thomas Ayivi. After his conversion he sold his lorry and bought a taxi so he could distribute the *Challenge* and books as he drove through the streets. But he wanted to do more; so finally he joined the *Challenge* staff as a full-time distributor.

"I'm thankful I can serve the Lord this way," he told me. "We work as a team, not for what we can get but to spread God's Word." The "team" had distributed 70,000 copies of *Challenge* that month—a record.

On one of Bergen's trips downtown he took me to meet the chairman of the Government Cocoa Marketing Board. I knew he must be an important individual, because Ghana is the world's biggest producer of cocoa—over one-third of the world's supply. Unlike Liberian rubber trees, every single cocoa tree in Ghana is owned by an African. The Marketing Board is the "middle man" between the farmers and the overseas companies. It uses the profits to protect the farmer from fluctuating world prices and to invest in development projects. Consequently the Board is the nation's biggest financier, and the post of chairman is no small position.

But John Bergen told me some other interesting facts about the chairman as we waited for an elevator to his office. He was a founder of Nkrumah's political party, was locked up along with Nkrumah by the British before independence, and then was imprisoned by Nkrumah *after* independence. While in prison he found Christ as Saviour. The Liberation Council made him a member of the committee drafting the new constitution, and asked him to represent Ghana at the next session of the United Nations. He declined because he wouldn't have enough time for Bible study and preaching.

The elevator door opened and I was about to enter when a short, plump man in open sport shirt bounced out. I heard John chuckle and turned around to find him embracing the little man.

"This is the chairman of the Cocoa Marketing Board, Mr. William Ofori-Attah," John explained, introducing me.

"Praise the Lord!" said the little gray-haired man, grabbing me by one hand and John by the other as he bounded down the steps to his waiting Mercedes Benz. "I'd like to talk with

The author began his journey at ELWA Radio Village, a 100-acre site carved from the jungle along the Atlantic near Monrovia, Liberia. *ELWA*

A proud owner of Africa's latest status symbol gets instruction from a shopkeeper in Monrovia on how to use his new transistor radio. *ELWA*

Incredible
Safari:
West Africa

"You are dead without a radio!" declared a Liberian official. Villagers gladly
accept a set pre-tuned to ELWA from David and Mary Naff.   *Heinz Fussle*

As part of ELWA's training program, Al Snyder schools staff members in
news reporting. Liberians outnumber missionaries at ELWA.   *ELWA*

At a school in Ghana, *African Challenge* representative John Bergen is welcomed by a distribution team of teachers and senior students.

... of ELWA's many African voices, ...in Kayea, grandson of a Muslim ...mount chief, airs Gio broadcasts ...y to his people inland. *ELWA*

Reading *African Challenge* while in prison under Nkrumah helped lead Mr. Ofori-Attah, chairman of Ghana's Cocoa Marketing Board, to Christ.

In the northwest corner of Nigeria, travellers waiting their turn to cross the Sokoto River watch the barge being pulled and poled to shore.

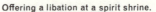

Offering a libation at a spirit shrine.

Yoruba girl

Fulani girl

A local Muslim official who has come to see the Roni Boys' School in northern Nigeria, discusses the farm program with Ralph Balisky.

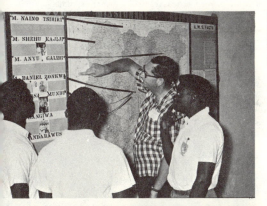

Nick Vander Dussen locates student-supported evangelists on map at Kagoro Teacher Training College.

ECWA churches (SIM-founded) sponsor grade schools reaching over 26,000 Nigerian children.

Commissioned and supported through the missionary arm of the national churches, an evangelist witnesses by the wayside in northern Nigeria.

Baptism is in public at Rinjin Gani.

Leprosy patient

Church elder
Young believer

Nigerian church leaders meet with SIM general director Dr. Raymond Davis (center) and West Africa director Bill Crouch.

A pastor displays fetishes, amulets, and Islamic prayer beads given up by people who have turned to Christ.

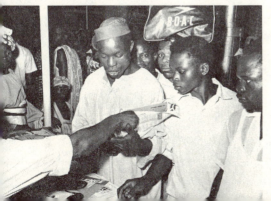

Hungry for reading material, eager young men buy Christian literature at an SIM stand in Lagos, Nigeria's capital.

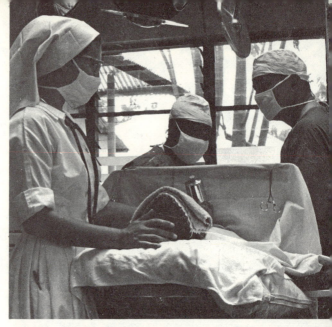

ABOVE: Dr. Don Edwards and staff perform surgery at Kaltungo Hospital.   BELOW LEFT: A camel herder has his eyes tested at Kano Eye Hospital in Nigeria's far north.   BELOW RIGHT: Sue Hooge and midwives do a brisk business at Kagoro maternity center.

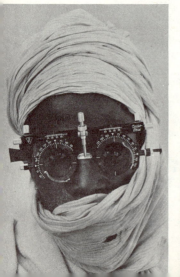

On the edge of the Sahara in Niger Republic, "Zeb" Zabriskie witnesses to veiled Tuareg, desert nomads of unknown origin.

Jean Playfair makes friends with a Kanuri woman in Niger.

Tuareg woman

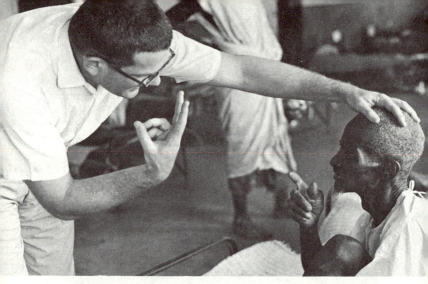

ABOVE: Dr. Jim VerLee tests the results of eye surgery at Galmi Hospital in Niger.   BELOW LEFT: Author Fuller visits a nomad's home.   BELOW RIGHT: M. Oumorou Yousoufou, Protocol Officer for the President of Niger, received his early education in SIM schools.

In Upper Volta, a converted spirit medium shows how he used to divine the future by writing in the sand.

Women pound grain in the shade of a tree in a typical Gourma village, Upper Volta.

Gourma children flock to admire the SIM airplane in which the author travelled.

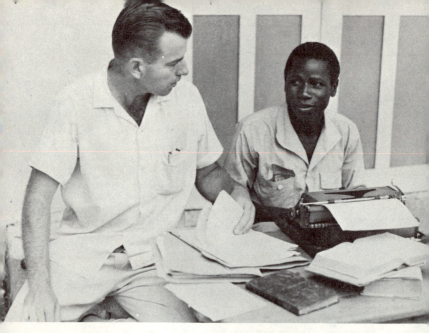

In Dahomey, Roland Pickering and an assistant he taught to type, translate the Scriptures into Dompago.

Burly, well-armed soldiers of the Dahoman army.

you, but I'm on my way to a Board meeting. Look . . . I'll come around after prayer meeting tonight."

With that he swung into the back seat of his chauffeur-driven limousine. A book he had been reading was open on the seat. He picked it up and waved it at John. "Great book this *In His Steps*, Bergen. Order me 24 more. I want to give them to my friends."

Sure enough, Mr. Ofori-Attah dropped into the Bergens' home that night and chatted while he sipped tea.

"I'm thankful for what Nkrumah did to me. He put me in prison, where I met the Lord. The guards let me have only the *African Challenge* and the Bible—I guess they figured those were non-political and wouldn't affect *me* anyway. Since I had nothing else to do month after month, I read and read. The Holy Spirit began to work through His Word. Like a slow-motion camera every sin I ever committed came before me.

"I became so miserable I refused to take my spectacles and the Bible from the prison guard each morning. I was in a mental hell. Then one day I took the Bible, and God made me turn to the story of the penitent thief. I confessed my sins and trusted Christ like the thief did. My whole life changed; I had peace and joy. I began to study the Bible in earnest. The authorities refused my request for a commentary; so I searched the Bible by myself.

"Then one day I was released. I sought out other believers to worship with. At a Scripture Union meeting I heard this man Bergen challenge us to reach others for Christ. I've been busy doing that ever since. By the way, John, I have to be in London next weekend—can you take my Bible class?"

The conversation turned to the spiritual state of some of the other prominent political prisoners now released. "I hear that X— has become interested in the gospel since he returned from Peking," said Ofori-Attah. "I must go to visit him. It is only when a man has come to the end of himself that he sees his need of a saviour. Some of us have been at the edge of it, and we know we've been saved from hell."

Talking with this man was about the most refreshing experience I've had. I wouldn't have guessed that some folk wanted him to be the next prime minister. I was only conscious that he had a consuming love for Christ and a desire to bring others to know him.

* * *

My itinerary was pushing me on, and we took off for Lagos, capital of Nigeria and the West Coast's busiest seaport. Before crossing Ghana's eastern border we flew over the industrial city of Tema, linked to Accra by 12 miles of superhighway. The 535-foot smoke stack of an aluminum smelting plant poked up at us. Under a project initiated by the British before Independence, Ghana had harnessed the waters of the Volta River to provide the greatest hyrdo-electric power source in Africa.

We flew across the border into Togo, a former German possession whittled down to 48 miles of coast but extending 350 miles inland. The tiny nation, population 1,620,000, had just survived an abortive coup and was trying to overcome the embarrassment of losing its entire army payroll. An army pay officer lost it to a fast-talking "magician" who promised to double it and split the net gain. Soldiers were asked to help restore the nation's honor and the loss by foregoing one-third of their salaries for the next two months.

Next we flew over Dahomey, another finger of land pointing to the sea (75 miles wide at the coast). It had been a French colony. We flew past the magnificent presidential palace, larger than Buckingham, built with $6,000,000 of French money intended for development projects. Resentment over this squandering was partly responsible for an army take-over there.

Along the coast I was seeing the show window of these countries. Until 1956 there were only four independent states in Africa. Now there were 36. In one year 17 were born. African states now constitute 32 per cent of the UN General Assembly. More Africans became independent in the last 10 years than there were people in the entire Roman Empire.

Their governments are run by intelligent, ambitious men who want their nations to take their place in the sun—now. They have taken on a gigantic task, for the further back from the coast the people live, the more isolated they are from the mainstream of world progress.

Inland the populace is largely content to be born, to live, to die in its traditional tropical somnolence. The progressive young men must push and cajole and dictate in order to get things done—dam a stream to provide enough water for a village; pipe it into the market place; build a school, a dispensary, a post office; get farmers to use fertilizer and better seed; talk cattle owners into allowing their herds to be inoculated; educate peasants to use latrines and mosquito nets, women to cover market food from flies, mothers to eat protein and give their babies milk and medicine.

A colossal task. A thankless task, whether for the former colonial power or for the new nationalist government. It must also be a depressing task at times, as these leaders look at the statistics. One nation reports that out of every two children born, one dies before the age of two. UNESCO says that Africa has the lowest literacy rate of any continent, the least number of newspapers and radios per capita. The World Bank states that African labor is not cheap, because its productivity is so low. The UN forecasts it will take Africa 200 years to raise her living standard to the 1964 level of Western Europe.

Unless a man is unusually mature in his thinking, such figures are bound to frustrate him. If a person feels that somehow the rest of the world has gone ahead and left his own people behind, he can become resentful of the progress of others, suspicious that the best-intended actions are discriminatory, and antagonistic even to offered aid because it again implies backwardness.

Balancing such a gloomy picture and giving hope are the bright spots one sees: the Christians who have risen above all the downward trends of their communities; the intelligent scholars who have won top honors in competition with Western minds; the unselfish individuals who quietly do their utmost to uplift their fellow citizens; the men of character—Christian character—who refuse to be corrupt and immoral, and who become pillars in the nation. I met such types on this trip; they are the ones who made the greatest impression on me. They proved to me that Africans are not an inferior race.

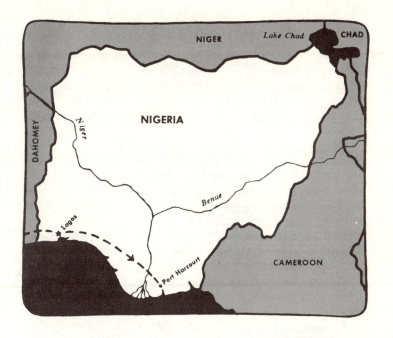

4. Traffic Jam in a Pirate Port

Africa's largest "African" port city, Lagos, sprawled below us 90 minutes after we left Accra airport. Lagos had been Eko, a fishing village on a 150-mile long lagoon, when the Portuguese found it and renamed it after one of their own fishing villages in Portugal. The natural harbor gave their slave ships protection from the coastal squalls and also from the British warships trying to break the traffic in wretched humanity. Lagos became such a notorious pirate port that the first missionaries had to enter through a smaller slave port 36 miles west.

The British attempt to stop the slave trade was a factor in Nigeria's birth. The king of Lagos, caught between rival slaving factions, ceded his island domain and a strip along the mainland to Queen Victoria in return for protection by her sailors and soldiers. That was in 1861. Since then the Colony of Lagos has grown into the 356,669-square-mile giant of Nigeria with a population of 55 million. The fishing village that became a pirate city is now a bustling metropolis of 750,000.

The rowdy spirit of the city's early history lives on in modern forms. Here is all the best and all the worst of urbanization crowded on to an island and a strip of swampy mainland. The city throbs with people. Uninhibited people, friendly people, loudmouthed arguing people. City slickers in the latest movie fashions, girls in mini-skirts or in flowing robes. Recently-arrived country cousins carrying their goods on their heads. University students, business tycoons, doctors, lawyers, market mammies, fishermen, factory workers. Muslims, pagans, Christians, Communists, Jehovah's Witnesses, Rosicrucians, Cherubims and Seraphims. Good men, bad men; bishops and dope agents.

At night the heavy humid air is shattered by the rhythm of combos doing the High Life—a modern African dance in which anything goes. Up the next street a group of relatives may be singing doleful hymns at a "wake"—a vigil for a member who died last year or several years before.

Driving into the city we hit a traffic jam that took an hour to crawl one mile. Thousands of cyclists swarmed past us—Nigeria is the world's largest importer of bicycles. We saw the ultra-modern University of Lagos overlooking the lagoon, and across from it on the island the 25-story Independence Building.

We were impressed with the modern department stores and tall blocks of offices. Turning my head, however, I suddenly realized that this was only an artery of modernity cut through lanes filled with oozing mud and garbage, and lined with ramshackle shanties. The city council is clearing some of the slum area, but it is a colossal task because of the thousands of job-seekers and relatives who pour into the city.

Passing from one suburb to another we came across palatial homes, some costing $100,000, surrounded by lush lawns and flowers, TV aerials on the roofs. Here some of Nigeria's elite drive their Mercedes Benz cars, quaff imported wines, and entertain call girls who may be wearing blonde or red wigs over their black hair.

I also saw the spot where slaves used to be sold under a breadfruit tree; now it is the site of Breadfruit Street Anglican Church, surrounded by modern offices and shops. I saw the place where SIM pioneers Rowland Bingham, Walter Gowans and Thomas Kent landed in 1893, and the CMS (Church Missionary Society) compound where Bingham later lay wracked with fever while a devout bishop prayed for his recovery. Kent and Gowans died of malaria on their trek inland, and Bingham had to return to Canada broken in body but not in faith.

That was only three-quarters of a century ago, but it was a daring pioneer venture. Timbuktu to the northwest had been taken by the French only that year. Northern Nigeria had not even been created; it became a political entity under Lord Lugard in 1900. Seven years later 87 percent of a British military expedition up the Niger had died or been invalided home because of tropical diseases. The leader of a mission told the three SIM pioneers in Lagos, "You'll never see the interior. Maybe your grandchildren will."

Now 75 years later some of the results of Dr. Bingham's faith could be seen right in the city where defeat had seemed so certain. In the city are five congregations which have sprung from the work of the SIM, meeting under the name, The Association of Evangelical Churches of West Africa (ECWA). And on the outskirts of the city are the offices of Niger-Challenge Publications, a literature project which not only reaches the new Africa on its doorstep but also has made an impact right across the continent.

I attended the 15th anniversary celebration of the *African Challenge*, the largest publication of NCP. Shaking the hands of program participants, checking that the loudspeakers worked, and detailing ushers to look after last-minute items was 43-year-old James Kayode Bolarin, Managing Editor of the *Challenge*.

My mind went back to earlier *Challenge* anniversaries, when those things had to be looked after by missionaries. Ten years ago missionaries did the writing, the photography, the illustrating and layout, the typesetting, the proofreading, the counseling, and even the mailing, assisted by a few Africans. Now every one of those tasks is carried on by capable African Christians, assisted by a skeleton missionary staff.

"When *African Challenge* first appeared on the news stands of Nigeria on July 1, 1951, it was very much a venture of faith," Editor Bolarin told the large crowd at the anniversary thanksgiving service. "The first copies were carried to the post office in a wash tub. But in the past 15 years the magazine has left an indelible mark on the pages of Christian history in Africa.

"Today 125,000 copies in English are distributed per month, with a Yoruba edition of 40,000 and a French edition of 20,000. The magazines are sold in nearly every country of Africa as well as in some overseas lands. And since the *Challenge* started, 12 other gospel magazines patterned on its format have been started by Christian leaders in other lands around the world."

We heard something of the results of this literature crusade as two of the *Challenge* counseling staff stood to read excerpts from readers' letters. A convict in Nigeria, a Muslim in Ghana, a self-declared pagan from East Africa all told how they had found Christ as Saviour through reading the *Challenge*. A Muslim in Sudan asked for "more information on how to become a child of God." A Kenyan girl studying in Denmark wanted to know how she could get it there, "to hear God's voice." A Cameroonian said the *Challenge* had taught him he should not take bribes. A factory worker in Eastern Nigeria told how the magazine had shown him and his friends the evils of Communism, so that they did not send in their membership forms to the Communist Party.

At the NCP compound the staff showed me current figures

for circulation and finance. The magazines are aimed at student readers, because 60 percent of Africa's population is under 21, and most of Africa's 25 percent literate population is school age. These readers have no earning power and most can scarcely find the pennies needed for their daily diet of yam or cassava. Therefore the NCP has to sell the magazines below cost.

The monthly subsidy comes to about $5,000 (£1,400). This is a considerable sum to be found issue after issue, but it works out to one of the cheapest forms of evangelism; because every magazine sold in Africa is read by at least 10 readers, and religious magazines by possibly 15, according to a research agency. That means the combined magazines reach around two million readers per issue—and it therefore costs only one third of a penny to contact each with the gospel. Funds for the magazines come in miraculously month after month from faithful supporters around the world who see this as an investment with high dividends for eternity.

Every month over 2,000 readers enquire about spiritual matters—from marriage problems to fears about ghosts. These letters are carefully followed up with further literature and counsel. Seventeen percent write back a second time to assure the Counselor they have now trusted Christ as Saviour. Many of the others are strengthened in their previous stand for Christ.

An African studying in Moscow appealed for a Bible, to show his Russian classmates that "Christ died for our sins on the cross." The *Challenge* was able to airmail a Bible, which, to everyone's surprise, reached him.

I could see that these Christian magazines are not only an instrument for spreading the gospel and teaching the Scriptures, but they also hold up a standard of righteousness in a continent convulsed with changing standards. They provide a channel for African believers to apply the Word to the needs of their people in their context.

The existence of Christian journalists in Africa's wild press world is a powerful witness. When James Bolarin, who first studied journalism in London under an SIM scholarship, took a refresher course at the University of Lagos, fellow students soon found he was different. He studied hard, didn't come to class drunk, and never had girls sleeping in his dorm room. The others mocked him, but when a Muslim student was expelled for drawing a knife in a classroom fight, he first went to James in front of the other journalists and said, "Bolarin, I want to thank you for what your life has meant to me. Now I have seen what a Christian really is."

African senior staff and missionaries live on the *Challenge* compound, and I saw many examples of "togetherness." One afternoon eight African women, colorfully garbed in traditional "wrappers," crowded into the tiny suite of one of the lady missionaries; they were members of her Bible class who had come for tea. A Nigerian youth was eating supper with a missionary couple I dropped in to see, and a university undergraduate stayed for several nights with another couple.

The nation had just been through six months of tragic bloodshed. For weeks the *Challenge* staff saw and heard rioting in the neighboring suburb, as followers of one political party roughed up others, burning their cars and houses, killing opponents. Then came the army coup of January 1966, when southern junior officers assassinated northern politicians and certain southern leaders who were in league with them.

Everyone waited apprehensively for a northern reaction to the slaughter; it came months later in waves of blood-letting. Around two million Ibos fled to their Eastern Region on the coast. For a while it looked as if the Federation of Nigeria, independent only six years, was doomed to disintegrate. Then the army found an interim leader acceptable to the north because he was a northerner, and acceptable to the south because he was not a Muslim—Yakubu Gowon.

The turn of events was remarkable. Six months earlier there had been a Muslim Federal leader, and the nation's politics were dominated by West Africa's greatest propagator of Islam, the Sardauna of Sokoto, Premier of Northern Nigeria. But now at the head of the nation, to guide it to a workable civilian government, was a 31-year-old son of a Nigerian evangelist. Major General Gowon is a professing believer in the Lord Jesus, taking an active interest in the distribution of Bibles among his troops.

Most people overseas thought another Congo was taking place, but there are basic differences between the Congo and Nigeria. The terror of the Congo broke when Belgium, after refusing to prepare the 13 million people for nationhood during 75 years of colonial rule, suddenly panicked and left the country to anarchy. There were only 16 university graduates; there was not one Congolese doctor or lawyer. Communist-trained guerrillas put narcotics in the mouths of children and machine guns in their hands. Result: the Congo revolution.

By contrast, Nigeria was carefully nurtured toward independence over half a century. When the British first moved in, they saw there were actually three or four separate nations based on large tribal groupings. These had warred on each other for centuries, building up deep tribal hatreds. To get these factions working together, the British constructed a federal system of government. It was wasteful because of inter-regional rivalry and duplication of services. But it worked—until one Region felt another was trying to dominate the Federation. Then the bubble of national unity broke, and century-old hatreds once again gripped the country.

Although interrupted and hard-hit by staff shortages, services continued to operate; the police force remained stable. Mature, responsible men headed up tribunals to look into national ills. The goodwill left behind by the British gave no grounds for anti-white feelings. As one Nigerian said to me, "Your white skin is the safest in the country." White car drivers were allowed through barricades while Africans were held up by each other. There was no unusual feeling against missions, even in the Islamic North, although southerners were sought out in churches and mission institutions during the tragic inter-tribal massacres.

SIM work in the south is chiefly through literature, not "stations." The pioneers headed into the unevangelized North because the coast already had a number of Protestant missionary societies: Anglican, Methodist, Presbyterian, Baptist, Lutheran, and several independent groups. Pentecostals came later. Many of those denominational missionaries preached the gospel. Nigeria's first President, Dr. Nnamdi Azikiwe, once publicly read a letter he received as a boy from a Scottish minister:

> *"My Dear Boy, I am delighted with your kind letter. Most of all because I see from it that you quite clearly understand that Jesus Christ is your only Saviour and that you have taken Him into your heart as such. Now yield to Jesus in everything and always. . . . The Lord bless and keep and use you."*

Since those days, however, a second and third generation of "Christians" has arisen, for whom the name means only progress, in contrast to being called pagan or Muslim. Actually pagan secret societies continue and claim many nominal Christians. Church members who find the rules too strict join sects which stress that they are truly African churches. Strong on visions and ritual, they also permit polygamy and concubinage. "Splinter churches" seem to be an African phenomenon. Throughout the continent there are 4,595 ecclesiastical schisms or groups which have broken away from the major churches. Their combined membership totals seven million.

Eastern Nigeria is especially fertile ground for these splinter churches. I visited the area for the opening of the SIM's bookshop and literature warehouse in Port Harcourt, a city 285 air miles east of Lagos. Along the roads I noted the names of splinter churches: The Holy Ghost Church, Apostolic Tabernacle of Christ, Church of the Redeemed Flock of Jesus Christ, True Christ's Association.

Some call themselves "denominations" but are actually the private means of support of enterprising individuals who style themselves "Reverend," "Bishop," or "Prophet." Others are groups which have left established missions after being disciplined for disgracing Christ's name. They are constantly corresponding with American churches begging for funds and supplies and even missionaries, which would add to their prestige. Yet they will not work with the many missions already there—several of them fundamental. I met two women who had come out in response to an impassioned request only to find the "Reverend's" 200 churches non-existent. I saw a large poster announcing that "the Church of Jesus Christ is now established on earth—missionaries are expected soon."

Through literature the SIM is able to reach readers among all this coastal hodgepodge of denominations and sects without entering as another rival white man's organization competing for membership. Many who have a nominal Christian background are saved after reading the way of salvation clearly explained.

ECWA national evangelists are opening up work, and have started a Christian Training Institute, which is being developed into a Bible College. Problems are increased by the fact that Eastern Nigeria is the stronghold of Roman Catholicism in the country.

The SIM's new bookshops in Enugu and Port Harcourt are further steps in reaching the most heavily populated area in tropical Africa. Since the discovery of oil, Port Harcourt, a sleepy town surrounded by swamps, has come alive. Shell Oil Company alone brought in 500 Americans who live in a self-contained suburb. Thousands of boys, whose primary schooling makes them unwilling to remain in their undeveloped villages but has not fitted them for industrial employment, drift into the city. Michelin Tire Company personally interviewed 22,000 before finding 500 suitable for employment.

Port Harcourt has the world's highest known net increase rate—11 percent per annum. That means its 300,000 population will *double* in seven and a half years. No wonder its facilities are inadaquate. I met an engineer building a refinery; he was preparing to make a telephone call to his head office overseas. In order to do so, he had to fly to Lagos, a round trip of 600 miles at a cost of nearly $100.

An official showed SIM Bookshop General Manager Trevor Ardill a thick file on bookshops in the Eastern Region. "Most of these are selling Communist literature," he said. "That's why we'd be glad to see you open up bookshops and bring in something helpful."

On the streets Communist magazines are laid out to catch the eye. Before the Army coup the Nigerian Communist Party advertised in a government paper: *"Wanted—highly disciplined, intelligent and well educated youths with organizational ability who are already Marxists-Leninists and those prepared to embrace the ideology of the Communists—to be trained as cadres for our mass work for every street in every city and every village in the rural areas. Join the Communist Party!"*

Bookshop Manager Mike Glerum drove me around the city in an SIM bookmobile, with "God's Word Is Light" painted on the sides. A small Ford passed us and stopped. Out jumped the driver and flagged us down. "I just want to tell you how happy I am to see the SIM over here! " said the smartly dressed Nigerian. "The literature I've bought from the SIM has helped me more than anything else."

Africa's ports and other booming cities are the storm centers of the continent today. The city people are awake and on the move. When Ardill and Glerum opened their mobile book display during a survey visit to a crowded city, a burly man pushed his way in to the crowd that immediately gathered. Without looking to see whether the literature was atheistic or religious, secular or spiritual, he shouted, "I don't care what you're selling—we want it! "

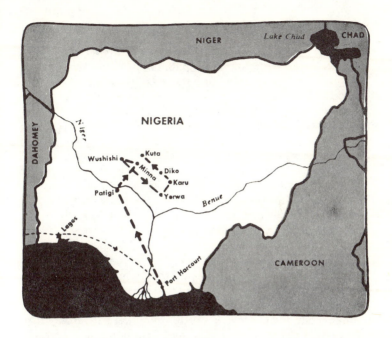

5. On Trek with Stanley

Pilot Dave Rutt picked me up in an SIM Comanche at Port Harcourt. As the tiny four-seater lifted off the steaming strip, we saw the burn-off flares of oil wells belching orange flame as if from dragons hiding in the dense jungle.

The vast Niger Delta stretched below us, a 14,000-square-mile mass of tangled mangroves and stagnant water. Here the Niger, Africa's third longest river (after the Nile and Congo) loses itself in silt washed down through the centuries.

Contrary to the way most rivers are discovered, explorers did not know where the mouth was for 100 years after they had discovered the source! At first they thought it linked up with the Nile on the other side of Africa. Although it begins only 150 miles from the Atlantic, just north of where my safari started in Liberia, the Niger wanders up to Timbuktu in the Sahara and back before it empties into the Atlantic in Nigeria, 2,600 miles from its source.

I was headed for a rendezvous with Stanley. The name reminded me of H. M. Stanley who found David Livingstone in East Africa and stayed on to help carve out an earthly kingdom, the Belgian Congo. But the man I was to meet was F. X. Stanley, who arrived in West Africa in 1909 only five years after explorer Stanley died. Francis Stanley came as a missionary to establish a spiritual kingdom in the hearts of men and women. After 56 years of service, he begged the Mission to let him stay out until his 80th birthday. Now he was to make his last visit to the work he had pioneered. It was to be my privilege to travel with him and his wife.

Down below, the countryside changed from swampy delta to luxuriant rain forests where giant mahogany and iroko hardwoods stood out among spreading cottonwoods. As these thinned out further north the hillsides were covered with plantations of cocoa or rubber trees. Lining the many rivers were oil palms, which supply the people with a beverage, vitamin-rich oil for cooking, and poles and thatch for roofing. In the markets villagers can also buy soap and margarine made in Nigeria from a palm-oil base.

"There's the Niger," Dave said at last. Through the haze ahead I could distinguish a light streak across the horizon. We had cut across the big southward bend of the river and were meeting it again. The verdant growth thinned out and massive black rocks protruded from the ground like granite bubbles. We were in Northern Nigeria. Descending for ten minutes, we flew along the river plains to the town of Patigi, site of the SIM's first mission station.

And there was Stanley. Not a feeble little bent figure, but a short, straight-backed gray-haired gentleman with a zip in his step and a twinkle in his eye. He playfully chided me for not keeping up with him as we went down to the river's edge to see the very spot where pioneer A. W. Banfield landed in 1901. Following the death of Gowans and Kent on their overland trek, Banfield and his companions sailed up-river to this place in a government stern-wheeler and talked the suspicious chief into letting them set up camp. Very few white people lasted more than two or three years before succumbing to the dread malaria—which was then thought to be a fever carried by "mal-aria" ("bad air") from swamps, rather than by the *Anopheles* mosquito.

Stanley said the majestic river looked exactly as it did when he first saw it in 1909. Even the mat-covered dugout canoes nudging the high mud banks were the same kind he traveled in to give the Word to the Nupe ("Noo-pay") tribe living along the banks. He once lived for 23 days on a dugout, traveling 460 miles up-river with building supplies for a mission station in French-administered Niger.

When we went to "salute" the chief, the 60-year-old Muslim ruler put a burly arm around Stanley's small frame and said, "This man is my father. He taught me how to read!" Stanley chuckled at the memory and reminisced about early days. The Nupe tribe had become strongly Islamic over the past century under political pressure, resisting the gospel. But Stanley told me that at a farewell dinner for him and his wife the week before, the paramount chief of another Nupe town had asked the District Officer why the north had not gone ahead like the south. Both of the men and the other distinguished Nigerians present were Muslims. "It is because we hindered the missionaries in the early days," said the D.O. frankly. "In the south the people welcomed the missionaries and became educated. Our people are only beginning to wake up."

Presenting traditional robes and other gifts to the Stanleys, the paramount chief pleaded: "Please ask your Mission to send other missionaries to take your place." It was the Stanleys' greatest disappointment to have to padlock the mission house door as they left with no replacement. There weren't enough missionaries to fill all the needs.

At Patigi, a town of 7,000, the gospel goes out through a school, a leprosarium, a dispensary, and a maternity home. Overlooking the graves of early workers, there stands a large whitewashed church which was overflowing with believers for the Stanleys' last Sunday there. The pioneer led the communion service, passing the elements to aged elders whom he had led to the Lord in their youth.

When it came time for the Stanleys to say goodbye, school children lined up at the edge of the grassy airstrip. Stanley couldn't resist giving the delighted boys and girls a farewell tattoo on the school drum.

Standing with tears streaming down his wrinkled face was a white-haired elder. Maidugu George was one of Stanley's first converts and the second Nupe to be baptized. On each side of him were two fine-looking young men, his sons. One was headmaster of the church school; the other was completing degree studies at Ibadan University to prepare for further service with the Mission. Elder Maidugu couldn't say goodbye as the Stanleys climbed into the plane. He just kept slapping the back of one hand against the palm of the other and repeating, "Our father has gone; our father has gone!"

Stanley rubbed his eyes as we took off and flew across the river to Gbariland. I was to see many similar scenes as I traveled with the Stanleys through a tribe which northerners used to consider the most primitive in the land. The Hausas point out that Gbari women don't even carry loads on their heads but stoop over with them on the back of their necks, where large callouses are raised by 60–100 pound loads.

We landed at Minna and for the next week toured the district in Albert Diamond's German Opel. The Gbari villages we passed were tight clusters of 15 to 20 round mud huts, their thatched roofs touching one another. A son builds huts for himself and his wives next to his father's huts, and so the cluster grows. Larger towns are made up of several clusters of families. Smoke seeps through the thatch, which is usually topped with a clay cooking pot up-side-down to shed the water from the very peak.

In clearings between locust bean and neem trees farmers hoed the red soil in the heat of the day. Peasants waved at us as we sped by.

We saw the oldest work in the district and also a brand new work. The oldest is Wushishi, where we ate lunch in the original house built in 1904—the oldest in the Mission. An orphanage with 75 girls between infancy and 16 years of age is operated there by two missionary ladies. We were greeted by a white-bearded patriarch, Inusa Samuel, 75, of the earliest pastors.

The Emir of Wushishi drove up in his Plymouth (flown over from Canada for independence celebrations) while we were there. He was a striking figure in his tall turban and gold-brocade cloak covered with rose tulle, but he plopped down in an arm chair and chatted away about his last visit to Scotland and Rome. "He often drops in for tea," the ladies told us.

"This orphanage is doing a great job," he told me. "Some of our leaders say we shouldn't send Muslim children to a Christian place, but I tell them that doing so doesn't automatically make them Christians. Christianity is a heart matter—the children have to believe in their hearts."

The Emir had some insight into what constitutes a Christian. He also had his own ideas about the way certain people were propagating Islam: "I tell them it is wrong to force people to be Muslims. Others will laugh at our religion in 10 years' time if we do that."

The new work we saw was in a little Bassa village down in the V formed by the confluence of the Niger and Benue Rivers. It is only four miles from Yerwa, a Gbari station opened in 1934, yet we were the first people to drive in to the village. Bill Johnston, an Irish missionary who with his wife had been trekking out from Yerwa among the Bassa people, piloted us in. Our car nearly stuck in the loose dirt of the new trail cleared through the bush.

This is the remarkable thing about Africa—pockets of untouched territory right in the midst of areas where the gospel has been preached for 30 years. The phenomenon is accounted for by the lack of roads, the extreme conservatism of the people, and their different languages, cutting them off from the rest of the world. The Johnstons were learning the Bassa language as they visited villages by bicycle, their three-year-old son strapped in a box behind.

At the sound of our approaching car, the women scuttled into their huts, but adventurous youths crowded around to cluck over the marvel of a vehicle in their village. Their front teeth were filed to a point and stained red. Generally the tribe is not interested in sending children to school. Sister exchange in marriage is officially outlawed but continues. The people do not believe in digging wells—spirits might come out of the holes.

We heard groans coming from a compound and found an aged woman lying unclothed on the ground. She had a strangulated hernia, and was in urgent need of surgery. Her family bluntly refused to let us take her for medical attention.

Finally we had to turn away, leaving her to die. As I looked back she suddenly convulsed with pain, her eyes bulging from their sockets. Two nights later the hopeless death wail rose over the village, and the woman was buried amid drumming and drinking. Her family threw coins and cloth into the grave; then they piled clay on top to prevent the spirits from disturbing the corpse.

A happier sight awaited us outside that compound. Fifteen believers (fruit of only 30 months' work) had gathered beside the "church" they had built. It was only an open thatch shelter supported on poles, with rough benches for "pews." But it was their place of worship, a brave witness right beside the beer-brewing pots, where women were grinding grain (two-thirds of the grain harvest is put into beer). The next week the Christians would have a Bible conference, after which they would go into surrounding villages to preach.

We drove back north to spend the night at Karu, rich with history of the Gbari church since 1911. There missionary Stanley re-met evangelist Yepwi and both fairly danced as they embraced and reminisced. The two had walked and cycled hundreds of miles preaching throughout Gbariland. They were about the same age, but Yepwi chuckled proudly as he learned he had 60 grandchildren to Stanley's 15.

In the early years Yepwi backslid, tempted by women and offers of position in the tribe. Patient prayer saw him restored, and like the Apostle Peter he thereafter strengthened his brethren. He told me that whenever he feels tired, he goes out to preach; that revives him.

The chief of Karu heard the gospel through Yepwi and believed. His son Panya is local pastor and also national Treasurer for ECWA. At Karu Bible School 100 students are studying the Word.

Passing the Gbari "Heaven," a gigantic dome of granite, we reached Diko mission station. From a hill capped with black boulders—formerly a spirit sacrifice shrine—we looked across lush green ridges and valleys. It was a peaceful land overlaid with a patchwork of little farms. Immediately below us nestled a Gbari village, with brilliant flame-of-the-forest trees here and there between the thatched roofs. Blue smoke hung over the huts, from which we could hear the thud of women pounding grain for the evening meal and the laughter of children playing. Farmers tramped home across the trails, some carrying on their heads bundles of grass for their rams.

Esther Anderson was rounding up her orphans when we arrived. She is an institution in herself—66 years old but still with a tinge of red in her hair. One pretty little girl was on crutches—she had been brought to Esther by a Christian aunt who snatched her from her mother's grave (Gbari custom had demanded that a mother dying in childbirth must have the infant buried with her).

The tall youth who served us at lunch was a twin who had been brought to Esther 20 years before. At that time the bigger one of a set of twins had to be killed, because it was certainly the evil spirit "eating" the spirit of the genuine baby. The "spirit twin" was usually starved for four days; then if still alive it would be poisoned.

A Christian mother sent this baby to Esther for safety. The father, son of a witchdoctor, found out and sent word that the spirits had cursed the boy and he would die. He was very sickly, but the missionaries nursed him back to health. They were warned never to allow him to return to his village. Now he was a strapping young man on holiday from the SIM's Christian Training Institute at Kwoi. One day Esther found him fairly dancing with joy—his father had just repented and followed Jesus.

Esther drove us furiously through town in her yellow car to the leprosy welfare center she runs for 17 patients who can't support themselves. One Fulani woman had been brought by relatives on a donkey, pushed off, and left lying on the ground. Another had been chased from her camp by her own children. The grateful look in the eyes of these patients as they watched Esther walk around the center was ample reward for her work. Queen Elizabeth had also honored her with a Member of the British Empire decoration.

"You've seen new work and old work," said Al Diamond as we left Diko. "Now you must see work which the church has taken over from the Mission. We'll go to Kuta Sunday morning—they've had quite an experience there."

We drove over a rough trail in a tropical downpour that stalled Al's car three times. In spite of the rain, 143 believers trudged into their mud-walled church, heads covered with baskets, cloths, and raincoats. There would have been three times that number present to meet the Stanleys, but for the swollen rivers which prevented neighboring congregations from coming in.

Kuta was opened in 1919. For the past 10 years the churches had been at low ebb spiritually. The younger generation did not know anything of the ridicule, privation, and suffering which their fathers went through when they first turned from their tribe's pagan traditions. They became more concerned about their farms and houses, and with material progress came selfishness, coldness, jealousy.

Then Islam moved in to the once pagan area. First came traders who fingered their beads and prostrated to Allah in the market. A few villagers followed this new way. At times a malam (teacher of Islam) came to teach them; then he came to live in Kuta. A Muslim chief was elected and a mosque built. A prominent politician visited Kuta and told the people that paganism was outdated; everyone should choose either Islam or Christianity. Pagans were quick to catch the point when he handed out gifts of robes and prayer beads. Within a few weeks 2,000 declared for Islam.

That woke up the church. The missionaries had left to open a new work the year before. The believers were on their own. They met for prayer for a week; then visited every compound in Kuta the next week. As Christians prayed and witnessed together, the Holy Spirit convicted of coldness and sin. Backsliders repented; nominal Christians found salvation; pagans turned to Christ. They visited surrounding villages. The pastor listed over 300 conversions in one month.

That brought reprisal. Muslim teachers spread rumors against the Christians. Several believers were fined for preaching to Muslims, on the basis of disturbing the peace. At night malams visited villages where Christians had witnessed during the day, and told the people that the chief had ordered everyone to become Muslims. They burned one church.

One day six villagers were arrested after they trekked in to Kuta to ask the way of salvation. One was released when he promised to become a Muslim. The others were held without bail. The believers met to pray that God would vindicate His name.

Things began to happen, and villagers whispered, "These Christians are praying!" A chief was nearly killed when his car unaccountably swerved off the road on his way to the trial.

One of the policemen who was to testify against the Christians fell under the wheels of the train which brought him to the nearest station. There were other evidences of God's hand of judgment.

The whole countryside was watching. The judge dismissed the case and released the five, who returned to their village rejoicing "that they had been counted worthy to suffer shame for his name."

The believers at Kuta had come through this period of trial purified and strengthened, with a greater missionary vision. Within six weeks of the initial week of prayer, 1,000 men, women, and children had professed faith in Christ.

On this trek with the Stanleys I saw the oldest part of the Mission's work. The seed has been planted, has struggled into maturity, has borne fruit. There have been the tares too, but the believers meeting that Sunday morning as the rain pelted down on the roof made me thankful that the gospel *has* taken root. I suddenly realized that the singing, the praying, the Scripture reading means something very special to these people. It is no longer a message brought by foreigners. This faith is theirs.

The Sankey hymn tunes now have an African rhythm and harmony in a five-note scale. The prayers are like the supplications of the Psalmists. Scripture has local significance. It is as if the "graft" has taken and a new branch has blossomed out. The candle is burning on its own, no longer dependent on the match which lit it.

The believers sang a song specially written for the Stanleys:

"Goodbye brother, goodbye sister,
If we don't see you any more.
We part in the body, we meet in the spirit,
If we don't see you any more.
May God keep you, may God guide you,
If we don't see you any more. . . ."

As the Stanleys later headed for their homeland, I flew back across the Niger into Yoruba country, where I would see something of modern church-mission relations—their joys and their problems.

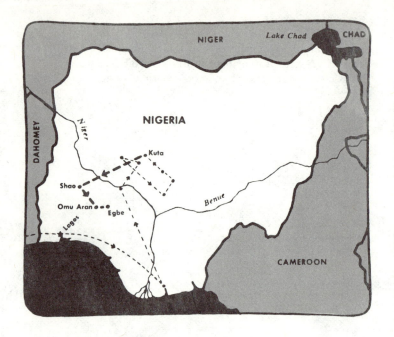

6. The Thunder God Strikes Again

Shao is a typical northern Yoruba village—relaxed, friendly, so different from the hard-faced noisy cities. A drummer and his little assistant nodded at me as they tapped on talking drums which they squeezed under their armpits. They were waiting to accompany the rhythmic movement of the farmers' hand hoes as they turned the soil, moist from the night's rain.

The lanes between the mud walls of family compounds were eroded by rain and daily sweeping, baring the gnarled roots of ancient wild fig trees and the stone foundations of mud houses. A lean cur slept on top of a bundle of faggots in the early morning sun. The night's droppings of goats were still around the pegs where they had been tethered in the entrance huts.

Women stepped in and out of low doorways, babies bobbing on their backs, as they did the morning's chores.

The Yorubas number 10 million, stretching from Nigeria's coast northwards to the Niger River, and spilling over into Dahomey. They are a closely knit tribe, with strong respect for family and chieftain authority, a contagious sense of humor, and remarkable business acumen. The tribe has an ancient culture; the glass beads and peerless bronzes of Ife are still a cultural marvel to anthropologists.

In the big Yoruba cities, like Ilorin, Ibadan (largest "African" city), Ijebu, and Abeokuta, traditional life is mingled with modern ways: shops, heavy traffic, and university students. In Shao I saw the charm of age-old traditions. Vic Carlson, SIM missionary there, took me to see the River God shrine.

Outside a rambling thatched house an old man greeted us. He was the chief priest. After we assured him of a tip, he bared his toothless gums, wrapped a dirty white cloth over one shoulder and around his waist, and rolled up a mat to reveal the shrine. At the entrance were three carved figures two feet high, their heads painted brilliant blue and their bodies covered with white cloth. These were the wives of the River God. A priestess slipped in behind the idols to make sure the white people did not desecrate them.

In a few months' time, just after the rains, the betrothed girls would all be married on the same day. Three days later a gay procession carries the idols down to the river. The brides are decked in new clothes bought with their earnings in the big cities. The fetish priest gives offerings to the River God to ensure fertility in marriage.

Reincarnation is a main tenet of Yoruba animistic belief. Because so many babies die from disease and malnutrition, pagan mothers believe that an evil spirit is being reincarnated to mock them. After a few deaths they will call the next baby, "Born to Die," believing it will go, too.

One mother brought her sixth child to nurse Louise Carlson —the other five had died from pneumonia. Louise left the mother to watch while the baby had steam treatment. The distraught mother pushed the child's head right over the steam to make "the evil spirit" suffer so it wouldn't return again after the baby died. When the child cried Louise rushed back and rescued it just in time. With careful nursing he has become a healthy three-year-old, and the mother is overcome with joy.

Shao is a relatively new work; one of the church elders told me how he had heard the gospel for the first time only 13 years before, when an SIM missionary preached in the market. "Every house in town that isn't a Christian's, still has an idol in it," the elder said. "And the light is only really beginning to dawn on the Christians. They need deeper understanding. Pray for us."

Although work at Shao was started recently, the SIM's work among Yorubas actually began in 1908, when missionaries from the first SIM station on the Niger trekked south into Yagba country. Yagba was one of several Yoruba divisions. The kingdoms nearer the coast quickly absorbed civilization and Christianity—at least nominally. Their relatives in the Northern Region, including the Yagbas, were cut off from coastal influence and long subjugated by northern tribes.

After slave raiding was outlawed, Yagba people filtered through to the coast and returned with stories about a God who loved the world. One man learned to read and brought back a Yoruba Bible. He begged missionaries to come to teach his people.

When a young fellow by the name of Tommy Titcombe arrived in 1908, he was sent off to live in the Yagba capital, Egbe. He needed every ounce of his youthful energy as he lived in a Yoruba hut and slowly pieced together the local dialect. Tommy lived to see Ilorin and Kabba Provinces become a leading church district.

Gordon Aro, ECWA Secretary for the district, told me about the work over a cup of coffee in his home at Omu Aran. There are 146 churches and 20 branch churches, with a total membership of 10,600. They support 98 pastors and a number of evangelists, some in other districts. Young men and women helped by missionaries now hold influential government and commercial posts, where many are witnessing for Christ. Wherever I traveled in the district, I saw larger churches being built to cope with overflowing attendance. One new church will seat 2,040.

The Yoruba churches have shouldered the responsibility for direct evangelism. Although every mission station has an evangelistic witness, the SIM's primary task in this area is now to strengthen ECWA to do a greater job than the missionaries could ever do.

I saw mission orphanages and girls' schools, where foundations for Christian homes are laid. I saw Teachers' Colleges where Christian teachers are prepared to reach pupils for Christ. At Egbe there is a high school, named Titcombe College after the area's pioneer, where the sons of Christians get the best training possible, academically and spiritually, to prepare them for Christian leadership. Also at Egbe is the Nurses' Training School, attached to Egbe Hospital, where trainees receive Bible instruction as well as medical knowledge.

Since medical work requires staff and finance which the young churches do not have, the Mission still carries on that aspect of gospel outreach. Besides Egbe Hospital, where Dr. George Campion and his colleagues treated 95,598 patients last year, the SIM operates two provincial leprosariums.

In the Yoruba area the Mission has made the transition from the role of a father to that of a brother. But even brothers have their misunderstandings, as I found out at a pastors' conference held at Igbaja Seminary and Bible College.

"Excuse my greasy hands," said Norman Lohrenz, acting principal, as we drove in at dusk. Since 6:30 that morning he had been overhauling the diesel-electric generating plant to get it ready for the first meeting of the conference. Before the evening service we sat down to a meal of wild pig in the

Lohrenzes' home, with some of the pastors. They were graduates of the Seminary, which trains men at degree level.

Over the next three days African pastors and white missionaries frankly discussed relations between the churches and the Mission. It was an eye-opener to see how minor misunderstandings could cause widespread resentments. Yet this is not peculiar to the Lord's work in Yorubaland, nor in Nigeria, nor in Africa. Wherever missions and national churches work together, the same problems arise.

The pastors said many of their young people were complaining about the Mission's education policy. "They say the Mission doesn't care enough about educating Africans," said one pastor. "Look at the big denominations down on the coast— they have produced doctors and lawyers; they have big institutions; they send many Africans overseas."

The missionaries patiently outlined the early history of the Mission—how evangelical Christians in Rowland Bingham's day had become apprehensive of the liberal theology of missions which had concentrated on education. They had seen large institutions, built with the Lord's money, taken over by non-Christians. They had said, "It is not our business to educate; we have been commissioned to preach the gospel. We want our money to go into direct evangelism."

The early missionaries also wanted the church to develop along its own lines, not to mimic Western civilization in the belief that it was Christianity itself. Some of them even discouraged Africans from wearing Western clothing; in one area the missionary in charge banned speaking in English and closed the schools. This outlook was not limited to the SIM. In 1913 a conference of all the Protestant missions in the North "deprecated the wearing of English dress by native Christians".

Such policy may have been born of sincerity, with the hope of preserving the spiritual purity of the church from the unsavory influences of coastal life. But the policy was short-sighted. Rowland Bingham saw that when he re-visited Nigeria.

"You may as well try to stop the tide coming in on the shore at Lagos," he told the missionaries. "Education is bound to come—your job is to channel it, to make sure it is Christ-centered." The early missionaries were zealous in winning souls to Christ, but some had forgotten that the next generation would have to live for Christ and spread His Word in a totally different Africa. Christian leadership had to be trained.

Realizing its initial short-sightedness, the Mission set up an education department, Christian schools, and a scholarship board to help worthy young men in preparation for Christian service. It can no longer be said that the Mission is neglecting education. Its schools have the highest standards and results in the North, and account for one-third of all Protestant education.

But there are two more factors today's young people should realize, the missionaries pointed out.

One was that denominational missions in the south have always reaped the benefit of progress from the coast, where people quickly embraced new ideas. The northern areas were often by-passed by colonial governments and by missions— partly because of the difficulty of living inland in the early days. When the SIM arrived it purposely passed by the areas already reached by missions and went inland, "not where Christ was named." They had to work against the opposition and conservatism of northern rulers, and overcome the lack of basic development of the area. The Mission in fact became "the development corporation" of many an area, as one African legislator recently put it, through the effects of the gospel.

The second factor was that denominational missions with church budgets often restrict their work to established areas, but invest more in those areas. The SIM, like most faith missions, has expanded to meet the needs of unreached areas even though it had no guaranteed budget. This meant that large funds simply were not available for doing all that some denominations could do in education, but it did mean that people like the northern Yorubas had received the gospel.

The pastors nodded their heads at this point. "I wish our teachers and students were here in this discussion," one said. "Then they would realize what the Mission is trying to do. We thank God that the gospel came to us."

"But I hear another common complaint from members of my church," spoke up a tall pastor in colorful robes. "My people say the missionaries of today are not like the missionaries of 25 years ago. They used to sit with the villagers; they were really part of the church. Now the new missionaries are too busy teaching and doing other things."

Here is a real problem, found in areas where the church has come of age, and where missionaries are more involved in the necessary work of training than of pioneering. New missionaries have trouble learning the language properly, because they are using English during the day teaching progressive young men and women. They are just as concerned about identifying themselves with the people as the early missionaries, but their ministry is different. The rural people notice the difference but don't understand the reason—they think the new missionaries don't really care about them.

Such criticism is hard for a doctor or nurse to take—after working long hours in the hot wards and operating room to save lives, then to be blamed for not spending time out in the villages. A teacher who works patiently all day with sometimes difficult students, and stays after school to mark their papers, is heart-broken to hear villagers say that he doesn't really love them, because he can't drop in any time of day like the early missionaries used to.

This problem requires communication and identification, and everywhere I went I met missionaries concerned about it. Specialists are needed for the gospel's outreach in the new Africa; the churches are constantly asking the Mission for them. Yet somehow they have to break down the impression of "professionalism."

The pastors mentioned other matters, like church-mission finances. How can missions help needy churches with projects without destroying indigenous principles and weakening Christian giving? Misunderstanding can arise here, as believers see a mission find funds for "mission" projects, but when the churches have similar projects which would advance the work, the mission can't help. To a national it looks like a form of apartheid. "That's your work, and this is ours," instead of saying, "This is the work of Jesus Christ—let's work together on it."

There were tears in the eyes of the missionaries and pastors as they realized how misunderstandings could arise over the best of intentions. They opened their hearts to each other in that conference, and the Holy Spirit drew them together in new understanding and fellowship. "The Spirit has poured water on the fire in our hearts," said an aged pastor who had seen the church take root and grow through early years of persecution. "We thank God for His working; we shall return to our people to help them understand the Lord's work better."

I, too, left the conference with a better understanding of the problems of church-mission relations, of the thinking of pastors, of the current problems missionaries face. Throughout the district I found teachers, nurses, doctors, technicians, and general missionaries devotedly sharing in "the care of the churches." Each one has a story I wish I had space to tell. But two diverse types taught me something about the kind of people God is using, and how He calls them.

Take Roger Anderson, for instance. School chaplain and a real "handy-man," he was servicing a vital water system for the Women's Teacher College at Woko when I met him. Roger's parents applied to the SIM 35 years ago but were turned down because of ill health. Before Roger was born, they dedicated him to be a missionary with the SIM in Nigeria, but they did not tell him, for they wanted God to call him. Roger went through school, finished with a major in Industrial Arts. The day Roger told his mother God had led him to apply to the SIM for service in Nigeria, she burst into tears and told him how she had prayed for that for 25 years.

Then there is James Kraakevik, B.S., Ph.D. When I saw him at Egbe, he was spending extra time with several sixth form boys in the science lab. Raised in a Christian home, Jim became a space research scientist with the U.S. Naval Research Laboratory in Washington, D.C. Later, while chairman of Wheaton's Department of Mathematics and Physics, he and his wife Marilyn felt the Lord wanted them to meet an urgent need at the SIM's Titcombe College for a year. Within two months they had packed outfits for themselves and their five children, rented their house, sold their car, and were in Nigeria.

This youthful research scientist found reaching African high school boys for Christ such a challenge that he stayed on to become acting principal of Titcombe College.

"Our friends thought we were crazy—and we had 101 questions," his wife Lynn told me. "But we're convinced we are in God's will. We worried specially about the boys' education, but they are well looked after at the Mission school—in fact, they figure they're lucky to get to study in a foreign land! Isn't it wonderful when you obey the Lord, how He works out the details?"

Jim had some penetrating thoughts on missionary adaptability: "I mean the ability to adjust to the local people, their different social and cultural standards—holding tenaciously to what is spiritually and morally absolute but exercising much give and take in what is culturally relative. In one's personal life, there must be a willingness to accept constantly-changing conditions. For me this has meant adapting to a more varied, sometimes menial, but really more meaningful life, than the specialized well-regulated one at home. Adaptability is indispensable for successful missionary service—and the best preparation, regardless of age, is having lived under the steady rule and discipline of a loving Lord."

Jim and Lynn Kraakevik demonstrated that, I felt. They were not just specialists; they were missionary specialists—the kind the young church needs.

As I saw the work in the Yoruba District, I wondered what would happen when a young church clashed with the deeply entrenched forces of evil surrounding it. I found out one Sunday, when a pastor asked me to preach in his church.

Over the past six months God had brought him and his members through an experience that had shaken the whole community. After the service the pastor asked if I had heard about the recent murder of one of the believers.

"Come and I'll show you the place," he volunteered. On the way he told me what had happened. One night lightning struck the hut of a village elder. The followers of the Thunder God said their god was angry and must be placated with a sacrifice, whom the god himself would claim.

The next night the fearsome whir of the cult whips sounded through the village, the signal that masqueraders—dressed to represent ancestral spirits—were around, and no woman must venture outside. Amid drumming and dancing they placed a fetish on a path leading to the village. The next night, a 30-year-old Christian walked along that path on his way home, accompanied by a relative. At a lonely spot surrounded by trees, 10 men sprang out and knocked him to the ground. The relative begged them to let their victim go, but the cult thugs dragged him to a nearby house. There they pierced holes under his eyes and ears to drain the blood for a libation.

"See?" the pastor pointed as we reached the spot. "Here is the path, there is the house, and over here is the deep hole where they threw the man's body. As soon as the relative told us what happened, we called the police and searched everywhere until we found the body down in here. In the past the cult leaders haven't been afraid of being caught—they are so powerful they have been able to cover up any evidence. But this time the Christians rose up in a body and said it was the end of their evil work. We had the body and other evidence."

Every Christian in the area met at the church. From there 400 marched to the fetish house and smashed it to pieces. The pastor took us to the site. The roofing lay around in twisted sheets; the mud walls were broken down. We could look right through the shrine and see bones hanging from a sacred bush in the middle. Scattered around were pieces of the ritual drums and carved panel doors from the main entrance. With the entire Christian populace aroused, no cult member dared put a hand even to clearing up the debris.

The Christians reported to the District Officer in the provincial capital, himself a believer. He had seven men arrested and committed for trial. Later I visited the D.O., who told me, "Without the Christians, these men might not have been apprehended." He allowed me to see the seven men awaiting trial. They were between 40 and 65 years of age. One was small and wizened, with a short white beard. Another had a pock-marked face. Their hardened, evil eyes narrowed as they looked at me with suspicion. The warder interpreted for me as I gave them the simple story of Christ's sacrifice for sin and His love for sinners.

"We thank God for the power of the gospel, which has saved us from doing this type of thing," the pastor told me. Fourteen members of the secret society had been converted, including the leader for the area. Church attendance had increased by 25 percent. What impressed me most was not the ritual murder. That was committed out of fear by misguided, superstitious men, and therefore made more sense than the inane killing of 14 people by a university student in the United States, reported around the same time. What was most significant was that in the lives of these believers the gospel had triumphed over evil, and there was a strong voice immediately raised against the works of the devil.

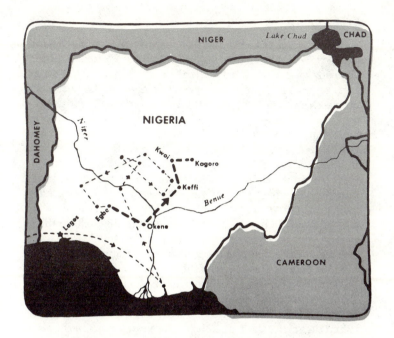

7. School for Headhunters' Children

My safari now took me by road northeast through the heart of Nigeria, my goal being Jos on the lofty central plateau. It was through country men feared to traverse in Bingham's day.

Before crossing the Niger, we stopped at Okene, center of the 300,000 Igbirra people. They are isolated from their Yoruba neighbors by volcanic ridges. In 1953 the Mission moved in, the first task being to translate the Scriptures into Igbirra.

The SIM's five-bed maternity center handles an average of 30 deliveries a month. I saw one patient with a hemoglobin blood count of only 18 (instead of 100). Her skin was yellow instead of brown. She should have been dead, according to the books. Anemia is the most common ailment among Africa's mothers, resulting in abortion and death. It is often caused by intestinal parasites and by tribal taboos which forbid an expectant mother taking meat, eggs, cheese or milk—just when she needs extra protein. Malnutrition among both mothers and babies is increased by the rigid custom of breast-feeding infants for two years. A local Igbirra treatment supposed to ensure fertility and childbirth has the opposite effect instead: it is a strong caustic mixture which leaves extensive burns.

Driving toward the Niger River we passed through steaming rain forests, where twisted vines looped like festive garlands from palm to mahogany to teak trees. Lush ferns and "elephant ears" graced their feet. As the car wound along the trail we caught the cries of forest birds and the warm smell of the forest gratefully responding to a gentle rain. A stalwart farmer, his muscled torso glistening from the sweat of hoeing yams, walked home, a short hand-hoe hooked over his shoulder.

In Nigeria there are two bridges across the Niger, 350 miles apart. We crossed the half-mile-wide river about half-way between them, on a flat barge pushed by a small tug. On the other side we headed on to Keffi, one of those mission stations where the results are out of all proportion to the investment of personnel.

Down in Lagos I had met Christian students at the University and other colleges who told me they found the Lord at Keffi Government College. The name Kleinsasser kept coming up. Now I met the man behind the long name—a prematurely gray extrovert who talked with a lecturer's vigor. Virgil taught the Scriptures to 380 students at the high school and teacher training college. His wife, Edna, had classes in government primary schools.

The 600 post-primary students from all over Nigeria soon got to know Kleinsasser—who was accepted as one of the faculty but didn't draw a salary. Five of them dropped in for lime juice and a singsong around the Kleinsassers' folding pump organ the afternoon we were there. Virgil and Edna reap a harvest through these contacts—40 professions in the last term. Converts become active witnesses among Muslim students and teach Sunday School classes in the town on weekends.

Virgil keeps track of those who make profession after the students leave Keffi—or rather, they want to keep in touch with him. One boy who got a good job in a bank sent his tithe each month to help the ECWA church in Keffi. When he gave up his job to train as a pastor at Igbaja, Virgil sent some of his own tithe to help support him. When the chapel needed a roof, Virgil let 40 former Christian students know—they sent in enough money to put on the roof.

A Christian lecturer at Ibadan University traveled 363 miles to see the Kleinsassers. "I just wanted to tell you that Christian students from here are the spiritual leaders at Ibadan," he said.

"We were feeling a little sorry for ourselves last week," Edna told me, "because we couldn't be home for the graduation of our daughter. But the Lord encouraged us through several letters that came from past students—some in overseas universities."

Perhaps the most encouraging letter came from a Nigerian Army officer serving in the Congo: "I told my soldiers how I was saved at Keffi 10 years ago, and I sang a hymn for them. Tell the students there that only Christ can give us strength in the difficult situations our country faces. I plead with them to accept Him as Saviour!"

Turning north we reached Kwoi, which in 1910 represented a daring advance "into the interior" before the British administration had officially declared the area safe for travelers. The Holy Spirit worked—and I saw His working still, over half a century later.

The missionaries took me to see an aged villager who was just one week old in the Lord. He hobbled out of his smoky hut, a hand clenched on a gnarled staff, and showed us the town's fetish rocks. Until last week he had been one of the fetish leaders, worshiping the spirits in the flat, six-foot-tall rocks which supposedly walk around the village at night.

The old man showed us the scars on his arms from tribal warfare. He had seen the first missionaries arrive, and he remembered how the villagers looked on as one pioneer buried his bride of 18 months.

"Now," they said, "we'll see if what he preaches is true. He says Christians will rise from the dead!" When the missionary's body stayed in the ground, they called the bereaved husband a liar and refused to listen to him any more.

But for nearly 60 years the Spirit patiently wooed this pagan. A week ago when his Christian son once more witnessed to him, he said, "Yes, I will believe." It was a big decision at the end of a man's life; he would forego all the pagan death rites, including the prestigious post-mortem bean feast in his honor. But the patience of God had been victorious. The old man now looked forward to the resurrection.

To train Kwoi Christians for service and leadership, there are now the Kwoi Bible School, a Girls' Secondary School, and a Christian Training Institute, where boys and girls too old to enter high school can get practical training.

The early missionaries at Kwoi had heard much about a ferocious tribe of headhunters living on a rocky promontory of the central plateau. European travelers were warned to carry arms when in the Kagoro area. This was a challenge to the missionaries and national believers. Young Tom and Grace Archibald trekked 37 miles to Kagoro for short visits, finally went to live there in 1927. They carried the Word of God, not firearms. At first the people wouldn't listen to them or sell them food.

One day the witch doctor was forced by pain to ask if Tom could pull a rotten tooth. Tom took it out with a pair of pliers. Then the word got around: "The white man can take out teeth without making your face swell up!" (Until then sore teeth were levered out with an arrow head, badly infecting the gum.) After that Tom was busy pulling teeth and preaching the gospel.

One of the little boys who heard Tom preach was Gwamna.

He believed the gospel and today is the respected Christian chief of Kagoro, an orderly community of 5,000. His jurisdiction extends over a wider area with a population of 30,000. The gospel revolutionized a tribe of headhunters in one short generation, and today Kagoro, peacefully nestling at the foot of a granite escarpment overlooking fertile plains, is a center of progress and education.

Decorated by the Queen of England and made a life-time member of her Privy Council, sought after by Muslim leaders for his advice on non-Islamic matters, Chief Gwamna Awan, M.B.E., is nevertheless a humble believer who gathers his family for Bible reading and prayer each evening.

"Forty years ago we lived in complete darkness," he told me. "Eight out of 10 babies died. No one could read. Our one thought was warfare. Now look at us. Our people are clothed and gentle. They are leaders in other communities. Fewer than two out of 10 babies die. You will even find pagans copying the way of living of the Christians, because the light of Jesus is strong. That is what the Bible says—'If any man be in Christ, he is a new creature.'

"We are grateful to God and to His messengers who came to us. Please tell the supporters overseas who helped them come, and who are praying for them and us—we are grateful to God for them too. Tell them to send others to help train our young men to take the light to other areas."

On an office wall in town I saw a large calendar published by the Kagoro Progressive Union. A bold-faced notice on it proclaimed:

KAGORO ENLIGHTENMENT DAY

'A day in May each year shall be observed by all Kagoro as being the Kagoro Day. This Day reflects the day when light was brought into Kagoro by the first missionary, Mr. Archibald, that's in May 1927. There shall be activities to commemorate the Day, as shall be deemed fit.

Although others were now leading the work, pioneer Archibald was still there, aged 70. He gave me a guided tour in his Land-Rover, punctuating everything he said with a finger jabbing the air while we bounced through mudholes. It is less than 40 years since the Archibalds saw their first convert at Kagoro, but the town is now a major center for preparing men and women to take the gospel to others. The white-haired veteran showed me the Teachers' College, where students support six African missionaries, the Hausa Bible College, and the Girls' Hausa Bible School. We also saw the busy dispensary—the major reason for the big drop in infant mortality mentioned by Chief Gwamna.

Four miles away is the SIM's new Kagoro Secondary School. Although the first class had completed its course only the year before, it had the highest results ever achieved by any high school in the North—a result of the devotion and hard work of missionary and Nigerian staff. However, shortage of missionary teachers made it necessary to use some young African teachers lacking the maturity needed to cope with the high-spirited boys.

As we drove up to the school, a national teacher was being taken to the hospital. He had become mentally unbalanced, temporarily, through an overdose of anti-malarial medicine with which he had treated himself, and had to be held back from climbing over the front seat. Part of his problem was extreme tension—not unusual among people leaping 100 years in a dozen years of schooling.

It is difficult for students to bridge the gap between the old village life and the new world of science. Most have no science background; they have never played with a mechanical toy, nor turned the leaves of a book until they go to school. At school they do not read for pleasure nor even for the satisfaction of enlarging their knowledge; the only motive seems to be to pass the next test. Only 12 students bought copies of the *National Geographic* magazine when a teacher offered 60 for sale at two pennies each. He put a nominal price on them to make sure they wouldn't be thrown away.

I met a fifth-year student who had not been doing well the previous year. He blamed it on the fact that his father, a church elder, had not followed the tribal custom of cutting out his uvula as an infant. After having the throat operation secretly performed in town, he rushed to the school nurse, afraid he was bleeding to death. When I saw him his grades still had not improved.

Newspapers sometimes report a student's going insane after drinking a potion bought from a local "medicine man," to give added brain power for examinations.

In the context of these schoolboy attitudes throughout the nation, a Christian school like Kagoro Secondary has strategic potential. At a recent school conference 23 boys gave their lives to Christ.

Kagoro is an up-to-date demonstration of what the gospel can do—not only in the life of an old pagan or a spirited young student, but also in an entire community, a tribe, a people. Everything, from the size of their huts to the manner of farming, from delivering a baby to burying a grandfather—everything has felt some influence of the new life in Christ Jesus.

The future spread of the gospel will not be uncontested. There was pagan opposition before; now it will be Islamic. Traveling through the North I had heard about the crusade for Islam by a prominent politician. At Kagoro I got more details.

The uncommitted pagan tribes lying between the Islamic north and the nominally Christian coast are termed the Middle Belt. They had generally been bypassed in the strategy of British administration, which favored Muslim chieftaincies as a useful means of indirect rule. For the gospel, the Middle Belt had been the most productive area in the North. To Muslims, the remaining uncommitted animists are a promising field.

As he had done in many other parts of the Middle Belt, a political leader sent a message to the chiefs of the Kagoro area saying he was going to visit their people, and he wanted all the population to turn out. Word passed around the countryside that pagan religions were to be outlawed, and that everyone must choose to be either Muslim or Christian. It was implied that Muslim officials would more readily grant such amenities as post office, dispensary, and more schools to an Islamic community. And how else could one expect promotion and position in a predominantly Islamic land? Besides, wasn't Islam much easier to follow than the strict Christian religion? A polygamist could keep at least four wives after becoming a Muslim.

The believers around Kagoro met for a whole week of prayer prior to the politician's visit. They had heard reports over the government radio station telling of thousands turning to Islam after the politician's visit to other towns—although some of the reports belied themselves by listing more converts than an area had population. They knew that beads, robes, and promises had been handed out to these people. One bed-ridden Christian had heard the politician himself talking to Muslims over the radio when he thought all Christians would be at church on Sunday morning, explaining plans to spread the Islamic faith. So in prayer they committed all this to the Lord and waited to see Him work.

The day arrived, and the politician's entourage drove into the village. The chief, his councillors, and the mission school-children politely greeted him. The students sang a hymn after the national anthem.

The politician spoke to the people about the day of progress. Finally he came to the matter of religion. Paganism was back-wardness, he told them. Every pagan must decide whether to be a Muslim or Christian.

"The Christians have their way," he continued, "but the way of truth is Islam. The Koran is the Word of God. All who wish to follow the way of truth, cross over to my right hand. All who wish to follow the Christians, remain on my left hand."

A handful of pagans walked over to the right under the appreciative gaze of the political leader. But that was all. There was no pre-primed mass "conversion" as there had been in many towns through the Middle Belt. The politician looked crestfallen. At last he stalked over to his waiting limousine.

As the population watched him get in, the car suddenly burst into flames. The politician leapt out just in time. It was unaccountable—no one had been near the vehicle, except his driver and personal bodyguard. And yet it *was* accountable, as far as the people of Kagoro were concerned. As the politician drove off in another car, leaving his limousine a charred pile, they talked quietly to one another about the One who sits in the heavens and vindicates His name.

Within six months the politician died.

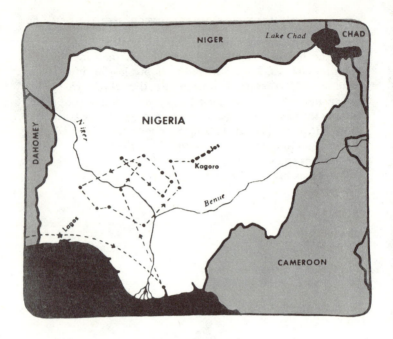

8. Beehive on a Plateau

Forty miles from Kagoro the road starts winding up through a pass on to Nigeria's central plateau, over 4,000 feet above sea level. It is a different world up on top. The scrub-covered hills and the sultry oppressiveness of the lower country suddenly give way to grassy plains swept by light breezes. Little wonder that Europeans take their annual leave up in the highlands if possible.

Giants undoubtedly once played here, I thought, using mammoth boulders for play blocks. Scattered around on the plains are granite rocks balanced in fantastic piles; it amazed me that some of them didn't topple over. There are also man-made giants around—tall mechanical shovels standing against the skyline, surrounded by dumps of earth. They mark the site of tin and columbite mines. The plateau is the world's biggest producer of columbite, used in hardening metals for jet engines.

The miners created the town of Jos, attracting people from all over the North to work in the mines, sell to the workers, repair their clothes and shoes, write in the miners' ledgers, teach school, and live with their relatives. Jobless boys wander the streets stealing mangoes (peach flavor, plum texture) from lush trees planted by thoughtful British officials.

On the mowed lawns of Hill Station—a government hotel with the atmosphere of an English country inn—you can relax among poinsettias and fragrant frangipani. But across the granite rocks in the milling town, you see a different world. Macabre vultures perch like bundles of burnt newspapers on the roofs of market stalls, watching for offal to pounce on. Butchers sell meat which still quivers (or is that caused by the swarms of flies?) at around 28 cents a pound—a price set by printed order of the town council's chief butcher. The hitch is that scales cannot be found anywhere; the butchers make money by guessing the weight on the high side.

In the market I could buy nearly anything—from scarce car parts to dried monkey skulls for fetish "medicine." One trader sold rolls of colorful floor linoleum; at the next stall a man had piles of old bottles and tins, which housewives bought for food containers. A Hausa dandy was having his fingernails manicured by a man with a chewing stick protruding from his mouth. Smoke rose from the head of a woman having her hair straightened with a sizzling hot comb.

Beggars held out their hands for alms. Some had their limbs bent backwards; I was not able to verify the report that this is done to unwanted children by parents, to give them a profitable means of livelihood through begging. A man was selling magic rings which could protect from all danger. To prove it, an accomplice "bought" one and then chewed up a razor blade and let two large scorpions crawl over him.

"Op art" seems to come naturally here. The Coal Corporation boasts a cement-block facade painted in horizontal bars of jet black and fire-engine red, with doors in Nigeria's flag colors of vertical green and white bands. Next door a bottled gas company shop is painted in vertical blue and white stripes.

Jos became West Africa headquarters for the SIM in 1921, after continued illness among missionaries in the lowlands made it necessary to have a center where they could find some relief. The area also became central to the whole work as stations opened further east and north.

The United States' Ambassador dropped in at SIM HQ one day, and I joined in a quick tour of the buildings covering two city blocks.

"This is his first visit to the North," the Consul leaned over to explain. "I want him to see for himself that your Mission is no fly-by-night outfit. You know how it is . . . no matter how many reports you read, you can never really grasp the magnitude of a work until you see it."

See it we did. Signs on office doors read: Director, Secretary, Treasurer, Education Secretary, Medical Secretary, Publications Secretary, Bookshop General Manager, plus assistants and secretaries.

We saw the ELWA Recording Studio (for Nigerian languages), the Guest House (gratefully used by a number of missions), Bingham Memorial Hospital (assignment: keep the missionary team operating in top gear), Headquarters Pharmacy (last year handled $200,000 worth of medicines for hospitals and dispensaries), Business Department (supplies building materials and groceries for other stations), Bookshop and Literature Mail Order Department. In other parts of the city are Evangel Hospital, the Dental Clinic, SIM Medical Auxiliary Training School, Aviation Department, and High School Hostel.

After that whirl, as the Ambassador was leaving, the Consul whispered, "He's convinced!"

I went back to some of the departments to ask questions.

In Sudan, the author's boat glides past Shilluk villages along the Nile.

Sudanese young people enjoy a game after an SIM Bible study in Khartoum.

Incredible Safari: East Africa

A typical Dinka
village on the Nile.

Charcoal on the way
to market.

The road across the
Nilotic plains.

In Ethiopia, young "deacons" of the Orthodox Church use ornate umbrellas to shade a sacred picture and ceremonial cross during public procession.

Africa Hall, Addis Ababa, Ethiopia—headquarters of the Organization of African Unity.

Haile Selassie I, Emperor of Ethiopia.

Ethiopian Airlines flew author Fuller to Bulki airstrip in 45 minutes. From there to the mission station took four hours by muleback.

Bulki station, deep in the mountains of southern Ethiopia, is the center of a flourishing spiritual movement.

A Tigre family of northern Ethiopia. The wife's ornaments are gold.

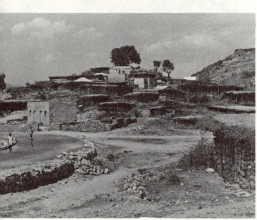

Typical village of stone houses in Eritrea province of Ethiopia.

The primitive balsa-like canoes of Gidicho island, southern Ethiopia.

A Wallamo believer gives what she can—her boots.

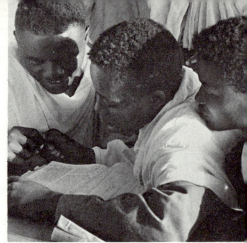

Young Wallamo men listen to a school friend read from the Bible, available only in the Amharic language.

Meeting at the annual conference, Wallamo believers greet each other in warm Ethiopian manner, exchanging kisses on the cheek.

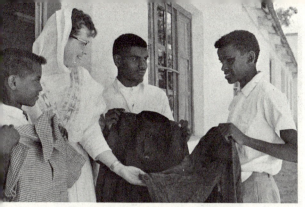

Students at Decamere Waifs' Home show Laura Steele the clothes she has taught them to make. Boy on right has only one hand.

Village elders look on approvingly as Ethiopian schoolboys explain their books.

Children at SIM's Durami school start the day with the national anthem.

Ethiopian student

Gujji woman

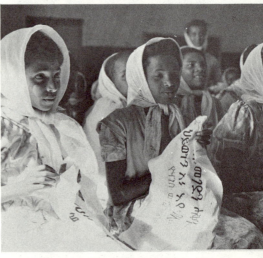

Bible classes and sewing lessons go together at Asmara.

Ernie Giles in the science room of the SIM's first Teacher Training School in Ethiopia, at Wando. Stuffed birds on the wall are his hobby.

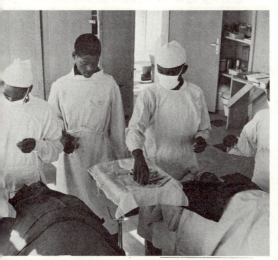

Orthodox priest

Amhara landowner

Supervised by skilled senior assistants, Ethiopian trainees at Soddo Hospital do eyelid operations.

Students at Grace Bible College, Jimma, receive advanced Bible training.

George Middleton discusses the gospel with students from government schools at Jimma, which has one of Ethiopia's largest student populations.

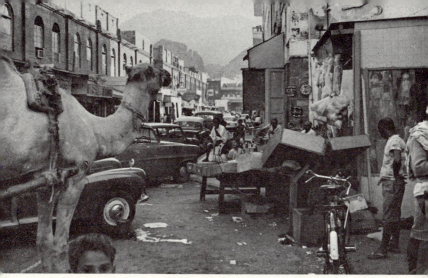

Crowded side street in the Crater district of Aden, in South Arabia.

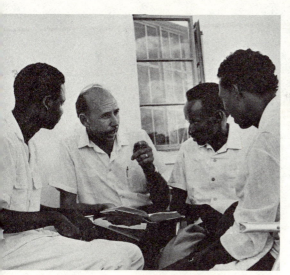

Adeni Arab

Howard Borlase gives young Somali believers intensive personal instruction in the Scriptures.

John Miller conducts typing class in Mogadishu, Somali Republic.

Muslim Somali woman with netting veiling her face waits for traffic signal.

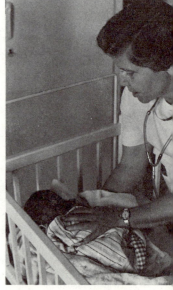

Dr. JoAnne Ader checks new arrival at Bulo Burti, Somalia.

How many missionaries are assigned to West Africa? Around 800—with one-fifth on furlough at any time. How many "stations"? One hundred and eight, in six countries. No wonder these central services and administration are needed.

I collected more statistics from the Publications Department and Bookshop. Last year the SIM distributed in Nigeria the equivalent of two million six-penny (10 cent) pieces of gospel literature through 26 bookshops, nine bookmobiles, five literature evangelists, and by mail order. Publications Secretary Phil Osbourne told me the Mission has published in 41 West African languages.

Medical Secretary Ken Tracey showed me a list of eight hospitals, 76 dispensaries (22 operated by ECWA churches) and eight leprosaria. SIM has had more leprosy patients under treatment than any other single organization in the world, but recently the government has been taking more responsibility for leprosy patients.

Doctor shortage is the biggest problem—a problem in every newly developing nation. Whereas doctor-population ratio is one to 790 in America, and one to 730 in West Germany, Nigeria's is one to 35,000. Since most government doctors like to stay in the big centers, there are areas where the ratio is actually one to 100,000.

An interesting sidelight on the doctor shortage is the large number of leprosy patients who cannot be discharged because there is no doctor to examine and declare them symptom free. But no one seems to mind. The patients are happy—it means another year of living in better conditions than at home. Some ask to stay and even build huts near the leprosarium after discharge; they might not be allowed back in their villages anyway. And missionaries are glad that patients will have longer to hear the gospel.

The SIM Medical Auxiliary Training School (SIMMATS) in Jos is a wise investment for the future, training young men as dispensary and lab attendants. But SIMMATS does more than train them medically. In areas of rapid change, corruption is the most prevalent disease. Medicines regularly disappear from government hospitals and turn up for sale in the markets.

Leprosy, I was told, could be eradicated with the new sulphone drugs, but because of corruption people are not being properly treated, and leprosy may actually increase. One million tablets for leprosy treatment were missing from a government supply of six million. These can be bought on the blackmarket by people ashamed to come for treatment; but improper dosage can cause insanity or death.

Peasants bribe sleeping sickness teams *not* to inoculate them, for fear of being stigmatized as a sick person. Injections for cattle are free, but some teams touring the country charge a shilling a head.

To strengthen their medical students against corruption and to prepare them as witnesses wherever they go, one-third of the SIMMATS course is spent in Bible study. This builds moral character, and as a result these men are in high demand.

One student really integrated the medical and devotional aspects when he led his class in prayer: "Lord, this medical course is not easy. Help our cranial cavities." He was quite serious; after all, the teacher had told them to make use of the medical terms they learned.

Students write some interesting answers to test questions:

It is more dangerous to die in an automobile accident than in an operating room.
TB is liable to cause miscarriage, especially in pregnant women.
A monk is a person who goes into seclusion to medicate.

Not only medical students have trouble with the confusing English language. The Education Department once received an invoice for a school's new generating plant, across which the Customs Department had marked, "Bicycles—60 percent duty." Since school equipment is duty free, Education Secretary Howard Dowdell protested, explaining that it was not a shipment of bicycles anyway. The Customs officer disagreed, took him to the warehouse, and showed him the generator's huge packing case clearly marked: 60 CYCLES.

I had seen many schools on my way up from the coast, but the Education Department helped me to understand the overall picture. In the North, one-third of all education has been carried on by Protestant missions. Although Northern Nigeria is only three percent Christian, the Christian student enrollment in government post-primary schools is 50 percent, and in the university is 85 percent. SIM/ECWA institutions have 27,785 Nigerian students enrolled in 133 primary schools, six high schools, four teacher training colleges, and several Bible and special schools. The Christian Education Office prepares material for day schools as well as Sunday schools, youth groups, and church fellowships—materials designed to relate scriptural truths to daily living.

All the teachers I talked with were thrilled with the opportunity for the gospel through the schools; their only complaint was the shortage of staff. It is not an opportunity without its problems. Education in a rapidly developing country holds amazing contradictions and frustrations. Awakened youth clamors for the chance to enter school. Each year the SIM gives an entrance examination for mission/church institutions. Last year only 1,025 places were available, but 20,000 boys and girls took the examination. When a government technical institute invited applications to fill 100 classroom seats, 18,000 young people applied, some camping on the streets for a week to try to get in.

A degree is almost worshipped, and even failing a degree examination carries prestige. I saw a sign on a shop: "Proprietor Samuel Oko, B.A. (Failed)." Total enrolment in Nigeria's five universities is under 10,000 but 25,000 Nigerians are studying in overseas institutions.

In spite of the stiff competition to get into a school, once a student is there he acts as if he had been paid to enrol. And he may well have been. Because the nation wants to develop rapidly and can't wait for lads to work their way through school, in some cases it pays all their bills and gives them pocket money besides; 40 percent of Nigeria's budget is spent on education. A student is singled out from thousands in his community; he has new liberties and vistas, and doesn't know their limits. The world is at his feet. So he may demonstrate or riot on the slightest pretext. Probably every post-primary institution—government or mission—has had a student revolt. Now educators have caught on. They simply close the school or the offending class and make the students sign a form of repentance before they can get back in. The young kings are quickly cut down to size.

In a newspaper I saw an interesting indication of students' feeling that the rest of the world owes them an education—prepaid. One hundred Nigerians on scholarships from the African-American Institute received their Bachelor's degrees. They then demanded that the AAI, a philanthropic organization, finance them to get their M.A. and Doctorate degrees over another three to four years. When the AAI explained that finances had to be shared with other countries needing scholarships, the students were furious and planned a "march on Washington." Shouted one: "To ask me to return to Nigeria with only the Bachelor's degree is to nip my talent in the mud" (sic).

Student ungratefulness can embitter an educator, but the missionary teacher has to remember that he might think the same if he came from a similar background. He has to swallow hard, smile, and plow ahead with his opportunities for turning bumptious spirits into Christian character.

I learned something which few people realize. The Nigerian government gives salary grants for teachers in recognized schools, but missionary teachers turn in every penny of their grants to help finance other Christian education projects. They live on a missionary allowance. So a B.Sc. missionary teacher, for instance, not only teaches Nigerian schoolboys but also helps finance the training of pastors, or a scholarship to prepare a Christian teacher for future leadership, or a dozen other projects. It has been a marvelous provision for a lot of gospel work. I sat in on a committee meeting where these funds were allocated. The only problem was that needs for finances were double the funds available—and many urgent requests had to be turned down.

A Bible School Coordinator administers the SIM Bible training program for West Africa. Nineteen vernacular Bible training institutes in seven languages, three Bible colleges in English, and a Seminary train men at different levels from lay evangelism to theology degree.

Jos is also headquarters for the Association of Evangelical Churches of West Africa (ECWA). The church leadership faces an exacting task of trying to bring about a sense of oneness among 300,000 adherents in 900 churches spread over an area of 356,000 square miles. These churches support 89 African missionary families in their Evangelical Missionary Society.

Nigerian pastor, David Ishola Olatayo told me how church/Mission partnership worked. "It's like a child and an adult," he explained. "The child needs the adult to reach the cookie jar on the top shelf, but the adult needs the child to put his small hand inside the jar to bring out the food."

I saw the Mission and church working together during the West Africa Council meetings, held twice a year. Looking on from the walls of the council room were photographs of the four General Directors of the Mission since its inception: (1) founder Rowland V. Bingham, 1893–1942; (2) Guy W. Playfair, a relentless warrior who saw the missionary force grow from 385 to 1,260 during his years in office from 1942 to 1957; (3) Albert D. Helser, 1957 to 1962, a remarkable Ph.D. who probably shook more hands in Africa than any other missionary; (4) Raymond J. Davis, who started out as a general missionary in Ethiopia in 1934, helped develop a boys' home and school in Northern Nigeria after the Italians ousted missionaries from Ethiopia, became West Africa Director in 1952, and General Director in 1962.

The 16 men seated around the table made an interesting cross-section of missionary life and work. Their average age was 46, with an average 21 years of service in Africa. At one time they had been a dentist, printer, engineer, pastor, home missionary, sailor, telephone linesman, salesman, jewel setter, farmer, and journalist. In Africa their work included medicine, linguistics, radio, teaching, trekking, evangelism, and administration. These men were elected by missionaries to represent their districts on the Council.

West Africa Director Bill Crouch chaired the session. Bill came out in 1938 armed with a Bachelor of Theology degree, a tropical medicine injection permit, and the ability to see things from the other man's viewpoint. The last time Bill and his wife Edith returned from furlough, they both knew it might be at the cost of Edith's life—she had suffered many years from a heart condition.

"But I won't be any worse than if I stay at home," Edith insisted, "and we're needed back in Africa." She died six months after they got back. At her funeral, a Nigerian pastor said, "If another chapter is ever added to the Bible in heaven, Mrs. Crouch's name should be included."

The Council members waded through discussions which included the expansion of Radio ELWA to reach the Arab world, how to interest doctors in missionary service, overall strategy for the work in changing conditions, the need for spiritual revival, youth centers to reach urban youth, liberal ecumenical pressures—and the request of an elderly missionary to be allowed to stay in Nigeria. All her ties were there, she said, and anyway, "funerals cost much less than at home."

Each of the nine days of sitting began with one-and-a-half hours of Bible meditation and prayer. During discussions of problems, a member would sometimes open his Bible and say, "Let's see what the Word says about that." These were spiritual leaders seeking the leading of the Holy Spirit in His work in Africa.

Seated with his fellow church executive members around

the council tables was a 58-year-old Nigerian, Gin Maigari, then President of ECWA. He had come to the Lord as a lad at Kwoi 35 years before and had since preached his heart out in the villages of the North. He put before the Council the needs of ECWA for missionary assistance. But as the Council went over the list of needs and personnel, there was no one available. The list had to be stretched to meet the most urgent needs, and still there were hospitals understaffed, school teachers overworked, stations that would have to be closed.

I watched pastor Gin's head sink lower and lower. I knew he was thinking of the tiny, struggling groups of Christians dotted across Africa, surrounded by hostile forces. He thought of their poverty, of their struggle to support pastors and evangelists, to build churches, to provide Christian education for their children in the face of paganism and Islam, to train their young men in the Word.

Then he must have thought of the churches overseas—rich in trained sons and daughters, rich in experience, rich in resources. I had heard African church leaders visiting overseas countries express amazement at meeting so many Christian men and women already trained as teachers and nurses and doctors. It is incomprehensible to them that there isn't an army of volunteers coming out to help the young churches of Africa in their need.

Tears spilled out of pastor Gin's eyes. He rubbed his hands over his face and sat looking down at his list of needs. He wasn't blaming anyone; he had often expressed gratefulness to God for all that missionaries had done in his land. But the size of the task and the shortage of help were too much for him. "God help us!" he said softly. "God help us!"

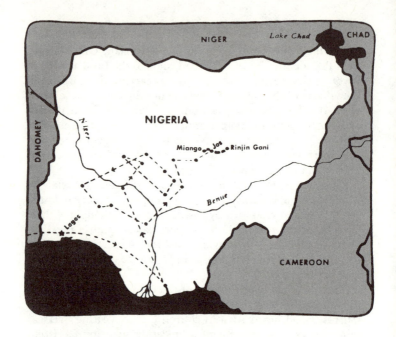

9. Heroes Without Haloes

Jos is a kind of missionary Grand Central Station, with all
kinds of people passing through. As I walked across the compound one day I noticed a pair of boots sticking out from under
a four-ton mechanical monster. The boots belonged to Harry
Elyea. He was repairing his home-made mobile house—"a
twentieth-century covered wagon, pioneering for the Lord
Jesus," he told me. He and his family make forays out from
Bursali into extremely hard Muslim areas, "gossiping" the
Word while they give emergency injections, pull teeth, deliver
babies, and teach elementary hygiene.

"It's tough slugging," said Harry as he wiped grease off his
chin. "But it's rewarding—like two weeks ago when a man

knocked at our back door at night and said he wanted to follow Jesus. He's taking lots of ridicule, but standing true."

Helen Griffin, most of five feet tall and aged 66, was climbing aboard a Land-Rover which boldly proclaimed in red letters, in Hausa: "Jesus Christ Is the Only Way to God." Friends were driving her to the end of the road at a river, she explained. She would then walk nine miles, sleep overnight in a village hut, and next day walk the other nine miles to her station, Gure.

"That's the best I can do these days," she apologized. "I used to be able to do the 18 miles in one day." The day before, she had sent a message by radio (the SIM makes daily radio contact with isolated stations), asking her evangelist to have load carriers at the river, "with my blanket and kettle." A nurse who arrived in Nigeria in 1927, she is one of those pioneers who doesn't want to go home—not even for furlough—and the Africans don't want her to leave, either.

Outside the Business Department an employee was trying to show a new laborer how to move a big packing case by using a two-wheeled cart. The man wanted to carry the case on his head. When at last he saw how easily it could be handled on wheels, he said in Hausa, "Surely cleverness is greater than strength!"

A carpenter gripped a board by placing one leg across it, and worked with the saw straight up and down, teeth away from him. I tried it, and found it was actually easier to follow a straight line that way. The wood was hard, beautiful *mahogany* —used for making anything from chairs to fence posts because the termites won't eat it, and it doesn't cost much.

That night I came across the Pharmacy's night watchman, a most necessary defense in a mining town. He was a colorful figure in a Hausa cloth cap, a woman's secondhand Persian Lamb winter coat (used clothing is big business in Africa), with his bow, arrows, and spear propped at his feet. He was occupying his time by drawing a lion on a piece of cardboard box. I asked him about all the cars parked on the other street. "Ah!"

he shook his head, "that's the white man's fetish house. The Europeans go there to drink beer, dance, and make witchcraft. Very bad." I later learned that the place was the local European club!

On Sunday night we had special prayer during the chapel service. John Ockers had rushed down from Niger Republic to the bedside of his wife, Evelyn, dying of jaundice and kidney complications. John was in the service as Dr. Jeanette Troup sang a meaningful solo: *"No one understands like Jesus."* Here was a doctor whose spiritual ministry to the Mission family was just as real as her medical ministry. Evelyn passed away next morning.

It was evident that the Mission constitutes a great family. The lives of missionaries are enriched by working together with others from 13 different nations and at least 23 different church backgrounds. This follows the pattern God gave SIM founder Rowland Bingham: "Our fellowship must be on horizontal, not vertical lines."

The result has been a great gospel advance which could never have been if the founders had waited for one denomination to do it. This is the Body of Christ at work—international and inter-denominational. Yet it is not "ecumenical" in the liberal sense of any compromise of fundamental theological views. The SIM has remained true to God's Word in doctrine and practice.

Just about now I can almost hear someone say, "So the SIM is one big happy family! But if I know human nature, it can't be *that* good. Didn't you meet any problem types?"

Yes I did—only they weren't the ones who made the greatest impression. Living with missionaries soon takes the halo off their heads. You find out they are real people. I saw two or three blow up—but apologize after. I saw some discouraged, critical, complaining. A few were built that way; they were the same before they came to Africa. Others were that way because they had been up for the past three nights trying to keep a new mother alive, or because they had filaria, or because they needed a furlough.

I saw selfishness, pride, comfort-seeking, lack of cooperation, self-will, cantankerousness, inconsiderateness. I guess I saw all the same human foibles which were in quarrelling Paul and Barnabas, in pig-headed Peter, in hot-eyed James and John Zebedee.

I saw that missionaries aren't made by crossing the sea. Missionaries are not born. They are made in the crucible of service; by the school of God's discipline; by running while the sun is hot. Those who turn out to be real missionaries are those who stick it out long enough to go through as many fiery furnaces as God sees they need.

The missionary halo may slip, but that halo should not be there in the first place. An ordinary Christian goes to do the Lord's work in another land and immediately becomes the epitome of sainthood: "So you're a *missionary!*"

The result is that we set the missionary up on a pedestal and don't pray for him as if he were human with mortal foibles. And we become terribly disillusioned if he suffers spiritual defeat or acts like a cantankerous church member at home.

In place of artificial missionary haloes, I would place something else on the heads of the missionaries I met. I'd place laurel wreaths—the hard-won laurels of victory. These are laurels won by very ordinary people in the face of every human weakness within and every diabolical plan of Satan without. They are won because of godly determination, perseverance, courage, obedience, and often sacrifice. In place of adulation for haloes I developed admiration for heroes—laurel winners —of the cross.

Talking of laurels, I think most missionaries would place them on the missionary staff at Miango, 23 miles from Jos. Their work isn't spectacular, but that is just the point. They have the untrumpeted task of looking after the children of missionaries at Kent Academy and of operating a rest home so that missionaries can be refreshed and do a better job back on their stations.

I drove out to Miango and found Jack Phillips, principal of Kent Academy, looking somewhat bedraggled in the middle of the playground, with 239 boys and girls between the ages of six and 14, running in every direction.

"Term's just started," explained Jack. "The last batch of kids came in this afternoon."

One little tyke got off to a bad start. He stood beside his empty wardrobe drawers in the dormitory, crying because his trunk hadn't arrived. "I only have pajamas to wear!" he sobbed.

Tears come easily when a child suddenly finds himself several hundred miles away from Dad and Mom, with no prospect of seeing them until the end of term. A 10-year-old from across the border in Dahomey was heartbroken because his three new roommates ate up the toffees his father gave him as a farewell gift.

Wiping away tears, finding lost articles, settling disputes, and just being "Dad and Mom"—this is the work of several "house parents" who look after the children as if they are their own. They comfort them in troubles, counsel them in problems, and rejoice when a child shows signs of spiritual growth. The 14 teachers, who teach six primary and three junior high grades, have the same dedication—every child is a challenge to shape a life for God.

A survey of "K.A. kids" reveals that 31 percent have made professions of salvation while at K.A., and 87 percent desire to enter full-time Christian service when they grow up. They easily fit into school life on furlough, often leading their classes. With increasing teenage problems in homelands, the Mission's provision of schooling in Africa enables many parents to keep at their work. Students can complete high school at a combined school in Jos.

Now "second-generation missionaries" are returning under the SIM. There are three serving as house parents at the very school they had attended twelve years before! Before K.A. was opened, children had to be left at home at the age of six. They would see their parents again when they were 10, next time at the age of 15, and then 20.

When I dropped in at the school later in the term, tears had dried up and all were having the time of their lives. A gang of "fellers" played cowboys and Indians; a little English girl skipped with a little Nigerian girl (a dozen children of senior Nigerian pastors and Christian teachers are enrolled at K.A).

In the dorm a boy held up his shoe with the sole ripped off, asking a distracted house parent, "What do I do now?" In the school, three grade nine boys were begging their science teacher to postpone tomorrow's test, and two 12-year-old girls practised "posture" by walking down the hall with books on their heads. From various rooms came the strains of trumpet and piano practice.

Five solemn little boys sat in the waiting room of the dental clinic, where the Mission dentist makes an average of 500 fillings and 20 extractions during the school year. He also cares for the teeth of missionaries.

Missionary parents can be with their children during their vacation at Miango Rest Home, on an adjacent compound. Grapefruit and orange trees were laden with fruit when I was there. The staff couldn't do more to make their guests feel "at home."

From the cottage in which I stayed I looked out across a beautiful panorama of green valleys and rocky hills on the plateau's edge.

"Look at all this well-favored land," I thought. "Plenty of good soil, rain, sunshine—and no winter ice. What couldn't be done with big farm equipment and proper fields instead of those short hand-hoes and weed-covered patches!"

I wasn't the first foreigner to have such mistaken ideas. I later learned that agricultural experts are coming to the conclusion that the African's hand-hoe and his little mounds are perhaps the best way to tackle some of the continent's peculiar land problems. There are exceptions, and in some areas farmers are benefitting from communal projects, using oxen or tractors. But in other parts there are abandoned projects (like Britain's East Africa Groundnut Scheme) which prove the folly of using big Western farm concepts.

Africa has the world's largest land mass in a tropical climate, and things just don't work as they do in other continents, except on alluvial plains laid down by annual flooding, and in the cooler highlands.

In lateritic soils, steel plow disks are quickly rasped dull by sharp quartz grains, and tires of heavy equipment have the same effect as a road roller, pressing the quartz into a hard mass. Bulldozers have difficulty clearing land because tree roots are fantastically long and deep due to their search for water in the long dry seasons. As soon as land is cleared, hot air turns humus into gas and makes the soil sterile. Warm tropical rain hastens chemical action, leaching out minerals and forming iron oxides which make a hard crust. Rainy season cloudbursts erode the top soil wherever it is broken and beat the residue harder. There is no deep frost to break up and aerate soil particles.

Maybe the "primitive" farmer isn't so far behind after all. His little hoe doesn't dig deep enough to expose the undersoil and increase erosion. He cultivates small patches between trees, piles the soil in mounds to keep the earth inside away from the air and to form troughs to hold rain, and lets weeds protect the topsoil. The thing he could benefit from is intelligent use of fertilizers—natural and chemical.

One way to get the feel of Africa is by going for a walk; so I set out across one of the volcanic valleys. It looked uninhabited until I started down the trail. Nestled between the rocks, camouflaged by grass thatch roofs, were picturesque huts surrounded by cactus hedges. A skinny dog yapped at me. A fat baby snoozed contentedly on his mother's back as she ground grain between two stones.

Farther along a farmer unbent from his hand-hoeing for a

moment to wave at me. On the hillside above him two boys
were shouting and throwing stones, to keep grain birds from
settling on ripening guinea corn. An elderly woman, slight as
a deer, carefully arranged sprigs of leaves as she walked along
the zig-zag trail; she tucked them under her rope girdle to
make her tribe's version of Eve's apron.

Over a hill I came across 30 hump-backed cattle, watched
by a lithe Fulani youth playing a plaintive melody on his cornstalk flute. Texans would have envied the horns on some of
those steers. In a stream a muscular peasant was panning for
tin, collecting the precious grains of black ore in a gourd.

These were a simple but outwardly happy people. Women
dandled their babies, children laughed as they swung on a rope
hanging from a baobab tree. A dozen of them were having as
much fun as children on a toboggan slide: sitting on small flat
rocks, they hurtled down a smooth rock face. In the market,
men played the world's oldest game—a kind of checkers with
marble-sized seeds in 12 holes (a frieze on a 7,000-year-old
tomb in Syria depicts the same game).

But the charms around the children's tummies, bulging from
worms and malnutrition, and piles of fetish rocks in compounds revealed the inner fears of these animists. Three witchdoctors were huddled over the remains of a goat in a juju hut.
They were trying to divine how to stop a leopard raiding the
town. The goat had been the leopard's latest victim; it might
be a child next. Outside, hunters armed with spears, bows and
arrows, and ancient muskets were preparing to track down the
beast in the sacred rocks behind the village. They had pow-
dered large red circles around their eyes in the belief that this
would make themselves invisible to the leopard.

In Miango town itself, I saw signs of progress. Government
posters pasted on walls gave instruction about using fertilizer
for better crops and being considerate of one's wife by helping
lift her load on to her head. One poster stressed hygiene—flies
carried germs from a boy defecating on the ground. Another

graphically showed how flies carry disease from one man's eyes to another's.

The chief of Miango, Weyi Sanfara, is one of the visible results of the gospel's power. Both pagans and Muslims of the tribe elected him chief, even though he was a pastor at the time, because they knew he would rule them justly. He withstood pressures from other chiefs to become a Muslim. "I would sooner give up my chieftaincy than Christ," he told me. "In myself I do not have power to rule. I only pray that God will enable me to serve Him faithfully."

Chief Weyi at times preaches in the big mud-walled church built by the Christians. Believers have moved out of the squalor of the pagan town and built cleaner, larger houses on the surrounding plains, near their farms.

The Miango tribe is only one of 35 tribes within a radius of 50 miles. Each has a distinct language or dialect not understood by the others. They can communicate only in the Hausa trade language. The largest has 100,000 population; the smallest 100. Many of these groups still live as their ancestors did when they fled to the craggy plateau to escape from slave-raiding horsemen of the plains.

I saw something of the great contrasts among these people when Harold Hide took me out to Rinjin Gani. Beside the highway is a government teacher training college, where Harold gives instructions in the Scriptures to bright young men during the week. A mile back from the highway is a Ribina village living practically in the stone age.

Harold had won his way into the villagers' hearts, and they hailed him as a brother when we approached. The men wore clothes; the women wore only bustles of leaves—they believe clothes will make them sterile. Yet they didn't really seem naked as we sat on a rock while Harold chatted with them. They were not savages. They were personable, friendly, with a quiet dignity. Their way of life is different from ours, but that isn't the point—they need Christ.

Some have believed. At a nearby stream on Sunday morning

I watched the baptism of a teenage Ribina girl; she is studying at the SIM's girls' school at Zambuk and is engaged to a Christian Ribina youth who is a student at the government teacher training college.

Two things impressed me at Rinjin Gani. There are still pockets of people like the Ribinas—within only a few miles of a city, isolated from the progress around them. Secondly, in the Mission there is such a wide range of ministry. Here is one young missionary straddling the centuries: reaching modern students (in English) and also a primitive people (he had to decipher their language) with the unchanging gospel of Jesus Christ.

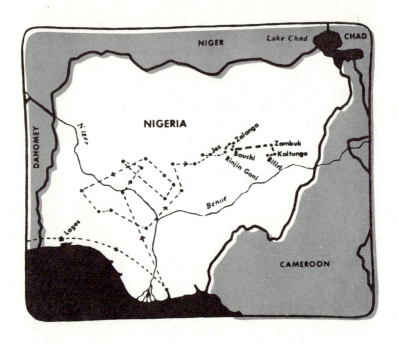

10. "Then the Elephant Charged . . ."

"I thought it was a big black boulder—then it moved. I couldn't imagine an animal being so big!" Bernard Clymer was telling us how he shot his elephant. Bernard doesn't look the "mighty hunter" type, but you can never tell what these missionaries have been up to.

I was visiting Zalanga with District Superintendent Charlie Rhine. The SIM's Area Representative for Eastern Canada, Harry Percy, was there too; he had come out to get an up-to-date picture of the work, and we combined our tours for the next month.

"The people of a village about 50 miles from here were bothered by a rogue elephant," Bernard continued. "So I put my Winchester rifle in the Land-Rover the next time I had to go up that way. The villagers showed me their farms. The place looked as if a tornado had gone through it. The sugar cane was all flattened and cassava uprooted. Their granaries had been emptied as if by a suction hose.

"Then I saw this big black object, at least 12 feet high. When it moved I knew I had found Mr. Rogue. I was down-wind, so he didn't smell me. I prayed, 'Lord, if You want me to get him, help me drop him with the first rounds.' I didn't fancy being chased by a wounded beast. I fired, and to my relief he dropped! What a bellowing filled the forest!

"But just as I was congratulating myself, I suddenly realized Mrs. Elephant had got wind of me. She had been grazing behind a clump of trees. Now she flared her ears and trumpeted shrilly. I knew what that meant.

"I barely had time to take aim when she came down the trail at me. I blasted away and she stopped. Then up went her trunk and she came at me again. I pumped another charge into her and again she stopped. I just had time to reload when she charged me for the third time.

" 'Lord, stop her this time!' I prayed as I emptied the rifle point-blank. Suddenly she pulled up, stomped the ground, and crashed off into the bush with a ferocious cry. The male lurched to his feet and staggered off, too. I raced back to the Land-Rover, where I found all my guides cowering."

"Didn't you get the male?" Harry and I asked.

"Finally," said Bernard, bringing out two ivory tusks to prove it. "That beast walked in a great circle for about four miles and finally dropped dead from internal bleeding. The female got away. There was big feasting in the town that night. We had to cut off the trunk to get the head in my box trailer, and then it took six men to lift it. The trunk was six and a half feet long. The rear feet were 18 inches across, and the front were 22 inches."

The tusks were nice pieces of ivory—the larger weighed

24 lbs. and was 43 inches long. The elephant was fairly young, for tusks can grow to twice that length.

Bernard later found a trophy more precious than the tusks, however. A man came to tell him he first heard the gospel when Bernard stood on the dead elephant and preached to the crowd that gathered. He accepted Christ as Saviour. Elephant hunting is not Bernard's usual occupation. He is principal of a Bible school, and his wife supervises the dispensary work in the area.

We set off for the next station, Bauchi, in Charlie Rhine's pickup. Charlie is unmistakably a Pennsylvania Dutchman, and during the next five days we never exceeded the plodding Dutch speed of 35 mph. His "parish" is larger than either Pennsylvania or Holland.

After seeing him at work, I have a better idea what a "general missionary" is. Charlie is one by current definition. His job demands some of the talents of an explorer, a pastor, a mechanic, a rural school supervisor, a visiting family doctor, the director of a corporation, and a foreign ambassador. Not being a "specialist" in these fields, Charlie rubs his large chin and admits that he depends on the Holy Spirit's in-fitting, 22 years of missionary experience, and a Dutchman's perseverance.

Charlie and Irene Rhine live at Miya ("Meat Gravy"), an interesting pagan town distinguished for its annual dog feast. The feast is not the grand affair it used to be, since the number of sacrificed dogs is down to 1,000 from 5,000. However, it still marks the central festivity of the tribe, the occasion when eligible girls are carried off to their suitors by masked "dodo" spiritmen.

We reached Bauchi around noon and drove right out to the SIM's leprosarium, where Henry and Rita Guenter made us welcome with a fried chicken dinner. The patients under treatment included several of the local "duckbill tribe," whose women insert a gourd disc the size of a silver dollar in upper and lower lips.

In Bauchi itself, a town of 20,000 and provincial capital, Jim

Lilly was teaching Scripture classes in government institutions. Jim was trying to carry the almost impossible load of 42 classes per week, plus marking papers, plus holding Sunday services.

"We could increase the number of classes to 56 if we had more help," Jim told us with a note of desperation. "Tell young men at home that this is one of the greatest opportunities God has given missions."

Jim listed his reasons on four fingers: "1. The schools I teach in are in a Muslim area. 2. I am allowed to teach the Scriptures unhindered. 3. Former students are now teachers, principals, government administrators, Members of Parliament. Some are passing on the Word to others in their professions. 4. Forty-one tribes are represented in my classes. Think of the impact they can have on their own people!"

A five-hour drive east from Bauchi brought us to Zambuk Girls' Bible School, where a staff of three missionaries and three Nigerians are preparing girls to be Christian wives. Commander-in-chief is effervescent Elsie Lavery.

She and the other women on this "women's world" station have hooked up a telephone system between buildings on the five-acre compound with old phones Elsie picked up last furlough. "The men laugh when they see it—but it works, and what's funny about that?" grinned Elsie. A variety of scrap wire went into this communication system, along with medical adhesive tape and an inner tube for insulation.

Some of the girls need elementary schooling before going on to the proper Bible course. I saw the neat Hausa writing of a girl who could neither speak Hausa nor write when she arrived six months before. She came from the hills to the east, near the Cameroon border, where a case involving cannibalism was recently tried.

Zambuk seems to have more than the average mission station's share of local irritations. Someone told me to ask Elsie for her list of Zambuk's Ten Plagues. Here they are:

    1. Earwigs—in *everything*, including the bottom of my cup *after* drinking the coffee.

2. Flies—they get behind your glasses, in your ears, eyes, and mouth.

3. Lizards—they leave their marks everywhere.

4. Spitting cobras—they specially like our storerooms.

5. Frogs—we swept out 12 from behind a cupboard in a *screened* porch.

6. Donkeys—there were 13 in front of my house one day; the owners drive them our way to feed on our precious shrubs and vegetables.

7. Goats—they wander all over and eat anything left by the donkeys.

8. Dust storms.

9. Cut worms.

10. Heat—one day last March it was 100° inside, 105° on the porch, and 135° in the sun.

Fortunately the ladies have a good sense of humor, and we took our hats off to them for a great job done in difficult circumstances. In fact, I would take my hat off to all the 300 single girls in the Mission. They have to cope with a lot they shouldn't have to, because there aren't enough men to do the job. It strikes me that missionary service for a single woman takes the highest form of dedication. I think the Lord will have a special reward for them in heaven.

A church elder with 121 tribal marks on his face (60 thin parallel lines from forehead to chin on each side, and one down the middle of his forehead and nose) told us how he had been saved while helping build Zambuk's first mission house in 1930. When he asked the African foreman for time off to say his Muslim prayers, the foreman said he wouldn't be paid for the time.

"What!" he exclaimed. "The missionary is supposed to be a godly man, and yet he refuses me time to worship God?"

The foreman agreed to ask the missionary. The Muslim had mixed feelings when Gordon Beacham* looked at him kindly

* C. Gordon Beacham Sr., who has three sons and a daughter with the SIM.

and said, "We won't dock your pay, but we'll pray that one day you will come to know the Lord as your personal Saviour."

Gordon Beacham might have insisted the man give an hour's work for an hour's wage, or that he not say Muslim prayers while working for him, but he was wise enough to see how this looked to a Muslim in those early days. His kindness so impressed the workman that he began to attend Bible classes and at last gave his heart to Christ. He is one of the pillars of the Zambuk church today.

We spent the weekend at Kaltungo, heart of the Tangale tribe, where we saw the big pot in the sacred grove where twin babies used to be murdered and the heads of war captives were cooked. Those practices have long ceased, but there were fresh feathers and animal bones stuck in the branches of the nearby "spirit tree."

Harry Percy was most interested in nearby Biliri, because his brother Doug had been a missionary there for nine years before cerebral malaria invalided him home. Harry himself had been a missionary in Sokoto province, to the northwest, for 10 years before the Mission asked him to be an Area Representative in Canada. This was Harry's first time back.

The Biliri people had an ancient tradition that one day a creature with a red mouth would come with a message, which the people would receive. A little mother back on a New Hampshire farm in USA did not know this, but she had read about the Tangales and the way Islam was threatening to engulf the tribe. Mrs. Harling secretly prayed that God would use one of her strapping sons to take the gospel to them. Harry, studying Agriculture at university, felt a strong leading to be a missionary. When he wrote to tell his mother, she gave thanks to God and told her son her secret prayer.

In 1928 ruddy-haired Harry arrived at Biliri and began building a mission house. The people noticed he had "a red mouth" as they listened to his message. Some believed, but the witchdoctors opposed the stranger.

Since then the church has grown, until now there are 90

"out-stations." On Sunday morning we pressed our way into the huge church (the roof is supported by palm tree trunks), crowded out with over 1,000 believers. At Biliri Bible School local sons and daughters study the Word.

There is cause for rejoicing at Biliri, but there are also the usual problems. The younger generation takes the gospel for granted and does not quickly respond to instruction. The church has had to dismiss several Christian teachers because of sin. A Roman Catholic priest has moved into town and is trying to enroll ECWA members who have been disciplined.

Back in the town of Kaltungo we found another busy center for the gospel, with a 66-bed hospital and a Teachers' College. The 180 students at the College are taught by a staff of missionaries and Nigerians working under Nigerian Principal Simon Sayomi. When tribal warfare broke out, it was Sayomi who courageously held back the mobs in order to protect students of other tribes. Here is a Christian leader of character—the type who makes all the toil and problems of a mission training program very worthwhile.

At the hospital Dr. Don Edwards was doing ward rounds; so Harry and I followed him. He and his staff of five nurses and one lab technician treated 43,578 patients over the past year. Besides, the doctor makes monthly visits to do surgery at Bauchi leprosarium and visits 14 district dispensaries twice a year.

In the children's ward was a child with ashen-gray skin, suffering from sickle cell anemia. A tiny baby was in spasms from tetanus. In the male ward one man was recovering from cancer surgery, another from having a wicked-looking barbed spear removed from his abdomen.

The nurses were rejoicing over a double victory in the women's ward. A woman who had acted as if demon possessed was responding to treatment for TB of the spine. But more important, that Sunday morning she had testified to God's saving grace.

Every week several snake bite cases come in. Some are bitten by Nigeria's deadliest snake, the carpet viper. Dr. Edwards used to get the rare antivenom serum from South Africa, but when Nigeria banned all imports from there in protest against apartheid, the doctor had to hunt for another source, and finally found it in Sierra Leone.

The Christians at Kaltungo were being stirred up to witness by a crusade known as New Life for All. Three thousand marched around the town to publicize an evangelistic campaign. Five hundred conversions had been recorded during nine such campaigns in the surrounding Tangale Waja area, and 15,000 believers were now studying a handbook in preparation for systematic hut-to-hut evangelism. One group prayed specifically for a Muslim, who finally came to tell them, "For 40 years I have said Koranic prayers without finding peace. I want the new life you talk about."

Was New Life for All God's instrument to stir Christians from their complacency? It started in the burning heart of Jerry Swank, an energetic Bible school teacher at Kagoro. In 1963 evangelicals from a number of missions and churches caught the vision and formed a committee with the objective: "Total Evangelization."

Wishing to safeguard NLFA from the dangers inherent in cooperative evangelism, the committee laid down safeguards, including participation on an individual (not denominational) basis, a doctrinal statement, and careful follow-up by the committee itself.

These men—missionaries and nationals—are aware that in West Africa and former French Equatorial Africa there is an annual population increase of 1.6 million per year—30,000 per week. Divided into religious communities, every week there is a population increase of 15,000 among Muslim families, 10,000 in the pagan community, 4,000 in the Roman Catholic community, and only 2,000 in the Protestant community. The total Protestant community for Africa is listed as 7.33 percent.

The encouraging thing about NLFA is that it is "grass roots" and indigenous. Farmers who think they haven't enough money for their own needs find that by extra farming they can raise funds to buy gospel tracts for free distribution. Young men take a month off work to go to other districts where there are too few Christians to visit every village.

In one year believers met regularly in 7,000 prayer groups in Northern Nigeria to pray for unsaved friends, and 30,000 attended instruction classes in witnessing; 202 men volunteered for gospel teams, supported by their churches. Conviction came on entire communities, so that pastors couldn't cope with the requests for counseling. Witchdoctors burned their fetishes, Muslim priests turned from the Prophet to the Saviour. Was God preparing the North for the holocaust of tribal violence which lay ahead?

Our tour of the SIM's Eastern District of Northern Nigeria ended, and SIMAIR picked up Harry and me at the Kaltungo grass airstrip. We rose above the massive Tangale peak—a granite monolith shaped like an up-side-down jelly mold rising 1,000 feet above the plains. To the east was Tula Wange, where the Mission ministered to a pagan tribe of 14,000—most living on a terraced plateau four miles wide. In the whole Tangale Waja area beneath us there were 90,000 believers, half of them baptized or in baptismal classes. (In order to be sure that a new convert really understands what he is doing, and to enable him to grow in the faith, the churches require him to become literate enough to read the Scriptures before being baptized.)

"It's thrilling!" Harry said, looking down on town after town where there is now a witness. "After the years my wife and I struggled up north in Islamic territory without seeing more than 10 converts, it is absolutely thrilling to see how these pagans have turned to Christ. Thank God the gospel got to them before Islam."

I was to travel with Harry to those hard parts where he had worked—where Islam got in first. It would be very, very different.

A bright sparkle of light, like a diamond on the ground,

caught my eye as the sun glinted off a metal roof 5,000 feet below us.

"That's Bununu," said pilot Bob Swingle, banking the plane so we could just make out through the haze a little cluster of mission buildings. The station had been turned over to ECWA. When Harry and I were at Bauchi earlier, we had taken a quick drive out there and were delighted to find the grounds neatly kept and the pastor, school teacher, and dispenser busy carrying on the work in spite of opposition.

"We're keeping one house ready for when the Mission can send us a missionary again," the pastor told us. But the Mission was happy the church could man the station, releasing a missionary for a more needy area.

As we flew back to Jos, that tiny, isolated light down there on the ground spoke to me. The church was surrounded by forces which sought to engulf and extinguish it, but it blazed on bravely, reflecting the light of the Son of God. *"His life is the light that shines through the darkness—and the darkness can never extinguish it"* (Living Gospels, Paraphrase of John 1:5).

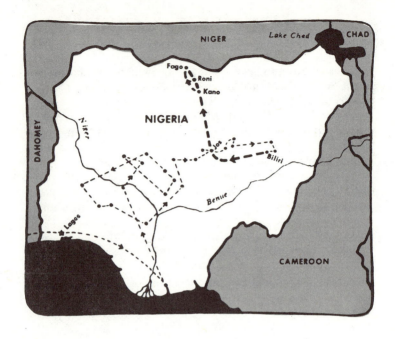

11. Wind of the White Horsemen

"Harmattan dust is thick this morning," said the pilots, squinting skywards. "Don't know yet if we can take off."

Harry Percy and I were at the SIM hangar at Jos airport, ready to fly north to Kano. The small planes save the Mission money and time in travel, and frequently save lives. Department Head Bill Tuck told us the four Comanches and one Aztec had flown over half-a-million miles in the past year, without mishap. The pilots all take a hand in servicing the aircraft to the highest flight standards, but the men also commit each flight to the Lord as they fly in unpredictable conditions.

Talking about the weather is not just making conversation

for these pilots. And they believe God's hand is in the storm—even if it means changing flight plans. Like the day the Education Secretary and two Nigerian supervisors were flying back to Jos. A heavy storm over Jos forced the pilot to land 70 miles away at Kagoro for the night. They noticed the look of surprise mixed with relief on the face of the newly appointed high school principal. The fourth year students had just gone on strike because one student was under discipline. The Lord used a storm to bring advice and authoritative help just in time.

Then there was the miraculous Lupwe flight. A little boy had been in a coma for two days. His parents, in a sister mission near the Cameroon border, in desperation tried the radio transmitter that hadn't worked for two months. God made it work that morning. The SIM picked up the weak signal and radioed Rich Schaffer to change his flight plans.

Rich had no maps of the area, had to find gas on the way, but slid in on the Lupwe bush strip just before a tropical deluge broke. Through the night he joined in prayer for the boy's life and for a miracle to clear the fog which usually covered the airstrip till mid-morning. Again God worked, and at sunrise Rich took off into a clear sky. Two weeks later he flew a perky boy back home.

Now we were in the dry season. Dust had taken the place of rain. Harry and I took off at last, after the Jos control tower called to say visibility was O.K. Jim Weener was at the controls. "I used to think missionaries were a bunch of squares," Jim told us. But after his conversion while in university, he knew God wanted him to be a missionary—"square" or not. Knowing Jim Elliot and Nate Saint before they were killed by the Auca Indians gave him an interest in South America.

While studying in Wheaton College he met the dark-eyed daughter of the Overseas Missionary Fellowship's Candidate Secretary. Julie Whipple told Jim that God was leading her to the Far East; Jim told her he was called to South America. They both decided that nothing should interfere with God's will for them; so they didn't date again. Jim trained as a pilot.

Going west for further studies, Julie started praying for a missionary in Nigeria and became so burdened for the needs there that she finally applied to the SIM. Only after she was on her way to Africa did she discover that a dashing young pilot named Jim Weener was already out in Nigeria—which had a more urgent need for pilots than South America just then.

"You guessed it," said Jim. "It didn't take long for us to get engaged then. It all confirmed God's leading in our lives."

We were at an altitude of 10,000 feet, level with the top of an ashen-gray veil covering the land.

"That's harmattan," Jim explained. "It started last week, and we'll have it for the next three months. Doesn't help flying at all."

"Up in Sokoto I've seen it so thick you couldn't make out the road when driving," added Harry.

It was dust, yet you couldn't feel anything—not like a dust storm. The name "harmattan" comes from an Arabic word for "evil," and the Hausas call it "The Wind of the White Horsemen"—because it looks like white ghosts sweeping across the sandy plains. It starts in high-pressure areas of the Sahara. Thermals carry the silt high into the sky, and desert winds sweep it southward, where it slowly filters down, covering everything with a film of dust. The dry wind sucks the last ounce of moisture from soil and foliage and flesh, cracking one's lips and nostrils. Its rapid evaporation does lower temperatures, but harmattan season is also the time of plagues and epidemics, carried in the wind-blown dust.

"Kano is below us," Jim said about an hour after take-off. But we couldn't see it until he swooped in over the ancient walled city. Then I blinked twice before I realized what I was looking at. The jigsaw puzzle below was really a mass of rectangular mud houses interlaced with mud walls and mud streets. Most of the roofs were flat and also mud. Shadows cast by the yellow sunlight further increased the honeycomb effect.

Driving in from the modern international airport, we entered a different world—"as different from the South as China is from Europe," said one Nigerian politician. This is the Hausa North, the Islamic North. There are more donkeys than bicycles on the streets. Flowing white Muslim robes are everywhere. Few women are around, except little girls selling kola nuts, or unsavory women of the street (faces dabbed with vermilion paint), or older women with their cloths covering their heads and hanging down like tents. Most other Muslim women are shut up in their compounds.

Within the old city's mud walls are 100,000 people. Within a 50-mile radius four million live. Kano was once the cross-roads for camel caravans. Camels can still be seen, but now jets thunder in and out, and around the city are light industries: canning, soap, textiles, canvas shoes. Kano's ancient blue dye pits are famous, but so are her modern "pyramids" of bagged peanuts—760 tons in each. Nigeria is the world's largest exporter of peanuts, and Kano is the largest export center: one half a million tons annually, valued at 40 million dollars.

It was Friday, the Islamic sabbath, and Harry and I wanted to see what took place at prayer time at Nigeria's largest mosque. So we headed off to the old city. Although it has a written history dating back 1,000 years, Kano was not seen by a white man until 1824, and it was 1903 before the British captured it. To prevent further slave trade and rebellion, the British allowed the Hausas to keep only their city gates in repair, not the walls. Goats now run along the top of the 13-mile remains of Kano's walls, punctuated by 13 massive mud arches.

We followed a stream of white-robed men through one. A sign declared: "No cars allowed during Prayers on Fridays." Ahead of us lay the blue-green dome, as high as a four-story building, flanked by twin towers surmounted by crescents. Beggars were out in full force, for almsgiving is meritorious. An enterprising boy sold water in clay pitchers for the faithful to wash their hands, feet, eyes, and mouths before praying.

They converged on the mosque from all directions—young and old, on bicycles, on donkeys, most on foot. Hundreds increased into thousands and their pace quickened as the hour of two came near. There was no talking, only the shuffle of feet, until the multitude had filled the mosque, the courtyard, and the large open space all around it. At least 10,000 gathered, and this was not the only mosque in Kano.

Right at two the muezzin's voice crackled over loud-speakers so that all within a mile could hear: *"Allah ho ak-barrrr. Allah ho ak-barrrr! There is one God and Muhammed is His Prophet."*

We could sense the strength of this Christless religion, the feeling of togetherness, as the 10,000 went through their genuflections in unison—bending three times at the waist, then sinking to the ground, fingering their beads while reciting the 99 names of Allah, bowing their heads to touch the ground. The muezzin's call droned on with passages from the Koran, responded to by a chorus of 10,000 voices. It was an ominous, overpowering sound.

Then suddenly it was over. They had fulfilled their ritual duty for another week, although each day they must also pray five times towards Mecca, finger their beads, and give alms to the poor.

The sound of those feet shuffling away from this empty ritual filled me with a sense of despair. The devotees had just worshiped a relentless vindictive deity, and they had no assurance of acceptance with him, until the Day of Judgment when their good deeds would be weighed against their evil deeds. The hopelessness of it. How could we ever communicate the plan of God's love to this close-bonded brotherhood, with its millions of devoted zealots? Harry and I walked away from the mosque that afternoon with a great ache inside.

Rowland Bingham had that same ache in 1929, when he visited Nigeria and met with leaders of missions in Northern Nigeria.

"Unless we unitedly do something to open the North to the

gospel," declared Bingham, "I shall go up to Kano and preach in the market—even if I'm arrested. That might prove to the world that the British government is not insuring religious liberty!"

The other missionaries, who were just as concerned, managed to hold back the intrepid Bingham by promising to send a delegation to the British Colonial Secretary. At the same time a sympathetic man became acting Lieutenant Governor, and by 1933 the SIM was granted a site in the "strangers' suburb" just outside Kano city. Other stations in Sokoto, Katsina, and Kano Provinces were opened, and in 1936 the doors of welcome were pushed further ajar when the Mission started leprosy work under the enthusiastic drive of Albert D. Helser. The largest number of Muslim converts has come through leprosy work, where men and women have absorbed Scripture teaching over a long period.

But the institution which has probably created more good will for the gospel than any other single project in Nigeria is the SIM Eye Hospital started in 1943 by Dr. M. D. Hursh. It is the only one of its kind in all West Africa, and patients come from great distances. Beyond the personal contacts with patients, it indirectly arouses a receptive attitude to the work of missions.

Outside the Eye Clinic, Harry and I found a long line-up of patients from city clerks in shirts and ties to desert Tuareg swathed in blue-black muslin. Some were blind, led by children. Each was courteously and quickly examined by a team of missionary and Nigerian nurses, who directed patients to the departments which could help their problems.

Dr. Gerry Hewitt was examining patients who needed glasses. I was startled to see a camel herder, with only his nose and eyes showing between his turban and veil, peering through a modern optical testing device—like something out of a flying saucer.

The Optical Shop looks after the prescriptions. Key man here is a humble Nigerian Christian, James Kugbiyi, whose professional training in Britain as an optician was sponsored by the Mission. In the well-equipped lens laboratory Kugbiyi moves around the staff to check on the precision grinding and fitting of lenses. He also examines eyes and prescribes glasses.

Handling customers in the reception room with professional efficiency was "Char" Bruce. She had been an optician's secretary in America until Dr. Helser passed through her office one day and characteristically said, "Young lady, we need you in Africa." It was like the Lord's calling Peter and James from their fishing nets. "When I go back on furlough I see others with everything they desire," says Charlotte. "But I wouldn't trade this ministry for their life for anything."

Harry and I were amazed at the surgery being done at the hospital. An eye specialist in America or Europe would do perhaps eight to 12 operations a month. Dr. Ben Kietzman with a staff of four missionary and five Nigerian nurses did 6,000 eye operations in one year (27,000 patients were treated in hospital and clinic). Measles causes the most blindness, followed by trachoma, an infection spread by unsanitary conditions. "River blindness" is also prevalent, transmitted by a fly breeding in water. There are many tumors, cataracts, and eye injuries.

With that number of patients, the small staff has to operate with assembly-line efficiency. A Nigerian nurse wheels in a patient and gives local anesthetic to the affected eye, pausing for prayer with the patient. After surgery, as the doctor starts on the next patient, the operated case is wheeled to another nurse to apply dressings, or perhaps work on eyelids. A Nigerian assistant does that. In this way three operating tables are kept filled with cases being prepared, operated on, or having post-operative work done.

I knew that one nurse, Delta Bond, has been there since the hospital was opened; so I asked if she had done any cataract operations—with a doctor around of course.

"A few," she grinned; "—maybe a thousand."

As we watched the doctor's deft hands, little did we realize how much we would thank God for them in a few days' time.

Acting District Superintendent Jim Jacobson took Harry and me on a quick tour of the district. A book could be written about the Lord's work in each place. There are joys, there are sorrows—there is the constant struggle against spiritual forces.

Fago is one illustration of that struggle. Several men and women have been saved through the dispensary ministry there, but there is only one Christian family in the whole town. The first convert at Fago was poisoned by relatives; so thereafter the missionaries arranged for converts to get away from the area to take Bible training. Today they are scattered all over the North witnessing for the Lord.

What does a lad do when his relatives put him out of the village, when his parents won't pay his school fees, and when he has no training to enable him to live on his own? The Boys' School and Farm School at Roni have a practical answer. The staff teach modern agricultural methods along with school subjects and Bible study. They produce such astonishing results that the boys not only are able to earn a good living—they earn the respect of hostile neighbors.

The missionaries start by demonstrating to the boys that fertilizer can double peanut harvests. Enthusiasm increases when the students see that planting at the right time with improved seed can yield 250 percent more.

One of the students ran his hands through a pile of peanuts and told me how he had been able to earn enough to pay his school fees, working after school. He first gave a tithe to the local church, then bought a present of cloth for his mother and clothes for himself. He was a Muslim before; now he is looking forward to returning to his village to witness while he farms.

Whenever a Nigeria Airways plane flies overhead, the boys wonder if Paul Thahal is at the controls. Paul was a student at Roni when SIM General Director Raymond J. Davis was a teacher there. He went on to the Sudan United Mission's Gindiri Secondary School, and was one of seven Nigerians chosen from 1,000 applicants for pilot training. He has maintained a faithful witness in the world of pilots, even representing his nation at international pilots' conventions overseas.

We had to head back to Kano at last. "Only 12 miles more now," Jim Jacobson said as we came to the beginning of a new highway leading into the city. "No trouble from here on in."

It was dark; the headlights of a truck blazed at us. Suddenly a donkey appeared in our own headlights. It had stepped out from behind the truck, and there was nothing to do but hit its rear end. After the initial thud, there was a shattering crash, and we were all showered by broken glass. Apparently the donkey's head had swung around and smashed in the window on the passenger's side.

"Help!" shouted Harry, clutching his throat. "I'm bleeding!" Blood was spurting from a wound in his neck and pouring down on to the car seat. We raced into Kano. Harry was losing blood quickly and several times nearly passed out. We pulled up at the Eye Hospital and within a few minutes Dr. Kietzman had Harry on one of the operating tables we had been looking at the day before. A bullet-sized piece of glass had cut a major artery, and it took six stitches to sew up the damage. Harry had a sore jaw and a badly sprained shoulder for the rest of the trip.

While Harry was recuperating, Jim Jacobson took me to a village 12 miles from Kano. We had to follow a cattle trail across the harmattan-blown plains to reach it. "This is what we call a Magazawa village," Jim explained. "That means pagan Hausa. A few pockets of Hausas have resisted Islam for centuries and still worship idols. We're trying to reach them with the gospel. I want you to meet a man who has withstood pressure from both his pagan relatives and Muslims in his stand for God."

We met Molo on the trail leading to the village. As we sat together he told us what God had done for him. A few weeks before, he was returning from witnessing in another town when messengers met him with the news that his baby had died. He hurried home and asked a visiting pastor to give the body a Christian burial. The villagers stood around in surprise that there was no wailing or beer drinking—only reverent praying and singing of hymns.

The next day Molo was summoned to the local court, where a Muslim priest demanded why he had called a pastor to bury the child, instead of a priest.

"I am a follower of the Lord Jesus Christ," replied the bereaved father stoutly. "Therefore I wanted a Christian burial for my baby."

The priest tried to intimidate him by alleging that he would be tried for the offense. The father trudged home, only to find that a second child was in convulsions from fever. Next day she died too. This time the father called a few other believers and together they prayed, read the Scriptures, and placed the body in the ground.

Again the authorities threatened him, without regard for his broken heart.

"But God gave me grace," Molo told us. "He gave, and He took away. Through this I was able to witness to the court and the villagers."

It was costing Molo something to step out for God. By the side of that dusty trail, as "the white horsemen" swept around us, we bowed in prayer and committed each other "to God and to the Word of His grace."

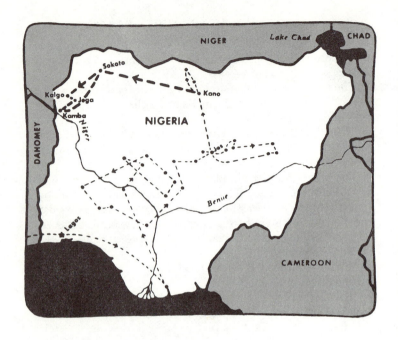

12. A Sultan and a Saint

"How do you greet a Sultan?" I whispered to Harry as we
approached the palace. "Does one bow or prostate flat on the
ground?"

"He'll probably shake hands," said Harry. "He's well educated."

Harry and I had flown northwest from Kano to meet the
Sultan of Sokoto. Alhaji Sir Abubakar is Nigeria's most powerful feudal ruler and also religious head of West Africa's
Muslims. The District Officer, a very courteous Nigerian, made
the arrangements and escorted us to the Sultan's palace. We
walked between crimson hibiscus and purple jacaranda toward
the modern buildings ornamented with arabesques.

Apparently no Muslim noticed that the contractor had made all the blocks on the palace facade in the form of Maltese crosses. Another incongruity I noted in Northern Nigeria was the Star of David (abhorrent to Arab Muslims) on government buildings and penny coins. I learned it was the emblem of Lord Lugard, first British Governor General of Nigeria, and became the nation's official seal.

Under an extensive yellow canopy Sir Abubakar sat in an armchair looking through documents, which he handed to a bowing attendant. As we approached, the Sultan poked his feet into his sandals, adjusted the folds of his white brocade robe, and rose with quiet dignity. Between the voluminous wraps of white gauze wound around his turban and his neck, there appeared a kindly face with soulful eyes. Sure enough, he extended a warm hand and welcomed us in a cultured Oxford accent.

The Sultan turned and swept grandly up the steps into his council chamber, where an aide pointed us to some of the 24 upholstered chairs. In filed his retinue as well, like a line-up from *Arabian Nights*: the bearded Shehu (chief Koranic scholar) in a blue robe; the court judge with the end of his orange turban dangling down past his waist; a portly vizier in a robe embroidered with brilliant red sabers and crescents. All wore turbans but no shoes.

The Sultan sat at the head of the council tables. In a room behind him we could see a resplendent gold throne. On the far wall of the council room was the tattered flag of Sokoto's army, captured by the British at the turn of this century but later restored to the Sultan.

"We are thankful for the good work of people from your lands," said the Sultan, avoiding direct reference to missions. Harry reminisced about his friendship with the Emir of Gwandu, one of Sokoto Province's important rulers.

The Sultan chatted so amiably that I asked if I could take his photo. After the Shehu muttered something, the Sultan gave permission as long as I didn't use it in a Christian publication in Africa. He even lined up his retinue for photographs and chuckled as I apologized for taking so many. He had seen newsmen before.

As we were leaving, the Sultan asked if we had seen the tomb of Othman Dan Fodio, his Fulani great-grandfather who conquered the Hausa people in an Islamic holy war. We said we were going there next. We found the historic tomb preserved in a large new shrine financed by Saudi Arabia.

Othman rode triumphantly into Sokoto on an Arabian charger in 1804, and the province has been famous ever since for its small, wiry horses and horsemen. He was a Fulani, a tribe with aristocratic bearing and Roman noses, which became the ruling class in Hausa country. Fulanis are lighter in color than the Hausas, who in turn are usually lighter and taller than their southern neighbors. (The term "Hausa," however, is like "Latin American," covering a number of groups now related by a common language.)

When the Fulanis arrived they found little culture among the Hausas, but a well-developed language, the second most widely used in Africa. Its Hamitic origin makes it easier for a Caucasian to learn than the more complex-toned negroid languages. The Fulanis also found Islam laid like a veneer over animistic belief and practices. They set to the task of purifying the faith and making more converts. Today Northern Nigeria and Saudi Arabia have the purest forms of Koranic law— drunkards can still be punished with 40 lashes. In the large towns some Muslims do drink, though, and they may marry up to four wives at a time.

The northern strongholds of Islam were a constant challenge to the early SIM missionaries. Guy Playfair, then West Africa Director, heard a rumor that a chief in Sokoto province had a Bible, and set out to track him down. He discovered that the Sarkin Gobir had 25 books, including a Hausa-Arabic Bible.

"He had read it through several times, so that he even knew the dimensions of Noah's ark!" Playfair reported. This chief later became the Emir of Gwandu, an enlightened ruler sympathetic to missions.

Before taking us to some of the SIM's stations, District Superintendent Wally Braband showed us a map of Sokoto Province, an area twice the size of Holland. Vast distances of dismal scrubland separate the lonely outposts. Several stations are closed for lack of staff. There is no spontaneous turning to God, such as we saw in the Middle Belt. Islam is openly militant; local Christians are a handful.

Yet the missionaries refuse to be discouraged. As we traveled we saw them busy in a wide variety of ministries—rural trekking, city evangelism among factory staff, Scripture classes in government schools, medical work—including the SIM's largest leprosarium, at Amanawa.

As we drove across the scrubby plains, I couldn't erase from my mind the sight of a cattle herder who typifies the world that these missionaries have to penetrate—somehow.

His skin is scaled and dusty from standing in the sun and wind all day. His cloth has rarely been washed. His stomach is full of worms, his blood full of malaria, and his mind empty. He has no concern about time or schedule or organization, except to get his cattle back to the circle of grass huts by nightfall. Then he will eat the same starchy food he has eaten every day out of a gourd and lie down on the ground or on a cornstalk stretcher and sleep till sunup and another day of the same unvarying life.

Unvarying but for a birth or marriage or death or the unwanted intrusion of another world when an overloaded truck roars along the distant road. But even it is gone in a moment, and any vague thought aroused by it dissipates as quickly as the cloud of dust left behind.

I saw all this; then I saw our own world at home in another perspective. Until now this simple herder was the odd one. Now I was. I used to think that our well-ordered life of tables and chairs, of running water and refrigerators, of supermarkets and traffic lights, of hi-fi records and swimming pools—that was the norm. Life was supposed to be like that, I presumed, and the herder lived in an unfortunate fringe world that should be changed by the UN.

Now for one jolting moment I saw him and two-thirds of the world as living in the norm. Theirs is the common existence. Ours is the unusual, abnormal life. Then I realized our privileged state—and our responsibility.

Harry Percy and his wife had lived in the midst of this kind of world at Kalgo. Although it was ten years since Harry left, the people remembered him and now kept him busy responding to a string of Hausa greetings.

"What my wife and I wouldn't do to be able to come back!" Harry exclaimed. I knew family illness prevented that, apart from the fact that he was filling a vital role at home. Harry is typical of the SIM's home personnel: Area Representatives, Candidate Secretaries, Home Secretaries, Treasurers, Directors, and other hard-working staff in offices and mission homes. Every last one of them would rather be out in Africa, as part of "the front line." But instead they are willing to work behind the lines, making it possible for others to carry on the battle.

And with them stand thousands of dedicated men and women who give and pray, to make it all possible. Everywhere I went I found missionaries very conscious of the sacrifices supporters make. This spurs them on to "run while the sun is hot."

The Chief of Kalgo greeted Harry profusely; we found him sitting on a canvas folding chair out in a field, listening to a transistor radio while watching three servants hand-hoe his farm. When the men shook their fists at us, they weren't saying, "White man go home!" They were welcoming us in the traditional Hausa horseman's greeting of waving his spear aloft. Even though there isn't a spear in a person's hand, he keeps his fist clenched as if holding one.

We stayed overnight at nearby Jega, the first site granted the Mission in Sokoto Province. I noticed that certain sounds and smells made Harry quite nostalgic. They were intangible things which spelled tropical Africa: on a sultry afternoon, a guinea fowl's plaintive dulcimer call; the hum of hornets and mud-daubers building their houses under the roof overhang; the fragrance of bougainvilia blossoms drifting in on the hot air.

At night, when we were stifling under mosquito nets (World Health Organization describes the area's mosquitoes as the most vicious anywhere), there was the steady "pink, pink" of stink bugs hitting the aluminum roof, attracted by the reflected moonlight. Now and then an armor-plated rhinoceros beetle crashed on the metal and tumbled noisily down.

Stink bugs are just what their name claims for them. The size of a lady's little fingernail and shaped like a medieval shield, they exude a skunk-like odor and hide in every conceivable corner, crevice, and article of clothing. One missionary lady had her househelp thoroughly clean her guest room for us before supper. The lad carted out a bucket of stink bugs. But when we went back into the room after supper, the walls, ceilings, and floors were spotted like chicken pox with the insects.

Lest I give the impression that all places are like Sokoto Province for flying creatures—they aren't. And one soon adapts until he enjoys the limitless variety of magnificent moths and butterflies, the push-ups of gaudy blue-orange outdoor lizards, and the excitement of watching small translucent indoor lizards race across the walls to gobble up insects.

One sound I could never enjoy. The braying of a donkey adds pain to the tropic's heat. It is something like a rusty pump being primed, greatly amplified. A variation sounds like the groans of a mortally wounded dragon. I even heard one moo like a cow, between wheezy gasps.

Missionaries have worked at Jega for 30 years, carrying on a trekking and medical ministry. Twice a week the clinic is reserved for Muslim women, whose husbands give them special permission to leave their compounds for this purpose.

"How many Christians were there when you lived here?" I asked Harry.

"Around 10," Harry said. "But only a couple were local people, and they have turned back. One was Danladi. He stood against terrific persecution without flinching. But when Satan changed his tactics and began offering him position and wealth, he became cold and stopped coming to services. We've heard he is saying Koranic prayers again. When I think of Danladi, I could weep."

There is only one local believer known at Jega now. Yet there isn't open hostility, like some places where evangelists are threatened. There is polite indifference, which in a sense makes the work more frustrating. In fact, when we went to greet the chief, he begged Wally to be sure the Mission sent another missionary to take the place of those going on furlough.

What were the people like in a village that could totally resist the gospel for 30 years? To find out, I walked through Jega in the evening. No one accosted me or hardly paid attention to me; I was as safe there as in my own hometown. (Apart from the big cities, this is generally true throughout Africa.)

Children laughed and played outside their parents' huts. Young men chatted around the front of little shops, the shelves illuminated by kerosene pressure lanterns. Along the lanes goods were displayed on rickety tables, lit by wicks burning in pots of oil. Boys and men squatted on mats, industriously embroidering colorful designs on Hausa caps, for which they would get £1 (three dollars) each in the market. I bent down to examine one, when a little boy who had been sleeping on the mat suddenly awoke to see a white monster hanging over him. He screamed in terror and took off like a rocket—while the whole street rocked with laughter.

Far from being "savage Africa," this remote village was a peaceful, well-ordered community, happy in its simple ways. But it also had the same spiritual needs as any other community. A staccato rhythm led me between mud walls to a clearing where young men stood around watching village girls dance to the beat of professional drummers. By tossing a coin at the feet of a bearded Hausa, a girl had the privilege of dancing to the rhythm. The crowd applauded as a young girl acted out a drama with the youngest drummer—a boy about 12. It portrayed a man bartering with a harlot, and the subsequent "affair."

To reach the remotest SIM station in Sokoto Province, we had to put the car on a flat barge to ferry it across a swift-flowing river. Ten men poled us up-river, then pushed out into the boiling current with the hope that we would drift near enough to the other side for their poles to touch bottom again. We made it before being swept down too far.

Kamba is three miles from the juncture where Nigeria, Niger, Dahomey, and the Niger River meet. The missionaries there are the only Protestant missionaries among 175,000 people—mostly tall Fulani and short Zabarma. Although officially considered Muslim, many of the people continue fetish rites.

On our way to Kamba we picked up Malam Kahno, an evangelist of ECWA's Evangelical Missionary Society, who treks out from a local village. Kahno once worked for Harry, and when the two met they embraced and prattled away joyously in Hausa for 10 minutes. A youth wearing a pair of shorts and a bright vermilion pixie cap, with red paint streaked across his face, stood around grinning. "He's just trusted in the Lord," explained Kahno. "He doesn't yet know we Christians don't mark our faces like the pagans."

As we bounced along the road toward Kamba, the evangelist told us about a recent victory. On a Muslim's farm beside the SIM compound at Kamba was a pagan fetish grove. There were terrifying stories of its demons' powers. The Muslim was afraid to cut it down—and couldn't find anyone else willing to do so. When Kahno said he was not afraid, the Muslim told him he could farm the spot if he cleared it. The villagers prophesied dire calamity when they saw him hacking down the grove, and the fetish priest was livid with rage. "You'll die before you finish clearing it!" he screamed.

"If you don't die, I'll believe in your God and follow him," said one farmer. Kahno didn't die, but when he reminded the man of his promise, he said, "Wait. I'll believe if the corn you planted comes up and you are still living."

The corn was a foot above the ground when Kahno spoke to him again, but the farmer postponed the date until the evangelist had harvested the corn. The demons would be angriest then. When the corn was safely harvested, Kahno again reminded the man.

"Yes, I know," said the farmer, "and if I had been as unfaithful to man as I have been to God in keeping my vow, I'd be in trouble now. Kahno, I believe. Your God is the true God. I give my heart to Him."

Kahno is one of several evangelists in the district, and no doubt the future outreach of the gospel in this province will depend largely on them. They are lonely men, but effective. When Muslims threatened to throw Kahno out of the village for "spoiling their religion," an elderly Muslim defended him: "He is the only one in our village who truly serves and fears God."

"Just think," Harry said to me. "When Kahno worked for us, we nearly despaired of him. We made mistakes in dealing with him—but Kahno is gracious, and has forgotten those things. There he is, living in that dark village with his wife and children, fearless for the Lord."

We had two happy days together with Kahno; then the time came to say goodbye. We prayed by the car. Harry said goodbye in Hausa, but Kahno didn't answer. I looked up and saw why. His lips were trembling, and tears welled up in his big dark eyes. He turned away from us, and we climbed in the car.

A mile down the road I said to Harry at last, "Kahno is a real saint."

Harry nodded. He couldn't talk either.

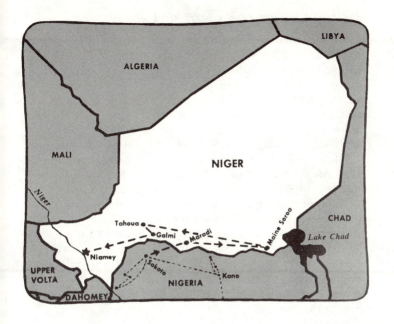

13. Crosses in the Sahara

Ostriches, camel trains straining into a dust storm, veiled Tuareg, swaggering career officers toasting their ladies with wine, and dervishes in baggy pants—this was the picture that came to my mind whenever I heard the term, "*Afrique francophone*"—French-speaking Africa. When Harry Percy and I flew across Nigeria's northern border into Niger Republic, we weren't disappointed.

Niger (pronounced "Neezhair") is a landlocked nation with its northern border smack in the middle of the Sahara. To the north are Algeria and Libya—countries with a Mediterranean coastline. To the south is Nigeria, with an Atlantic coastline.

Although Niger is larger than Texas and California combined (490,000 square miles), most of its three million people live on the southern edge, where a green film springs from the sandy soil as if by magic during the brief rainy period. Camels, cattle, and goats have room to wander endlessly, licking up the sparse grass and thorns. There are as many cattle as people, and twice as many sheep. Farmers cultivate rice, peanuts, and millet, especially in the Chad Basin in the southeast corner and along the tributaries of the Niger River in the southwest.

Niger Republic is one of the three states of former French West Africa in which the SIM has mission stations. Neighboring Upper Volta and Dahomey are the other two.

"Bon jour, messieurs," sun-tanned Newton Kapp welcomed us at Maradi airport. Born in Armenia but raised in Egypt and America, "Monsieur Kapp" arrived in Niger in 1934, speaks French with his hands, and can look at things like an oriental. He took Harry and me to see the mission work, with pilot Paul Rogalsky flying us. Paul looks like a proper bush pilot but reads classics like *The Campaigns of Alexander the Great* while waiting for the next take-off, and listens to long-hair stereo music at home.

As we flew east towards fabulous Lake Chad, pioneer Kapp outlined the Mission's strategy in Niger. The first outpost was opened in 1924 at Zinder, which was a staging point for armed forces crossing the desert during the World Wars. There was no further work started until 1940, when the Kapps opened Maradi as a central office. Then followed six other stations. In the sixties, trekking posts were opened to reach the Chad area, and a Hausa Bible school was started. The work at Maradi has grown to include a girls' home, a boys' home and agricultural school, and Niger's only leprosarium.

We landed on a sandy strip at Maine Soroa, only 80 air miles from Lake Chad. The missionaries live in a prefabricated sheet aluminum house set on an old sand dune. Since the well water has a very brackish flavor, they kindly let us drink the last of their precious rain water stored in a tank since the rainy season.

The missionaries are translating the Scriptures into Kanuri, spoken by three million people around Lake Chad. Most Kanuris live across the border in Nigeria. The missionaries personally know of only four Kanuri Christians; there is no resident missionary in an area of 25,000 square miles. Yet the people will listen to the gospel. When a survey team traveled to the lake, they found a man who had carefully gone over and over the words of a tract for the past two years. He had safeguarded it when Muslim priests told the villagers to burn any literature left by missionaries passing through. He trusted in Christ through this second contact.

"We are in darkness and need you to open our minds to the light," a swarthy Kanuri told the survey team through kola-stained teeth.

The missionaries had to grind through deep sand with four-wheel drive to get to Lake Chad. It is a vast shallow basin which collects the rainy season waters from the south. As the seasons change it doubles in size from 10,000 to 20,000 square miles, yet its average depth is only 13 feet. Scientists don't know how to explain its loss of water; there are no visible outlets and evaporation could not account for all the loss.

They are making tests to explore the theory that an underground channel empties into the Nile. Local fishermen are not worried about where the water goes, though. Their main interest is the catch of 60,000 tons of fish a year taken from the lake. The fish are cut up and dried in the sun right on the spot, then shipped to southern markets. The only problem: while the fish are drying, flies lay eggs which hatch during shipment. Larvae consume much of the flesh on the way to market.

Jean Playfair from Gouré was visiting Maine when we were there. She is typical of several widows in the SIM. When her husband Earl died 10 years ago in Dahomey, a friend counselled her, "Don't lay down your cross just because Earl has taken up his crown." She didn't, but stayed out with her three children. When the Mission prayed for staff to open up the new work in the Chad area, she helped to answer the prayer, moving from Dahomey to Niger and learning a new language.

Paul Rogalsky flew Harry and me northwest to Tahoua, a picturesque town that looks like a Christmas-card Bethlehem —except that there aren't any cypress trees around, and everything is the color of brown mud. A thousand cattle streamed in over the barren dunes to the water hole beside the town.

Leather-skinned "Zeb" Zabriskie works among the Tuareg in the area. Completely veiled but for eyes, hands, and feet, they are the proud nomads of the desert. Zabriskie himself looked part of the desert as he kicked off his sandals and sat with a group of Tuareg. They talked with Zeb in Tamachek, the world's oldest written language still in use.

We set out in search of a Tuareg camp site. On the trail we passed a family moving house. Their goat-skin tent and poles were rolled up and piled on a donkey, along with goat-skin buckets and other chattels. On top of the pile sat a shy Buzu woman of the former slave class.

In the shadow of a sand dune we spotted a camp. A Tuareg father was giving a drink of precious water to his son, perched on a camel. Another milked a goat. Their women spun cotton under a low tent made of 10 goat skins, which insulated them from the blazing sun. Tuareg women don't wear veils—only the men do.

"The camel that blats doesn't bite," says a proverb; so I took courage and tried to mount a white dromedary in spite of its complaining burbling and growling with bared teeth. Its Tuareg master gave a command and up it went on its rear knees while I shot forward on the hump. A second command and it got up on its front knees while I nearly slid off backwards. Then up shot the rear again followed by the front. The beast was on its feet at last, but I still had to go through the ordeal in reverse to get my own feet back on terra firma. In spite of its sanctimonious expression (because only the camel knows the 100th name of Allah, say the nomads), the camel is no saint.

But who *is* a saint in the Sahara? It is a frightening experience to fly over it. Silent, endless wastes stretch before the eye. The Sahara covers three and a half million square miles—an area larger than USA without Alaska—and is advancing 30 square miles a year in places. No wonder the desert dwellers, like all Muslims, are fatalistic. They are gripped by a relentless environment.

Over the Western Sahara there is an average annual rainfall of one and one-half inches, but there are vast stretches where it never rains. The blanket of dry air above it could absorb a lake 12 to 15 feet deep in a year. Even if clouds do build up and precipitate, each drop evaporates before reaching the parched ground. A man's body loses 25 pints of fluid a day in this climate, in temperatures up to 144°. But the nights can be bitterly cold, with frost, because there is no atmospheric moisture to keep the day's heat in. The difference of temperature between day and night can be 80°

Yet the desert is not all shifting sand. Millenniums ago it was a Congo forest, and the black ranges now pointing starkly to the sky still show the scars of torrents which once cascaded down their timbered slopes. Below, elephants and rhinos roamed the verdant plains. And did more recent Saharan dwellers once know something of the gospel? The Tuareg camel saddle rises in front in the form of a cross, and women wear a cross around their necks.

"We need young men to learn the language and trek among these people," Zeb said. Before we left the camp, the Tuareg presented us with a live, kicking goat, in appreciation of our visit—desert hospitality to people they had never met before.

On the way back to Maradi we visited Galmi Hospital. Why anyone decided to build a hospital on that rubble-strewn plain, I couldn't understand. There were no trees for shade or shelter from sand storms, the well water tasted terrible, and there didn't seem to be much population in the area. But then I saw the line-up of patients that Dr. Jim VerLee, Dr. Serge Bagda-sarianz, and six nurses were handling: up to 200 operations a month at peak times, and a total of 114,000 patients treated in the past year. At least 20 doctors would be considered necessary to handle that load in Western lands. Galmi hospital is located between a number of population centers, and people streamed in from all directions—including Tamanrasset and Timbuktu, both 700 miles away. The two other surgical hospitals in the country (both government) are 300 miles to the west and 300 miles to the east. Niger has the world's lowest ratio of doctors to population, with one doctor to 100,000 people.

Dr. Burt Long opened the hospital in 1950. Harry and I were impressed with the dedication of the doctors and nurses. When off duty they slip back to the bedsides to explain the colored pages of a "wordless book" again, or to pray with a distressed patient.

We were also impressed with the odor of the ulcer ward. The whole hospital is operated like a battlefield clinic. Since there may be over 300 ward patients at times, when the 120 beds fill up, the overflow sleep on mats between the beds. The staff aren't there for professional prestige, but to relieve human suffering and lead souls to Christ.

In visiting hospitals I found an unresolved debate between two viewpoints: whether medical staff should keep up the standards they had at home, or provide "grass roots" medical service. The answer probably depends on the local level of development. One doctor went home from East Africa with a nervous breakdown because he couldn't put up with such local customs as patients spitting on the walls. But most doctors and nurses learn to work within their context and do not expect ideal conditions.

"I wish doctors and nurses at home could see Galmi," said Harry. "They'd realize the importance of a mission hospital in opening a country to the gospel and keeping it open. Look at the people streaming in—missionaries just couldn't get out to reach them all where they live!"

Niger's appreciation of the SIM's medical work was shown when President Hamani Diori knighted Dr. Long and decorated three nurses with national Orders. Newton and Doris Kapp also were decorated.

"I'll take you to see the President," Newton said. "He's very friendly—I've known him since he was a student. I have to go to the capital to see about obtaining a new site. We'll go during the independence anniversary celebrations—then you'll see something of the nation's educated class."

Harry Percy had to leave us at Maradi, to continue his tour eastward to Ethiopia. Before he got back to Canada, he had the additional experience of a mule kicking him, a windshield popping out, and a Land-Rover turning over down a hillside.

*   *   *

Niamey, Niger's capital, was alive with festivity for the celebrations when we arrived. Students roamed the streets, singing and drumming. Everyone wore his finest robe—some women wore cloth with gold threads glistening in it, and locally-fashioned gold earrings and necklaces. Other states joined Niger in displaying their wares at a trade fair. Perhaps the most practical piece of equipment was an Israeli-made solar cooker. It boils a kettle of water in a few minutes, using only the reflected rays of the sun.

In a colorful pageantry, 200 caparisoned camels followed by a rumbling column of modern artillery paraded past the President's dais. Platoons of uniformed men and women marched smartly by at the salute. Behind them stalked traditional hunters armed with spears, and a village entertainer with two muzzled hyenas.

Newton got us invitations to the President's palace for a banquet. The palace and its lush gardens were ablaze with electric lights when we arrived. We watched while the ladies and gentlemen of the land rolled up in chauffeur-driven limousines. Then all the lights went out—too many light bulbs were plugged in.

When the lights came back on, we were feted at tables set

between tropical shrubbery. After hors d'oeuvres, uniformed stewards carried in whole barbecued lamb carcasses and set them on tripods between the tables. We joined the other guests, who wore evening gowns and dinner jackets, in tearing strips of meat off the carcasses with our fingers. Tomtoms beat a rhythm throughout the evening.

We were in the world of the *evolué*—a far different world from the goat-skin Tuareg tents. The French theory was to evolve (hence "evolué") an upper class to administer their colonies. The intelligentsia were supposed to be absorbed into French society without distinction—some took their seats in the French parliament. The emphasis was on culture, and French-speaking Africa has produced a number of poet-philosophers. President Leopold Senghor of Senegal is one.

One typical difference I noticed: here the educated class almost always wear Western suits and dresses, whereas in the former British areas educated nationals proudly display their traditional robes.

"Missionaries must understand the difference in background between the former French and English countries," Newton explained as we watched the banquet scene. "That's why we need more French-speaking missionaries from Europe who understand the approach."

I found other missionaries conscious of the almost intangible differences, and thankful for the increasing number of new workers coming from Europe. They have an immediate rapport which an English-speaking missionary does not have. The French-speaking states need more missionaries. Although representing about 30 percent of West Africa's population, they have only 11 percent of the total missionary force of all denominations.

God has His Daniels among the *evolué* in Niger as well as in other lands. Newton introduced me to a strapping young man, Oumarou Youssoufou, who handles the President's protocol arrangements. Monsieur Oumarou keeps his Bible prominent as he moves in high places. His background: the SIM's Roni Boys' School, and Titcombe College, before studying in Europe. His wife is a former SIM school teacher.

"Bon courage!" I said to Newton Kapp as I later left him to continue my safari. "Bon courage. The gospel is at work in palaces as well as in goat-skin tents."

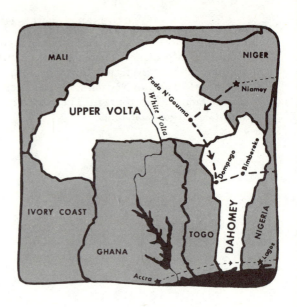

14. Initiation Ordeal

"There's big game down there on the other side of the river," said Bob Ediger. "Let's fly lower and have a look."

Bob was flying me from Niger Republic westward to neighboring Upper Volta, another of the three French-area states the SIM is working in. It is tucked under the great northern loop which the Niger River makes into the desert and is less arid than its neighbor.

We skimmed the treetops, keeping an eye on the dry bush below. A baboon loped off a boulder; a tiny dyker deer raced our shadow with graceful leaps. In the middle of a grassy meadow a herd of big roan antelope were startled at the roar of the plane.

"Elephant!" shouted Bob, pulling back on the plane's stick. Sure enough, there were seven of the gray mammoths feeding on shrubs. By the time we circled around they had crowded together under trees to escape from the strange Thing in the sky.

We later saw another elephant—a magnificent bull which flared its ears and threw up its trunk to repulse our "attack."

Upper Volta is another of West Africa's landlocked countries, with Ivory Coast, Ghana, Togo, and Dahomey for its southern neighbors. It is on a vast plateau about the size of Italy.

"We're thankful we have peace in this land," a missionary said to a visiting doctor.

"Yes," replied the doctor, "but that's *all* you've got!"

Actually this nation of 4,650,000 has plans for development, such as a factory for making soap from peanuts. Its capital, Ouagadougou, once had a TV station, Volta-Vision, operated primarily to help overcome the teacher shortage. It transmitted only two hours a day, and after the coup in 1966, the army closed it down to save money.

Upper Volta is the only independent state in West Africa officially classified as Roman Catholic. Actually the population is 80 percent animist, 18 percent Muslim, and the rest— around 70,000 people—are listed as "Christians." Most of those are Roman Catholics.

The SIM's work is among a large pagan tribe, the Gourma, in the eastern part of the country. I wondered how 250,000 Gourmas resisted the pressures of Islam that had surrounded their tribe for at least a century. Islam has in fact gone right around them in its drive southward to the sea.

"If you got to know the Gourmas, you'd see why," veteran Bill Strong explained. "These are some of the most independent people you've met. They don't even have the usual strong community ties. Islamic 'brotherhood' and prestige don't mean a thing to them. They say to the Muslim priests, 'You can believe what you want; it doesn't concern us.' So Islam has never made headway."

Of course that same independent spirit made them ignore the gospel for many years. In 1930 the SIM opened work at Fada N'Gourma in the middle of the tribe. It was 15 years later before a second station was opened, to the east at Diapaga. Then followed two more stations, south and north, at Mahadaga and Piela. After 30 years of slow, stunted growth, the work sprang into harvest in the sixties.

Then God used their independent spirit to *aid* the gospel. They individually made their decisions, not afraid to confess their faith in spite of opposition and persecution.

Old Yedipagiba is one I met. He had been a sandwriter—one who could tell the future through using marks in the sand as a kind of ouija board. He was squatting on a six-legged stool in his grass hut when we happened along.

"If you had come here before I was a follower of Jesus," he told us, demonstrating how he used to divine in the sand, "you would have seen people waiting around for me to tell their future. And I would have known you were coming before you left your house."

"Do those marks in the sand speak to you now?" I asked.

Yedipagiba's filed teeth showed as he grinned. "No. When I followed Jesus, I threw away the spirit stone which gave me power, because I knew it was from the devil. Now God speaks to me through the Bible."

These new believers are fearless and active. One young man had a vision in which God told him, "Go and witness—I have some people in yonder village." He went, and 15 villagers believed.

Before a youth can become a full member of the tribe, Gourma custom requires him to go through an initiation ordeal. The rites are officially banned but commonly practised. Because missionary John Klopfenstein is a male nurse, he was called by the village elders one afternoon to save the life of a boy who was bleeding to death.

"Guides led me to the secret camp site," John told me. "I could hardly believe my eyes. There were 40 naked boys

huddled in an enclosure of grass mats. They had just been circumcised in filthy conditions. I treated the boy they showed
me; then attended to others who were hemorrhaging.

"The men said I could come back to treat others; so I went
back several times over the next three months. The boys could
wear no clothes and at night they were tied down on the hard
ground, tethered by the hands and feet to four stakes. The men
taught them degrading sex perversions. Finally they were
cruelly beaten and made to drink urine."

"Did any die?" I asked.

"Not that year. They didn't call me in time this year,
though. Three boys died and another went mad."

Several years ago the Gourma area missionaries faced the
problem of helping Christian young men avoid the degradation of this custom which was basic to the whole structure of
the tribe. How could they retain the core of tribal culture but
place it in a scriptural setting? The answer may be unique in
missionary methods: a Christian initiation camp. The idea
was immediately welcomed by Christians, and now even some
pagan parents want to send their sons. They are afraid for their
boys' lives at the pagan camps.

Hygienic circumcision is performed, but the main purpose
of the camp is to give practical instruction and Bible study on
how to live the Christian life in a pagan community.

There were 20 boys in the last camp John Klopfenstein held.
Ten were not believers, but by the end of the two-week camp
all had come to know Christ as Saviour. Several married men
came for the instruction, and some became convicted they had
not been treating their wives as Christians should.

"This is strategic work," District Superintendent Alan
Swanson told me. "If we can build strong Christian homes—
an entirely new concept to these people—we shall be laying
foundations for the future of the church in Gourmaland."

I marveled that men who had once passed through the pagan
initiation rites could become pure-minded, zealous preachers
of the the gospel. Yempaabu is one such proof of the grace of

God. He and his six brothers believed in Christ, in spite of the raging of their father.

After training at the SIM's Bible school at Fada N'Gourma, Yempaabu and his young bride took the gospel to their people. For several years they stood in the center of a vicious storm as the gospel clashed with pagan culture. They were threatened with death; angry mobs hurled curses at them. But they stood firm, and today that area is transformed. Children run out to meet them; recently two village elders confessed Christ.

Other young men like Yempaabu are now in training. They and the missionaries in Gourmaland are praying that the whole tribe will soon hear the Word of God, and that there will be a great turning to the Lord. Baptized believers increased 30 percent in the past year.

*   *   *

I saw another example of the gospel's clash with a pagan culture across the border in Dahomey, the third "French" state in which the SIM works. Half-way down this long, narrow strip of a nation is the Dompago tribe.

When Roland Pickering arrived in Dahomey in 1952, he was assigned to this little-known area. His task was to reduce the language to writing, translate the Scriptures, win and teach converts, and see the Lord establish His church in the area.

"It was too much for me," said Roland. "I didn't know where to begin. I could only give myself to the Lord for Him to do it."

What happened would make quite a book. *Chapter 1:* Roland's hut burned down, which ironically "broke the ice" and made him accepted in the tribe. *Chapter 2:* He learned enough of the language to preach the gospel, and people began leaving fetishism and turning to the Lord. *Chapter 3:* Roland agreed to teach a Bible school which *they* requested and organized. Church leadership was forming. *Chapter 4:* Roland boned up on agriculture, introduced better strains of grain and poultry. **Christians, free from fear of evil spirits, moved** to better land, raised their standard of living from subsistence level. *Chapter 5:* The gospel made such an impact on the life of the tribe, spiritually and sociologically, that visiting French experts were amazed, asked how Roland had done it. *Chapter 6:* Roland said he hadn't done it; he had only been God's tool. When I last saw him he was having the time of his life helping the Dompago churches grow.

Roland has been careful not to impose Western social customs on the people, but to let them develop their own code of Christian conduct from reading the Scriptures. Without any prompting from him they decided, for instance, that they should wear clothes and stop drinking beer.

On this safari I sometimes heard uninformed white people say that missionaries have ruined African culture, whereas traditional ceremonies are forms of art. But when I asked believers if missionaries had "destroyed their culture," they protested.

"Not at all!" they said. "We know even better than the missionaries what the songs and dances and drinking mean. We know we can't continue in them once we belong to the Lord, because they are connected with pagan rites. They are the same as the pagan feasts of Corinth that Paul warned about."

Occasionally hyper-nationalists accuse missionaries of robbing Africa of her "heritage" and call for a return to "the good old days." I read an editorial in an African-owned newspaper which answered that cry:

> "We think Christianity has saved Africa. Think of any African leader you know. Minus very few of them, the rest were trained and brought up by Christian missionaries.
>
> "Our social customs and traditions have not been destroyed by missionaries. All that happened is that those evil aspects in them died a natural death when they came face to face with a new set of values and higher morals."

Dahomey itself was famous a century ago for its Amazon

warriors but is now noted more for bronze figurines. I watched these being made by the primitive "lost wax" method. A perspiring craftsman coated a wax figure with clay, then heated it over a fire. After the wax melted and dripped out through a hole, he poured in bronze which another artisan had smelted from old car radiators. When the bronze hardened, the craftsman broke away the clay and chiseled markings on the figurine. It is a tedious process requiring a new mold for every figure.

The SIM has nine stations in the northern half of this narrow strip of a nation; two and a half million people live in 43,630 square miles. I sensed the frustration of the missionaries over two closed ministries. One was the French Bible school opened in 1961 at Kandi, but closed after one year for lack of French staff. In preparing church leadership able to stand in the rapid development of the nation, it is essential to have Bible training in French.

The other heartbreak was the hospital at Bimbereke—the only mission hospital in all Dahomey. At the opening in 1960, the nation's President thanked the SIM for its Christian ministry. But for two years the hospital was closed. No doctor.

"One man even jumped in the well to commit suicide when he trekked all the way here and found the doors closed," missionary Jim Cail told me. "I have never seen anyone more the picture of skin and bones. We've had letters from the Government, too, imploring us to re-open."

And on top of the shortage of missionary personnel, two key leaders had been drowned. Why, why, why—the missionaries were tempted to ask. But God's heart is greater than any sorrow, any shortage, any need. His plans move on in the face of seeming tragedy. What he requires is obedience and faithfulness.

The SIM's linguistics center in Dahomey has helped produce a major breakthrough in the science of linguistics. Missionaries revising a translation of the Gospel of John in the Bariba language ran into a complex problem. The tribe didn't usually use the first person in telling a story. So they wouldn't understand the verse, "Jesus said, 'No man can come to the father but through me.' "

When a missionary read it that way, the people said, "All right, we shall follow *you*." So the missionary had to change it to their way: "Jesus said that no one can go to the father but through him."

Yet unaccountably there would be a switch to first person at times. National "informants" couldn't agree on a pattern; translation came to a standstill. Then opportunity came for one of the missionary linguists to take part in a linguistics workshop in Nigeria. Working with Dr. Kenneth Pike of Wycliffe Bible Translators, she was able to formulate a pattern which could be applied not only to Bariba but to other languages with similar problems. "A major step forward in the field of discourse," Dr. Pike declared.

Africa has 1,400 distinct languages, with 400 of them in West Africa. It takes an average of 15 years to reduce a language to writing and translate the New Testament. The SIM currently has translation projects in a dozen languages across Africa.

An evangelist was reading the Scriptures to a Bariba. The tribesman listened intently to Isaiah's account of God's wrath against witchcraft 3,000 years ago. He placed his hand over his mouth in surprise.

"How did God know all about the Baribas?" he asked.

15. "Let My People Go"

Our jet met the sun over the world's longest river, the fabled Nile. Through the night we had crossed Nigeria, the Cameroon watershed, and the scrublands of Chad and western Sudan. Now in the blaze of a tropical dawn we landed beside the river of the Pharaohs at Khartoum, capital of the Republic of Sudan.

At Khartoum, the White Nile, reaching the 2,000-mile mark in its journey from Uganda down through the southern Sudan, mixes with the Blue Nile, not so far from its rocky source high in Ethiopia's mountains to the east. On the waters flow, through nearly 2,000 miles of burning sand before reaching the Mediterranean. From Khartoum to Cairo the Nile crawls like a writhing serpent, with an average drop of eight inches per mile. Ten percent of the water is lost in evaporation; the rest supports a thin vein of life along its course.

In area Africa's largest country, Sudan stretches from Egypt and the Red Sea down to Uganda and tributaries of the Congo. It led the way in Africa's decade of independence when in 1956 it became the first African nation to receive independence from a colonial power. But this nation of 12 million is ruptured by an ethnological problem: most of the eight million living in the five northern provinces are Arab-related, while four million in the three southern provinces are Negro-related.

"Let my people go," cried Moses 3,500 years ago beside the Nile. Today the cry echoes across the plains of the Upper Nile in a tragic modern Exodus.

The problem was being aired in the capital's newspapers when I arrived. One quoted a speech the Prime Minister had given the day before: "It is not a simple problem of race and religion we are up against. It is a whole matrix of relationships that has been vitiated in part by lack of imagination on the side of our past colonial masters, and in part by professional religionists, who posed as benefactors to Southerners and advisers to administrators."

In an editorial headlined "Premier Attacks Churches," a sometimes-banned opposition paper objected to the statement that the Southern problem was created by imperialists and missionaries. "The Anglo-Egyptian occupation has been in the grave for the last 11 years and the last remnants of the tortured missionaries were deported early in 1964. One would like to ask the Prime Minister to compare the magnitude of the problem today with what it was only three years ago."

The missionaries were not "tortured," but 272 Roman Catholics and 28 Protestants were expelled from the South in 1964. The only Christian missionaries left in Sudan are a few in the Islamic North, where it is felt they will have little effect, while lending support to the administration's claim of religious liberty.

The problem is complex. Caught in the conflict of Arab against African and African against Arab, it is difficult for Southern Christians to keep neutral. Pressure is put on them by their own people to join the rebels. Pagan southerners sometimes "turn Christian" in their animosity to Muslim northerners.

A newspaper report estimated that perhaps one million southerners have died, and another 120,000 have fled the country. One village was wiped out because a couple of soldiers were killed in the area. To teach the whole area a lesson, soldiers shot all the men and boys, burned the huts, and took the women and girls captive.

While the government claimed that churches were sacked only because rebels were hiding in them, one paper reported African priests shot at, bullet holes in cathedral doors, seminaries attacked, and churches burned. "A law to curb the spread of Christianity by the military regime is still in execution. There is a government department catering for Islam and an Islamic Constitution is being envisaged."

This is present-day Sudan. Yet the remarkable fact is that it was once the site of two powerful Christian kingdoms. Recorded references to Sudan date back 4,000 years, to 2000 B.C. when Egypt subjugated northern Sudan, the land of Kush. Finally the tables were turned and the king of Kush overran Egypt from 744–710 B.C. The Assyrians drove the Sudanese out of Egypt in 661 B.C., about the time the prophet Jeremiah was prophesying Assyria's attacks on Israel.

The Ethiopian eunuch (Acts 8.27) was really from a city north of Khartoum and was likely the first Christian witness in Sudan (A.D. 34). At that time the term "Ethiopian" was applied to all dark-skinned people, whether in Africa or India. The eunuch was treasurer of Candace, the queen-mother, who looked after such secular matters because the deified king, child of the Sun-god, was considered too holy. Candace ruled from Meroe, between what is now Khartoum and Aswan. This was ancient Sudan's finest period of culture, but by A.D. 350 Meroe was in ruins and the people had lost even the art of writing.

In A.D. 540 the Empress Theodora of Byzantium (Turkey) sent Christian missionaries to convert the Sudanese, and two powerful Christian kingdoms arose. These Sudanese Christians fought off invading Egyptian Muslims in the seventh century, but one kingdom fell to Islam in A.D. 1323. The other Christian kingdom continued until A.D. 1504—just before Martin Luther confronted the pope in Europe—and finally fell to a tribe from the south. Pockets of Coptic Christians continued to exist, but for 300 years there was no evangelical witness in the once "Christian" Northern Sudan.

Now most of the mission work in Khartoum is among Egyptian-background Copts. The Coptic Church is similar in structure to the Greek Orthodox Church but is Monophysitic —teaching that Jesus Christ has only one nature, not two. Most of the Church's three million members are in Egypt and Ethiopia, although the Ethiopian Orthodox Church is independent of Egypt and dislikes the term "Copt". Many Coptic young people in Khartoum have shown an interest in the gospel, and the SIM holds weekly classes for them.

The tragedy of the Coptic Christians—even evangelicals— is that they have no vision for witnessing to Northern Muslims or Southern pagans. This isolated position can only result in stagnation. Few believe a Muslim can be converted. They don't want to identify with Southern Christians for fear of antagonizing the government. Meanwhile Muslims are pressing to make Sudan a completely Islamic state. Saudi Arabia has promised finances to propagate Islam in the southern provinces. Even the Red Cross Society is called "The Red Crescent" in Sudan.

There is no discrimination between Northerners and Southerners at the SIM headquarters. On Sunday afternoon two different language groups of Southerners meet for services on the compound. At night 21 nations are represented at the SIM's gospel service. When I was there, two Dinkas, black as shoe polish, dropped in for supper with the missionaries. One of them was president of the Christian Fellowship at the university. He was 24, in his second year, and hoped to become an anthropologist. He was six feet five inches tall in his socks.

"Do sit down," I begged him; "then I won't feel so inferior having to look up at you." He laughed and sat beside me. We were then the same height, for a Dinka's height is in his spindly legs. The lower half of a Dinka's face is compressed and the forehead extended; traditional Dinka tribal scars are cut horizontally in five rows from temple to temple, making a perpetual frown. These men had not heard from any relatives for several months, and it wouldn't be safe for them to return home to look for them. "Our people are hiding in the forests," they said, "—if they are still alive."

Missionaries are not allowed to visit the southern provinces, but I talked with a Christian university professor who had just returned from an anthropological survey. He met the pastor who now heads up the "little flock" left behind by SIM missionaries. He told me the believers were standing true against great odds.

I had met that pastor and many of the Christians during a visit before the expulsion of missionaries. The trip "up south" was like traveling backwards a thousand years. I went part way on the White Nile in an outboard motorboat. We passed clusters of mud huts on the banks, where people lived just as their ancestors did a millennium ago. A family floated past us on a raft piled with charcoal. They made charcoal up on the Sudd plains and lived on the raft for three weeks while they floated downriver 800 miles to sell it.

We had just spotted three hippos in the river when a pin in the propeller shaft sheared and we, too, began to drift. We paddled into a clump of tall grass, startling a mother heron from her nest. While we made repairs, the hippos became curious and swam toward us, their bulging eyes sticking up out of the water. Although I was happy to get a close-up photo, I was not too happy when they kept diving and surfacing closer to the boat. I could visualize the boat and us flipping into the air after the next dive. They finally satisfied their curiosity and swam off into midstream.

Great clumps of water hyacinth kept floating past us. It is one of the world's most prolific water weeds, multiplying itself one thousand times in six weeks.

When we turned up one of the Nile's tributaries, we found it choked with hyacinth. Finally we had to abandon the boat and walk the rest of the way to the station. We passed telegraph lines which had been raised to an extra height because giraffe were constantly tangling their heads in the wires on their way down to the river to drink.

This was Dinka country. Dinkas are some of the proudest people on earth. I wondered why. Those barren plains stretching back from the Nile are to them paradise itself. There are no trees to speak of; the earth is rent by deep fissures in the dry season and turns into an impassable bog in the rains. Their grass huts sit starkly on the bare earth, bleached by the relentless sun and swept by the dust-laden wind. Lions stalk through the rainy-season grass, and tiny grain birds darken the sky in the dry season, bent on consuming what little grain may be ripening. Away from the river, where women may have to walk several miles for water (for the men and dogs), the people dust themselves with ashes instead of bathing.

I could understand why missionaries think that Isaiah was describing Dinka country when he wrote: "Woe to the land shadowing with wings, which is beyond the rivers of Ethiopia: that sendeth ambassadors by the sea, even in vessels of bulrushes upon the waters, saying, Go, ye swift messengers, to a nation scattered and peeled, to a people terrible from their beginning hitherto; a nation meted out and trodden down, whose land the rivers have spoiled!"

Leaving the Nilotic plains, I had traveled further east, within sight of the foothills of the Ethiopian plateau. Here the SIM worked among several small tribes.

Anthropologists describe Koma and Mabaan life as one of

the most primordial on earth. A renowned ear specialist claims that Mabaans have perfect hearing, presumably because of the almost total lack of "artificial" noises. They do not use the wheel. They crawl through small holes to enter their roughly-built huts. Their bodies are covered with deep tribal scars and patterns made by an instrument like a crochet hook, which raises the flesh. Soot and mud are rubbed in to scarify the tissue. Their women's ears bristle with thorns pierced through; two bottom teeth are knocked out and a beaded ring inserted in the lower lip. In a neighboring tribe, twin babies are killed for fear of the evil spirits which must have caused their birth.

Seeing these people who have impassively borne torture from childhood, filled my soul with loathing for the devil, who has reduced God's magnificent creation into scarred specters. I realized that those vacant, frightened eyes could have sparkled with intelligence if the gospel had only arrived sooner to dispel the superstition, the ignorance, the cruelty with which Satan tyrannizes his slaves. Africans with brilliant minds and healthy physiques all across the continent prove what the Creator intended them to be.

An amazing transformation takes place as these people turn to Christ. They develop a respect for their bodies, now the "temples of the Holy Spirit." They want to be clean, to clothe themselves, to learn to read. They let air and light into their huts. They build an extra room so they can get away from the smoke of the cooking fire and the disturbances of children, to read and pray. Instead of wasting their precious grain in brewing beer, they store it to feed the family during the dry season. Their whole lives become changed, not by the white man's customs, but by the desire to please their Maker and obey His Word.

But then come the problems; their new lives clash with tribal customs based on the old life. Men are cast out of their clan for refusing to brew ceremonial beer and join in drunken orgies. Any change in the course of nature is blamed on

Christians for grieving the ancestors. Christian girls returning to their village from boarding school have been known to have their clothes torn off by shrieking women, fearful lest the spirits make them all sterile because of these foolish ones who dare cover themselves.

A major problem is sister exchange. Koma tribal custom demands that a brother give a female relative to marry a man in the family from which he wants his wife. If either man has trouble with his wife—for anything from not brewing enough beer to sterility—and returns her to her parents, the other man has to return his own wife to her parents.

In pagan society, where women's feelings are not considered and marriage ties are often loose, this is a useful form of security against marriage palavers. For a Christian, however, it can be tragic. It can mean that a Christian sister has to be given in marriage to a pagan member of the other family. It can mean that a Christian woman has to be wrenched from her Christian husband and children if a pagan relative decides to return his wife. When Christians refuse to continue these traditional arrangements, often contracted before conversion, there is real trouble.

So the gospel conflicts with pagan society, and there are no easy answers to the complex problems which arise.

It was at Chali, in the Uduk tribe, that I met one of the pastors during my visit before the expulsion. He was helping the missionaries rush to complete the New Testament in his language. No one knew how long the missionaries would have, and they wanted to leave the Word of God with the people.

A leopard had recently been killed near Chali, and according to custom the villagers must stay in their huts for one week, lest the leopard's spirit find them. The week was over, and a leopard dance was to be held that night. Veteran Mary Beam, whom the people looked upon as their "white mother," took me down to the village. The grass huts stood out against a full yellow moon. A rhythmic beating filled the air.

We found six men standing in a huddle, each beating a rod on a thick, yard-long piece of resonant wood gripped between his legs. Perspiration glistened on their unclothed bodies. The villagers had been drinking beer. They paid no attention to us, but one by one joined in a large circle around the drummers. They moved in a slow shuffle around and around, chanting a minor strain punctuated by glottal sounds like air trying to get into a rapidly emptying water bottle.

"Listen," whispered Mary; "they are singing about the pastor." She interpreted for me as they told of all the deviltry he had participated in before his conversion. They could not forgive the young evangelist for leaving their ways; his wife had even given birth to twins—surely the devil's judgment on him. Who was this Jesus, anyway? Was He not the white man's God?

As the thumping increased in tempo the dancers chanted other folk songs. The circle was full now with men and women, teenagers, and children swaying around—all entirely naked. Suddenly the thumping stopped, and the drummers made an evil sound. This was the signal for the males to jerk their bodies lewdly at the females. The thumping and swaying began again, built up into a frenzied crescendo, followed by more lewdness.

It was nauseating, and Mary and I turned back to the mission station. I wished I could take teenagers from our "enlightened" lands and let them see the truth about today's sensual dances.

The pastor they were ridiculing was one of three the expelled missionaries later left as overseers of the Church of the East-Central Sudan (SIM). They were like Daniel's three young friends in the fiery furnace.

One is bravely strengthening the believers in difficult circumstances. Another is currently overseas, where he had to go to have an artificial limb fitted. His family was in the chieftaincy line, and had he been at home, he too would have been slain with the others. He was bitter when he first heard the news, but God worked in his life and he stayed overseas to take Bible training. One day this man will return with the Word of God for his people—God making it possible.

The missionaries had counted on the third man, Gideon Adwok, to be a pillar in the young church. He was better trained than his fellow Shilluks, but he walked humbly. He farmed with them, he taught them how to read the Bible. He counseled and preached. After his ordination, he became secretary-treasurer of the SIM churches. Then all the missionaries had to leave the south. Gideon's eyes were wet but shone resolutely as he said he would see them in Christ's presence, if not before.

One day soldiers came looking for men rumored to be collecting money to aid the rebels. They found pastor Gideon's church offering box, with a list of names of members and their monthly church pledges. The soldiers would accept no explanation. While his friends pleaded and his family wept, they tortured him and took him bound to the river's edge. They shot him and two other church leaders. Crocodiles tore up their bodies thrown into the river.

My visit to Sudan left me with disturbing thoughts about our Western Christian philosophy. We have it all down so pat: believe in Jesus and all your problems will be solved. How can you tell that to a Dinka boy who knows he will have difficulty finishing school and getting a decent job—because he is a believer? How can you slap a Southern Sudanese on the back and say, "Cheer up, saint of God, there's nothing to worry about!"—when he has just heard that his family and village have been wiped out? Can you even sing that comforting hymn, "God will take care of you," as Gideon is led to the river and shot?

These thoughts shook me as I revisited Sudan and heard of the suffering of believers there. I realized my own Christian philosophy had been built on the security and affluence of a cozy Christian society. It seems we have picked out the Scripture promises about God's protection and provision, and have skipped over the verses about suffering: "All that will live godly in Christ Jesus shall suffer persecution. . . . We are joint-heirs with Christ if so be that we suffer with Him."

I thought again of the three young men standing before the king of Babylon and saying, "Our God is able to deliver us from the burning fiery furnace—*but if not*, we still shall not serve your gods!" The three pastors left behind by the SIM missionaries had an "if-not" theology as they faced the fiery furnace. All Sudanese believers have to have an "if-not" outlook on life and death and their faith. God *is* able to deliver them—but if He chooses not to, they will still be faithful unto death.

God used a seeming tragedy to bring the gospel to the people of Sudan's Blue Nile and Upper Nile Provinces in the first place. It was after Mussolini's army expelled missionaries from Ethiopia that the SIM redirected its personnel to the east-central Sudan in 1936. Anglicans, Presbyterians, and the Sudan United Mission worked farther south and west.

Twenty-six years later, God used a second expulsion to send the missionaries on to other areas. Instead of wringing their hands, they thanked God for 26 years of planting and trusted Him to continue watering.

During this safari I met in Khartoum with the seven SIM missionaries left in the north. It was the Mission's day of prayer, the last Friday of the month. We prayed for the believers in the south. They too would be meeting, because the government decreed that everyone observe Friday instead of Sunday as the day of rest. We sang a hymn by a French believer who had been imprisoned two centuries before, Madame Guyon:

> *To me remains nor place nor time,*
> *My country is in every clime;*
> *I can be calm and free from care*
> *On any shore, since God is there.*

My Bible reading that night was John 16: "The time cometh, that whosoever killeth you will think that he doeth God service. . . . These things I have spoken unto you, that in me ye might have peace. In the world ye shall have tribulation; but be of good cheer; I have overcome the world."

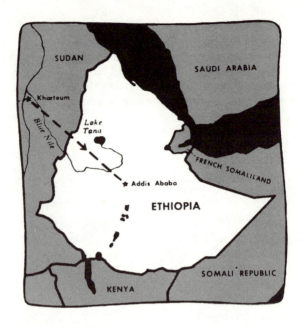

16. The Queen of Sheba's Land

I flew in to Ethiopia at 10 miles a minute in a luxurious Ethiopian Airlines jet. The svelte Ethiopian stewardesses and natty stewards made the flight a royal one. We landed at Addis Ababa's modern airport in the geographic center of the ancient empire. The cool breeze at 8,200 feet made me shiver for the first time on this safari.

One needs a word like "magnificent" to describe Ethiopia. The cloud-draped ranges are graced with eucalyptus trees which change from green to blue to silver as the wind combs their leaves.

In this exotic land, 22 million people live in 450,000 mountainous square miles. Even the calendar reminded me I had arrived in a different world: the date is reckoned eight years behind our calendar, and the year has 13 months—12 of 30 days each, with the remaining five or six in a thirteenth. Christmas Day is celebrated January 7th. The time of day is reckoned from sunrise, so that noon is only 6 a.m.

The nation's modern capital is the seat of the Organization of African Unity, with its imposing Africa Hall. The Ethiopian Tourist Organization speaks glowingly of "untouched beauty, the appeal of the traditional way of life," and describes "the country man trying to herd his donkeys and goats through a changing traffic light along the palm-fringed boulevards."

Addis Ababa (New Flower) was in full blossom with the annual Timkat festival when I arrived. "Of all Ethiopian festivals, Timkat is probably the most celebrated and beloved," explained the tourist folder I picked up in the plane. "The holiday commemorates the baptism of Jesus Christ in the River Jordan by St. John the Baptist."

I joined the people streaming toward the Jan Hoy meadow in the early morning—women dressed in lovely embroidered shawls and full white skirts; men in tailored shirts and Indian-style jodhpurs. Processions from the city's churches, their priests and "arks" in the midst, were converging in colorful display on the meadow.

An eerie chanting sound came from loudspeakers. Elbowing my way through to the blue-painted pool used for the ceremony, we saw a priest robed in gold and crimson brocade, intoning effortlessly into a microphone, accompanied by a chorus of falsetto-voiced novices. They were reciting ceremonial passages in the sacred Ge'ez, ancient Ethiopic language which the people do not understand. A functionary was trying to set a tray of lighted candles afloat on the pool but had to retreat in defeat when they kept toppling into the water. A Boy Scout sold me a Timkat tag which depicted John sprinkling Jesus in an ankle-deep Jordan River. An Amharic inscription exulted, "Oh joy—thus He has brought you to the light of baptism!"

Two hours after the appointed time the patriarch and his

high priest drove up in an Oldsmobile and swept into the enclosure, holding out their crosses to be kissed. The white bearded patriarch read the Scriptures—again in unintelligible Ge'ez—about the baptism of Jesus. Just as he finished, the industrious Boy Scout appeared under his outstretched arms and pinned a Timkat tag on him. Before the boy would leave, the patriarch had to pull up his black skirts to get a coin from his pocket. The crowd nodded approvingly at this priestly benevolence.

After further incantations, the patriarch blessed the water spraying out of an ornate fountain, on which were figures of John baptizing Jesus. The highest ranking VIP leaned forward and received the baptismal water on his forehead. Others followed.

Anxious to photograph the ceremony, I climbed up on the back side of the fountain wall, just out of range of the spray. All at once the quiet dignity of the baptismal service disintegrated, and I found myself looking down on a pandemonium of flailing limbs. I then realized that the archbishop, priests, and VIPs had disappeared, which was the signal for the local populace to burst past the police to get some of the holy water. A monk who hadn't got away in time stood in the fountain's basin and splashed water up into the faces of the hilarious crowd—and into the lenses of my cameras. To my surprise I felt water pouring on my head and through the back of my coat. The caretaker had thoughtfully turned up the water pressure so that the fountain spray would reach more people. I too was thoroughly re-baptized.

During this melée the dignitaries seated themselves on an elevation from which they could watch the ceremonial dancing of the priests. In front of them, contingents from the churches moved into position, each with its banner, sacred cross, and priest carrying a *tabot* (ark of the covenant) on his head. A stoic-faced holy man nearly stole the show, as far as the tourists were concerned, by standing with a large brazier of flaming charcoal balanced on his matted hair.

Novices held tassled umbrellas over the heads of priests who perfumed the air by gently swinging silver censers containing burning incense. Each church tried to outdo the others in vivid colors and ornaments. The meadow was a dazzling ring of blue, yellow, crimson, chartreuse, and purple, flecked with burnished brass and sparkling silver and gold. The zenith of splendor was reached in the line-up of chief priests, each bedecked in the richest vestments and balancing his *tabot* on his head.

A *tabot* is supposed to be a replica of the tablets of the Law from the ark of the covenant, which was stolen from Jerusalem, according to Ethiopic tradition. It forms the center of the Church's worship—in fact, the *tabot*, not the church is consecrated. The *tabot* sanctifies the church in which it rests.

In the middle of the semicircle two lines of monks assembled to perform the ceremonial dance. To the slow tempo of muffled drums, rhythmic handclapping, and the rattling of silver sistra, the monks swayed slowly back and forth in unison, keeping time with their prayer staffs. Throughout the religious dance the effortless sing-song chanting rose and fell.

My mind went back to the Old Testament days, when "David and all the house of Israel played before the Lord on all manner of instruments. And David danced before the Lord" (2 Samuel 6:5, 14).

In fact, there is a lot of Israel and the Old Testament in Ethiopian church life. Judaistic influences were strong centuries before the Christian era. The names of the days of the week reflect Hebraic derivation. Among all the world's cultures, only in Israel and ancient Abyssinia (as far as records show) were male babies circumcised on the eighth day. Through the centuries Ethiopians have resisted the customs of surrounding Muslims, pagans, and even Egyptian Copts and have retained the eighth day for circumcision, as prescribed in the Pentateuch.

The Queen of Sheba's visit to Solomon is an integral part of Ethiopia's link with Israel. Actually historians are not agreed on whether Shebaland was in Ethiopia or on the other side of the Red Sea or farther south on Africa's coast. But the Ethiopian tradition that the Queen had a son sired by Solomon, who became the founder of the nation's Solomonic dynasty is "one of the most powerful and influential national sagas anywhere in the world," states Dr. Edward Ullendorf, Professor of Ethiopian Studies, University of London.

Although Western Christians may look on it as an apocryphal perversion of the Bible story, it is accepted by Ethiopians without any sense of impropriety, fitting the context of Eastern morals. The legend affects the whole personality of Ethiopia and its attitudes to Africa's other major ethnic groups (Arab and Negro) and religions (Islam and animism).

Ethiopians certainly are unlike any other people on the continent. So opposed are these light brown people to being classed with Africa's negroid races that the government once banned a shipment of dictionaries which so defined them. Ethiopia's northern plateau was first inhabited by Ham's son Cush, or Ethiops. Semitic Arab tribes later crossed the Red Sea and intermingled with the descendants of Ethiops.

Christianity was introduced to Ethiopia in the fourth century. Two Syrian boys, who alone were kept alive when Ethiopians massacred the crew of their father's merchant ship on the Red Sea coast, became court advisers to the royal family. Through them the youthful King Ezana and his family heard the gospel and believed.

The king not only introduced Christianity officially but also, on the advice of his two Syrian courtiers, brought in Roman merchants and builders. One of the Syrians later became the first bishop of the Ethiopian Church, which then came under the patriarch of Alexandria in Egypt. Today it is independent of the Egyptian Coptic Church and appoints its own archbishop. Greek was the official language at this time, and Greek gods and culture were introduced to the Ethiopian plateau.

It has been a topsy-turvy world. In the sixth century a Christian king of Ethiopia rescued Christians in Arabia from being exterminated by a Jewish king—and tried to destroy the Kaaba stone, which was being worshiped by pagans. That same year Mohammed was born, and the Kaaba is now the center of Muslim pilgrimage to Mecca.

Added to the inevitable conflicts of Judaism, Christianity, and the Greek pantheon were remnants of animism among the original descendants of Cush. Ethiopians today state that initially part of the nation worshiped the serpent and part worshiped God. As I would be finding out in my travels, belief in magic, spirits, and the evil eye is deeply ingrained in Ethiopian life.

What I saw at the Timkat ceremony was symbolic of the remarkable syncretism found in the Ethiopian Orthodox Church. The Judaistic chanting, the Orthodox icon paintings, the magical power sought in the baptismal water by the delirious crowd—all resulted from the many influences upon Ethiopia through the centuries.

Later that day I followed the festive crowds as they paraded their churches' *tabots* through the streets of Addis. The sidewalks were filled with knots of dancers. It was the end of the Feast of Timkat, the annual commemoration of the baptism of our Lord. In the evening I walked away from the hilarity, back to the SIM guest house. The city lights were now on, and from the open doors of house after house streamed yellow light. Against the walls were bottles of beer and wine, and silhouetted in each doorway was a girl. The street dancers would soon be passing that way.

This is the context in which missionaries find themselves working today. There are 32 missions registered in Ethiopia, with a total of 900 missionaries. Some, like the Lutherans, work closely with the State Orthodox Church. SIM-affiliated churches, however, are members of the indigenous Fellowship of Evangelical Believers, which lists 1,214 churches. These support 200 Ethiopian missionary evangelists. The SIM lists

275 missionaries on 45 stations, but one-fifth are on furlough at any given time.

Most Orthodox people have resented the intrusion of non-Orthodox missions. Recently, however, their attitude has shown some change as they see Islam increasing. The population is divided into thirds as to religions: Orthodox, Muslim, and pagan. Evangelicals total roughly 150,000 church members, plus 100,000 adherents.

"Evangelical missions have produced some of our finest statesmen," His Imperial Majesty, Emperor Haile Selassie I, recently told a mission conference. His interest in the spread of the gospel stems from his personal faith in the Lord Jesus Christ. His inherited titles of Elect of God, Conquering Lion of the Tribe of Judah, King of Zion, and King of Kings are not looked upon as sacrilegious but the nation's inheritance from the Solomonic dynasty. The Emperor is "King of Kings" because there are other kings under him.

His titles may sound pompous, but His Imperial Majesty is a humble gentleman. Although only five feet four inches tall and weighing 100 pounds, he has held his troubled nation together for over 35 years; he towered morally over the heads of many other world statesmen when the League of Nations stood idle while Italy invaded his land.

Because of the Emperor's personal interest in the work of the gospel, and since nearly every detail of the nation's life comes under his scrutiny at some stage, SIM leaders in Ethiopia have always had very intimate relations with the royal household. The phone once rang at SIM headquarters with a royal command: The Emperor had seen a magazine photo of the President of the United States receiving a new edition of the Bible from the Bible Society. A palace official asked the SIM to get the Emperor one like it—and the telephone rang often until the Bible eventually arrived.

When the Empress Menen was ill, the palace asked the SIM to send a nurse. When the Emperor's son was dying, the SIM

Secretary gave a blood transfusion. When the Empress wanted to do something for orphans, she turned to the wives of SIM headquarters' staff and asked them to start and operate Her Imperial Majesty's Children's Home.

Howard and Ruth Borlase from SIM headquarters took me to meet their good friend, Her Imperial Highness Tenangye Werke, firstborn of the Emperor and first lady of the land since her mother died in 1962. In a humble little Volkswagen we drove up to the Princess's palace, surrounded with ornamental shrubbery and brilliant blossoms. A white-liveried doorman ushered us into the parlor, filled with exotic ornaments and furniture from around the world.

Her Imperial Highness was detained at an official reception, explained her daughter, Princess Sophia. Trim and tiny, her hair in the latest bouffant style, the attractive princess perched on the edge of an over-stuffed crimson armchair while chatting informally with us in a cultured English accent. The young Princess came to the Lord during her student days in England and is always ready to talk of spiritual things. She has an English Bible college graduate as governess for her five-year-old daughter.

We sipped coffee until H.I.M. the Princess arrived, apologetic for keeping us waiting. She noticed that Ruth Borlase was wearing the solid gold bracelet given her by the Empress in appreciation of her service at the Children's Home, and she asked about some of the children by name. She was delighted to know that a blind girl, who had been the first child sent to the Home by the Empress, was now teaching. Ruth told her that the girl had sung at her farewell, "Face to Face with Christ My Saviour"—with joy on her face at the words, "I shall *see* Him, face to face"!

I asked the Princess what she felt was the greatest need of the nation.

"The laying of a spiritual foundation is the greatest need," she replied. "If our people, particularly our youth, don't have this, how can they build a strong nation? Spiritual life is the most important aspect of a nation."

An attendant whispered a reminder about her next engagement, and we excused ourselves. It had been a simple, family-style visit with members of a royal family who would gladly lay their crowns at the feet of their Saviour and eternal King.

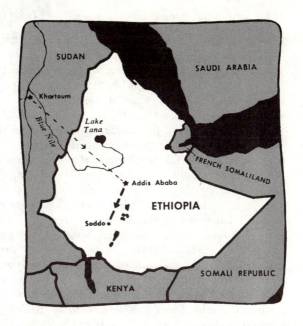

17. Boots in the Offering Plate

"We've arranged to take you down to the Wallamo conference at Soddo," said Walter Ohman. "It's an experience you'll never forget."

Driving the 220 miles south with Walter and his wife made the trip even more unforgettable, because they gave me background details that lent significance to what I saw. This was Walter's farewell trip before retiring from office as East Africa Director of the SIM. Thirty-eight years before, he and others in a pioneer party took two weeks to make the trip with a caravan of 20 donkeys and 66 mules. Now we sped over a well-graded road in six and a half hours.

The scenery moved by like a travelog film: eucalyptus

groves along the ridges of undulating hills; thatched huts huddled among lush banana-like inset trees; stately cedars planted by Italians of a past era; candelabra cactuses and flat-topped acacia trees, through which we caught glimpses of the lakes which rest on the floor of the Rift Valley. This is the same Rift Valley that ruptures the earth's surface for 4,000 miles all the way from Jordan through the Red Sea to Mozambique in southeast Africa. We crossed the arid Arussi plain where two of the Ohmans' missionary colleagues had been murdered by bandits while fleeing to Addis during the Italian occupation.

The struggling work at Soddo seemed doomed to extinction when the missionaries were forced out by the Italian invaders in 1936. But God was bringing His church to birth through the pangs of tribulation. When Walter Ohman left Soddo there were only 48 Wallamo baptized believers and only one church. When he returned after World War II, the believers had multiplied to 10,000 in 100 churches. Ethiopia's hands were out-stretched (Psalm 68:31), at least among the Wallamos, as untaught believers begged Ohman and his colleagues to teach them the Word.

The thrilling account of this amazing church growth would take a whole book to tell—and fortunately it has been told in *Fire on the Mountains* by Raymond J. Davis,* who started his missionary career in Wallamo.

"Unforgettable experience" was an understatement for the Soddo conference. It was more like a mixture of the apostle John's preview of the throng around the Lamb's throne, and Luke's history of the early disciples. As we drove up the mountainside, believers were coming in over the hills, a few on mules, but most walking barefoot. One group walked in from churches 55 miles away. As they wended their way down the trails that funneled from the green hills, they sang the hymns of Zion.

* Published by Zondervan Publishing House, Grand Rapids, Michigan. Obtainable through SIM offices.

There was no shortage of men—young, sharp-eyed men. Women plodded in with their babies on their backs, protected from swarms of flies by their cheesecloth shawls. Girls carried the family's food supply for the conference, wrapped up in broad inset leaves. A schoolboy arrived with a yard-long sugar cane for dessert over one shoulder, and a bundle of inset root for the main course dangling from the end. A white-haired man, with a black woolen mantle pinned over his shoulders, leaned heavily on a knotty staff.

These people are darker than the Amhara ruling class, but not as negroid-looking as the tribes farther south. They have high, broad foreheads and long noses. Most have a small circle branded on the side of the face beside the eye—done in infancy "to overcome bad eye sight or eye disease," they explained to me.

There were joyous reunions as believers from distant churches met again for the first time in a year. They kissed in gracious Eastern fashion, one hand on the other's shoulder or neck, first planting a kiss on this cheek and then on the other. There was no hasty "Hi!" or frantic handshake. Men kissed men; women kissed women; young men kissed elderly women —and each greeting took several moments.

During conference meetings the people sat in a shaded area between two stone buildings, built originally by the Italians as prisons and taken over by the Mission for Bible and grade schools. The shade was provided by a framework of poles covered by eucalyptus branches, silvery leaves drooping downwards. While everyone joined in singing, people slipped into the area and squatted on the grass, until there was a multitude varying from 3,000 to 5,000 through the week-long conference. The audience looked like a vast flower garden, with brightly-colored hair nets—red, blue, yellow, purple, chartreuse, orange, green, pink—among the dark faces and white shawls.

The antiphonal singing at the conference still haunts me. No organ, no piano, no hymn books, no choir, no special numbers. The leader didn't even wave his hands. He merely stood up and sang a sentence on two notes: do do me me. The audience replied with a chorus of two or three words on the same two notes. The leader continued with his next phrase. There was no variation of notes, only of the number of do's or me's.

The leader at times used familiar sentences, and at other times made them up. The words were a prayer or some burden he wanted to express. He put everything into those two notes and the few words of each line. The people hung on to each word intently and joined in with the response at the rhythmic moment. The intensity built up until there was no break between refrain and chorus. There was total participation, yet no swaying or handclapping. Teenagers, old folk, all were caught up in the words.

After 15 minutes of singing, Dana (chief) Maja got up and spoke over a microphone hanging from the fork of a eucalyptus branch. Dana Maja had once been the feared owner of 100 slaves. He had carried tobacco leaves in his pocket whenever he went to the Mission for medicine—he heard tobacco would keep the missionaries from "eating" him. Now as a leader of the Wallamo churches, this former slaver was seeking to break the bonds of Satan's slaves.

Dana Maja's tall, lanky son Markina then got up to tell about his visit to North America. Markina is Secretary of the SIM-related churches and Treasurer of the Ethiopian Fellowship of Evangelical Believers. He and Fellowship President Abagolie Nunamo took part in SIM conferences in the U.S.A. and Canada just the year before.

Markina told the Soddo believers some of the wonders of the New World. They laughed in disbelief when he said he had seen one cow give a bucket and a half of milk at one milking. In fact, he advised his father to sell his 50 cattle—which protestingly gave about a quart a day per cow—and buy one of the kind he had seen.

"We traveled in subways and came out of the earth like moles," Markina told the incredulous people. "We went to the top of the Empire State building—floor upon floor reaching into the clouds. We saw men playing ball in a big field where night was turned to day." Waves of laughter were the response to these tall stories. An astronaut returning from Mars couldn't have told the people anything more unbelievable.

Most amazing was a flush toilet—"you press a lever and everything disappears!" With unabashed Eastern frankness, Markina once confided to a missionary that two thoughts had come to him at seeing this wonder: (1) if he threw in his passport, perhaps he could stay in the U.S.A.; (2) the Lord had removed his sins as completely as the water flushed everything away.

Markina told his people about the missionary prayer meetings in America. "We here only pray for ourselves. Over there believers pray for others all over the world—foreigners they have never seen. And they even pray for us."

After Markina saw a missionary wipe away tears as she bade farewell to her aged parents at an American airport, he said. "Now I know it costs missionaries to come to our land. We used to think they came because our land was better and they had nothing to give up."

The one thing which burdened Markina most was the number of Christian young people there are in churches, "already trained as teachers, doctors, and pastors." Yet so few are coming to help the struggling churches in Africa.

Several Bible school students had told Markina they were interested, but since there were so many churches in Ethiopia, they felt they should go somewhere else.

"I explained that Wallamo, where we have many churches, is only one of 14 provinces," Markina told me. "In fact, most of our churches are in only three provinces. We are sending out some evangelists to other places—as many as we can possibly support—but we need missionaries to train pastors and evangelists and to open up new areas. Our people usually have more difficulty than white missionaries being accepted by other tribes—especially in the northern Islamic and Coptic areas. And there are probably eight million people in Ethiopia who still have not heard the way of salvation."

At that conference we saw just how much they did give to send out evangelists. In front of the platform were two signs in Amharic: "Follow Me," and "Go ye into all the world and preach the gospel." After his report, Markina challenged his brothers and sisters.

"When I see believers refusing to give to God their lives and possessions as they did when they first came to Christ, my heart is filled with deep sorrow. Whatever you hold tightly in your own hands will be lost. Whatever you place in God's hands will be kept safely for eternity."

As Markina sat down on the bamboo log bench, his father stood up and asked for the missionary offering. The elders moved among the people with sun helmets and felt hats as offering plates. After people had given their cash, they began to give clothing which could be used by the evangelists or sold for their support. A white-haired man strode up to the platform and took off the heavy army overcoat he'd need back up in the cold mountain air. A young mother took her child's boots off and put them in one of the collection hats. There were beads, hats, bright scarves, even precious soap. People who came in late or otherwise missed the offering hats called out to the ushers to collect theirs.

Then Dana Maja asked for promises, to be paid before next year's conference. People stood up all over the crowded turf, shouting out how much they would trust God to enable them to give. Elders moved among them, recording the amounts. Some gave land which would be sown and reaped by volunteers, the proceeds given to support the missionary work of the church.

I was watching a New Testament church at work. This is what characterizes the evangelical church in Ethiopia. Not only do the believers look and act like early disciples, but God also seems to deal with them in the same way. He speaks to them in dreams and visions. They wrestle with visibly manifest demon power. The Holy Spirit often deals with hypocrisy, deception, and disobedience as directly as He did in the days of Ananias and Sapphira.

One elder knew God wanted him to give his mule. Instead he gave a dollar. Back home he had no joy; the Holy Spirit kept urging him to give the mule.

One day an evangelist asked to borrow the mule to preach up in the mountains. Thought the elder, "If I lend it now, it will be just as good as if I had given the mule at the conference." A few days later a messenger turned up with an extremely apologetic note from the evangelist. The mule had died. The evangelist was afraid to come with the news himself.

"Don't worry," said the smitten owner. "Tell the evangelist it is I who have killed the mule. If I had obeyed the voice of the Holy Spirit, this would not have happened. I have sinned against God." He confessed in the church next Sunday and with repentant tears handed over the price of a mule to the pastor. His heart and his home were flooded with joy after that.

Sitting right under the speaker during each service was Wandaro, the man who had led slave owner Dana Maja to the Lord, when the latter was fleeing for his life from The Judgment. What Dana Maja thought was The Judgment turned out to be Italian war planes dropping bombs; but the scare made him realize he wasn't ready to meet God.

Wandaro fascinated me as he sat there hour after hour, his woolly hair frosted with gray, emotions flashing across his face as he listened. For most people, his posture would have been unbearable—squatting on the hard ground with his face turned almost straight up to catch every expression of the speaker. But Wandaro was inured to hardship. I was glad when Selma Bergsten invited us over to her house to drink coffee with him after one of the meetings.

The coffee, incidentally, was grown, roasted, ground, and brewed by Selma. I was grateful that, unlike the way most Ethiopians drink their coffee, Selma's was not doctored with salt and rancid butter.

Wandaro perched on the edge of his chair between the Ohmans and me, his big Wallamo head out of proportion to his slight figure. I knew that his khaki jacket and laced jodhpurs covered a mass of scars, for I had heard and read about this humble hero of the cross. He wouldn't have bothered to tell me about the stripes of the cruel hippo-whip lashed across his bleeding back, or of the hate-filled official who pulled out tufts of this simple preacher's beard.

This was the Wandaro who managed to gasp out, while one tormenter passed the whip to another to continue, "I will never give up my faith in Jesus Christ!" This was Wandaro, who likely has led more people to Christ than any other person in Wallamo.

I was unprepared for Wandaro's reaction when I told him I had heard of God's working through him. He put down his cup, got off his chair, knelt down on the floor, and bowed his head right down to the ground for a moment. Then he solemnly lifted his hands and eyes upward, saying in Wallamo, "We give glory to God. He has helped us greatly!" I realized then that I was not looking at just a man; I was looking at Christ Jesus in a disciple.

The Wallamo church was born in tribulation, and even today persecution is not unknown. I learned that 12 believers were currently in prison, charged with "slander." They had gone to another area to witness, and over 600 people had been converted.

The church continues growing. Two thousand believers were baptized in one area during one week-end. Wallamo Christians number 44,000. The main propagation is not modern mass methods, for few read or have radios. It is by the disciple's method of personal witness.

Today modern temptations more subtle than the former trials face the Wallamo believers, but they are standing just as resolute. The national tobacco company discovered that Soddo has the best soil for growing tobacco and laid plans for extensive cultivation. They were surprised when Christians refused to grow it, even though community pipe smoking is a favorite Wallamo pastime.

"The Bible says our bodies are the house of God's Spirit, and we should keep them clean," the believers explained.

Rather than shelve the project, the authorities sent a high-powered delegation to inform the people they must plant tobacco, insinuating that even the SIM had agreed to this.

"We don't care what the SIM says," replied the believers. "We still won't grow tobacco." They soon discovered that the SIM had agreed to nothing of the sort.

"Do you still need missionaries?" I asked Wandaro, thinking of the 388 churches in Wallamo.

Wandaro winced as he swallowed a piece of biscuit. Kicks in the jaw by Italian soldiers had left him with difficulty in swallowing.

"The gospel has come to us," he said, crowsfoot wrinkles deepening at the corner of each eye. "We have believed it, but our people still don't understand it properly. Even our young men who have been to Bible school don't understand the Bible properly, because the law doesn't allow us to have Bibles in our own language. We need missionaries to teach our young men so they can teach others."

Before leaving Soddo I had a guided tour of the station, a cluster of white-washed mud-and-wattle houses on a flat hill-top, with snapdragons, geraniums, and peach trees set against the blue-green backdrop of higher hills. I saw the primary school, Bible school, bookshop, and hospital. An Italian diesel truck was lumbering up the road with a shipment of medicine.

"Praise the Lord!" shouted Dr. Nathan Barlow. "We've been waiting for this order for six months!" When I walked through the rambling, 101-bed hospital, the doctor noted my surprise at the vinyl tile floors in an otherwise very rudimentary building. Four visiting American doctors donated it, he explained, after being shocked at the rough stone and cement floors.

Soddo hospital has patients with all the usual complaints,

plus one I hadn't come across in other lands. Ethiopians consider raw meat a delicacy. Once a month many peasants have a reckoning day with the intestinal worms that hatch from the fly eggs laid while the meat hangs in the market. The purgative the people use is made from the kousso leaf and is deadly strong; it can cause dizziness, blindness, and mental derangement. But it does kill off the worms—even if one has to go to a hospital or asylum to have the side effects taken care of.

Dr. Barlow and his missionary colleagues train the Ethiopian staff to do things themselves. For a photograph, I asked him to supervise some lads in white who were sewing up a man's eyelids. "That wouldn't be authentic," he demurred. "I don't supervise them—too busy. These second and third year dresser students do trichiasis operations by themselves . . . about 150 per year. They learn from one another." I took the photo without the doctor.

It was this shy, blond doctor who helped save a tribe from being wiped out by a "mystery disease." The world press and radio eventually reported a massive campaign to vaccinate one million tribespeople against yellow fever. But few heard of the missionary doctor who battled single-handed for weeks to discover the cause of the epidemic.

It first came to light when SIM missionaries down near the Kenya border appealed to Dr. Barlow. "People are pouring into the dispensary, but nothing we give them touches the fever. They're dying like flies."

The Barlows hurried south and found Shankallas dying in hut after hut. Down on the river plain 700 had died. Dr. Barlow took blood specimens, questioned patients, and gave injections. It sounded like several diseases in one. It even sounded like yellow fever, but it couldn't be—that dread disease didn't exist in Ethiopia.

Back at the airstrip, the doctor sent test tubes of blood serum back to Addis Ababa with the airlines pilot. The Pasteur Institute there returned the verdict: yellow fever. There is no known cure for this disease, carried by mosquitoes from monkeys to humans. Vaccination can prevent infection, but the vaccine keeps only a few hours unrefrigerated.

Nathan Barlow got all the vaccine he could in a portable icebox. Riding muleback, he pushed into the worst area down on the fetid river banks to try to save some lives while more vaccine was coming.

The missionaries were grateful when the World Health Organization took up the campaign, moving in with all the resources it could muster. And as the yellow fever scourge retreated, there was a mission doctor unobtrusively busy, carrying not only vaccine with him but also the Word of Life into the huts of thousands who had never heard.

It was thrilling to hear how God used the epidemic to open up that area to the gospel. The government asked Dr. Barlow to follow up the WHO work, and to organize teams to poison the colonies of monkeys and baboons which carry the virus and also destroy crops. Floating on calabashes across jungle rivers where hippos snorted at them, camping in clearings within sound of hyenas and leopards, Nathan and Doris Barlow directed teams of men who set out poison-filled sweet potatoes for the baboons. Everywhere they went they played gospel records, preached, and left literature for the few who could read. Colonies of monkeys and baboons met their death; hundreds of Shankalla villages heard of eternal life, and many people believed.

I was to fly with Mr. Ohman and pastor Markina to another conference deep in the southern mountains, near the area where the epidemic had started. But before we left, the other church leaders presented us with a handsome ox as a traditional gesture of welcome. The ox then participated in the conference as beef stew for everyone present.

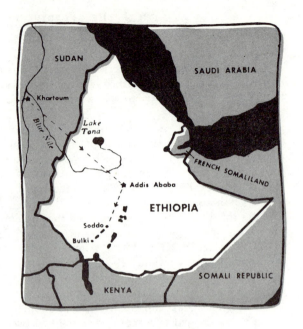

18. The Witchdoctor's Prophecy

"I feel like a Yo-Yo by the time I'm through for the day," the burly American pilot grunted. "We make 12 stops in 10 and a half hours between the time we leave Addis in the morning and the time we get back at night."

The pilot was climbing aboard the DC3 which would take us from Soddo to the foot of the mountain at Bulki. I looked forward to seeing for myself the land where a witchdoctor had prophesied that a Golden Book would one day come.

Soddo to Bulki is only 125 miles, but they are up-and-down miles, taking 12 to 15 hours of difficult driving. By air we'd do it in 45 minutes, including "Yo-Yo" stops. Ethiopian Air Lines, which employs several Americans, has done more to open up the country than any other factor.

When the pilot learned I was traveling for the SIM, he brightened. "We sure appreciate the SIM," he said. "Don't know what we'd do without their missionaries, especially when we get stuck overnight in one of these boondock towns."

Airborne, we were soon over rugged terrain. One moment we were several thousand feet above the ground. Suddenly it was only 100 feet below as we flew over a ridge—then it fell away again in a drop that made me gasp. We crossed ridge after ridge separated by lush valleys, as if the earth had been squeezed up into 6,000 foot-high wrinkles.

"Watch that gap there," Walter Ohman said, pointing ahead. "We have to go through it to get into Bulki."

Sure enough, we headed into a V-shaped cleft in a range, until I thought our wings were about to touch. Then the DC3 dropped quickly into a mammoth "well" on the other side, and we slid down on to the rough, sloping airstrip. With unfeigned admiration I thanked the pilot for the trip.

Waiting for us with mules to make the four-hour climb up the mountain was Bill Watson, a freckle-faced Australian with a real "down under" accent and a turned-up Aussie hat set jauntily on his head. It was already 10:45 a.m. and getting hotter by the minute as we set off on the trail, Bill leading on a roguish beast, water bottle swinging from the saddle; Markina, erect and silent on a brown animal; Walter Ohman, 65 and not feeling well but riding with the poise of a veteran; and myself, a journalist used to handling a typewriter but trying to look at ease handling my mule, which Bill assured me was the easiest of the four to get along with.

Outside the little town, at the foot of the trail, we passed a mule caravan resting by a stream before climbing the hills to bring down coffee. As we ascended the trail, our legs brushed against fragrant thorn bush blossoms. Wild bees swarmed around a cylindrical mat beehive perched in the branches of a tree.

When we stopped under a wild fig tree half way up to have a cup of tea and sandwiches, I asked Bill Watson how the Lord called an Australian out to Ethiopia. I knew that Aussies and New Zealanders outnumber other mission nationalities there. And I found they are home-spun folk who are ready to roll up their sleeves and pitch in.

Bill Watson emptied the tea leaves out of his mug and held it out for a refill as he answered my question.

"I was an electrician. After I was saved I began to feel I should do something to help others know about the Lord. I helped support an SIM Australian couple in Somalia. One day while wiring a church, I walked across some newspapers protecting the tile flooring. Part of a headline was covered by another page so that only two words showed: SUDAN . . . COME.

"Those two big bold words stuck in my mind. I went to Bible school, still praying for guidance. Surely the Lord didn't speak through newspaper headlines! Then as I was specially praying, the Scripture verse came to me, 'This is the way, walk ye in it.' I applied to the SIM and was accepted."

Not a very usual "call," but the main thing is that Bill was looking for guidance, doing all he could to help others go until he knew God's will, and God got him out to the place He wanted him.

Back on our mules, we headed higher. The air was cooler, so that we didn't feel the sun burning our arms and faces. Bill pointed out a clump of trees on a summit across a gorge: "The mission compound is in behind those trees, but it'll take us another two hours to get there."

Our ears began to pop as we followed the contour of the gorge. A vulture cocked an eye on us as he sailed past, 2,000 feet above the valley.

My mule didn't mind the dizzy height at all. In fact he kept as close to the outer edge as possible, even where the trail was wide enough for a truck. Did he know I was green? My composure did not increase when Watson pointed out the place where the building supplies for Bulki station had bounced down the cliff.

By 3 p.m. we had climbed 4,000 feet from the airstrip, to an altitude of 8,500 feet. I was surprised to find that even the highest hills are covered with grass; the annual rainfall is 112 inches. The people live in scattered huts and farm right up the steep slopes. There before us lay Bulki station, a welcome sight of white-washed bungalows graced with red roses.

Bruce and Betty Adams, in charge of the station, were busy with the conference, already in full swing, so nurse Dorothy Longmire brewed us an Australian cup of tea that helped overcome our saddle weariness. I heard about an Australian missionary—*not* Dorothy—who was grateful for tea bags given her by an American colleague, but complained, "It's such a nuisance opening all those little bags!"

Dorothy excused herself to attend to a father who appeared at her door with his sick son. As payment for medicine, he had two live hens, and nine eggs bound up in a long banana leaf like a string of beads. Bulki is too high up for malaria-carrying mosquitoes to fly, although peasants who go down to the humid valley to farm often return infected. But there are plenty of other ailments, including complications from local customs. Example: if a baby becomes ill with dysentery and vomiting, a village elder cuts out the uvula and the buds of the lower incisor teeth.

Next morning my reluctant ears were awakened at 4:30 to singing, as some of the 1,300 believers from 70 churches began to stir. By 6:30 most of them were in a prayer meeting; they all were on their knees and elbows, with their foreheads right down on the ground and their bodies covered from the cool air by their white shawls—looking every bit like a meadow of kneeling sheep as the sun rose over the peaks.

The clanging of an Italian bomb case summoned the believers to the main services held in the rustic conference hall which served as a Bible school the rest of the year. Sitting there, squeezed between several elders (and scratching furtively at times), I tried to analyse why this didn't seem like Christianity at home. There was nothing about the people that made you think they were reluctantly giving a little of their time to a Bible conference, before rushing back into their real world of self-interest.

Looking into those sincere faces, I realized that worshiping the Lord was the center of their lives. This is what they lived for. They were not wealthy people—the clothes of some were ragged, few wore shoes. They were not educated—most of the older folk could not read. They were not sophisticated—they ate the simplest meals of inset root from a common family pot. But they were redeemed children of God earnestly seeking to please the Lord and to witness to their generation.

Only one year before—or three, five, ten years—these handsome dark-skinned people were worshiping the devil. Now nothing else mattered but their love for Christ, who had delivered them from Satan.

The "Christian life" of my homeland suddenly looked very tinny beside this. I couldn't imagine some trappings of modern Christendom fitting in here: "traffic-tested aisle carpets in a choice of six reverent colors," dramatic lighting effects to induce "an atmosphere of worship, choir robes that lend dignity to your service." Things which are part of church life back home appeared artificial alongside this sincerity. I wished I could transplant the average church congregation into the midst of that conference.

Between messages people stood, stretched, yawned, and scratched. Then the conference secretary appealed to the people to remember all that God had done for them. Had they not been delivered from Satan? Did they not have food and shelter? Were not their children learning to read the Scriptures? Well, then, they should give to God's work to support evangelists to spread the Good News. They should send their young men to Bible school.

A youth from an area which had heard the gospel only three years before stood and said, "I'll go to tell others." As at Soddo, after the people had given their cash, they gave articles. An attractive 20-year-old girl walked to the platform, took off her new shoes, and walked back to her place smiling—barefoot.

There was a festive air between sessions. Some gathered in family groups, untied their little bundles, and ate. Several boys started a volley ball game with a small handball. Teenage girls got together and sang hymns. Young men huddled around a literate youth and spelled out the complicated characters of an Amharic Bible.

That was the Book which had revolutionized the whole area in the past 10 years. One of the elders, Ato Minota, told me the amazing story of how the Bible had come.

"See that grove of eucalyptus trees on the mountain side right across the valley?" Ato Minota started. "That is where Cheleke lived. He was the most powerful witchdoctor in all the land of Oida." As he recalled Cheleke's power, Minota's eyes rolled in his long, black face.

Cheleke had 30 wives and three large compounds. Although 30 years ago people would not normally travel from one village to another because of the dangers of being enslaved or murdered on the way, men would brave the risk of two days' journey to consult the witchdoctor. His prophecies always seemed to come true. He was the one who caused rain to fall. People spoke of him with awe and kissed his feet when they approached him with their large gifts.

Cheleke either had demon insight or else human foresight ahead of his day. As far back as 1930 the witchdoctor prophesied that foreigners would come into the valley, some of them flying in the air, and that the mountains would shake.

"We all thought he was crazy when he said men would fly," Minota said. "But this happened when the Italians came in their airplanes. And the mountains shook when they dropped their bombs. Today the plane from Addis flies through the valley down there twice a week."

Cheleke had a vision one day. "My god says he will give me a Golden Book under the wanza tree by my house," he told the people. "It will come down from above. Those who believe this powerful book will save their souls."

As time went on, the prophecy grew. Men carrying staffs with crooks (Oida walking sticks are straight) would come by way of the river with a powerful message. They would build a big house in each village, and whoever entered the big house would save his soul. In that day, old men would wish they were youths, and youths would wish they were babes.

So in a remarkable way, through the lips of men sold to Satan, God prepared the people throughout those hills and valleys with a great expectancy: a book, a power, a salvation was coming. Back in Wallamo, God was preparing His messengers. As the missionaries taught the Word, following their return after the Italian war, the believers around Soddo became burdened for their brothers in the southern valleys. It was forbidding country; there were tales of murder, slavery, dark magic power.

But one day a believer whose name means "Fair One" stood up and said, "I will take the Word to the Gofa people." The believers sent him on his way with a little bundle of food, his Bible, and his Wallamo staff with a crook in it. He traveled along the river course into the dangerous Oida valleys. When tribesmen stopped this stranger to ask his business, he told them he was seeking for a lost brother — spiritually lost brothers, he meant.

A messenger told Cheleke one day that a stranger was standing outside. Anticipating the usual request for divination, along with handsome payment, the witchdoctor went out to find a simple Wallamo holding a crooked stick.

"I have come with a message from God for you," Fair One told him.

"Eh, hey?" grunted Cheleke. "Sit here in the shade and tell me. I will soon know if it is from God or not."

Sitting under a spreading wanza tree, Fair One pulled out a "wordless book" which he kept tucked inside his Bible for preaching to illiterates. The witchdoctor listened to the stranger's tale about the black page and the red page and the green page. Then suddenly he leaned forward in astonishment. The next page blazed with gold!

"The Golden Book!" gasped Cheleke, clutching the fetishes around his neck. Things clicked in his mind. The stranger had a crooked stick; they were sitting under the wanza tree. But....

"You've come by the river!" Cheleke said to Fair One, who was still wondering why the witchdoctor had suddenly become so agitated. "My fetish told me about a Golden Book, but it would come from above."

"True," replied Fair One. "I traveled along the river. But this little book tells the message of the great God above. And this other big Book, the Bible, has been given to us from God himself."

Cheleke thought it over. Yes, the prophecy had said the strangers with the powerful message would come along the river. He slapped his thigh. The long-awaited Golden Book had come!

Cheleke professed to believe the gospel after that, but fellow witchdoctors, afraid of losing their power over the people, persuaded him to revert to his fetishes. They were aware of another prophecy. For several years the demons had told them their power would soon be broken by a greater power—the power of the book. Their time would soon be up. Within a year Cheleke had lost his power to prophesy as before, and three years later, in 1952, he died. In five years all his fellow witchdoctors had died. There are witchdoctors in the villages today, Minota said, but not powerful ones like their predecessors. Each one keeps a literacy primer in his fetish shrine—not to read, but to acknowledge that the power of the Book has come. And in many of their villages there is a "big house"—a church.

Households, villages, valleys have been revolutionized. The lying, adultery, and murder of centuries has given way to clean living. The changed status of women in many a compound is evidence of the power that has changed lives. Formerly women were treated worse than mules. After puberty they had to sit by themselves, and could not touch a cow or its milk.

An expectant mother had to wait alone in a grass shelter until her baby was born, allowing it to drop on the mud floor, leaving it uncared for for two days. She must not touch it, even if vicious driver ants should swarm over its body. In two days a low-caste midwife would come and take up the infant if it were still alive. And the mother could handle nothing for five more months, having to lap up her food from a gourd like a dog. Among some tribes, such as the Ara, pagan women still live in such degradation.

As Minota was telling me the story, I could hear the happy laughter of young mothers playing with their new babies on the grass. The gospel had emancipated the people of Oida. And as for Fair One, he was at that moment over on a distant range carrying his "wordless book" into other villages. He had been imprisoned since his first visit to Oida land—once in Wallamo for five years. But whether in prison or out, he saw the power of the Book working in men's lives.

Ato Minota finished his story, threw his red-bordered shawl over his shoulder, and chuckled.

"Truly, Cheleke's prophecies have come true," he explained, seeing my inquiring look. "Only this morning in the meeting we were talking thus—our elders wished they were youths so they could go to Bible school, and our youths wished they were babes so they could start learning to read in grade one!"

The Mission's strategy at Bulki is to train those who can train others. Missionaries are giving special advanced training to two promising young men who are helping them teach 19 district Bible school teachers. These return on weekends to their districts to teach 150 pastors, evangelists, and laymen, who in turn instruct hundreds of believers in 70 churches. More could be trained at Bulki if there were more missionary teachers.

The believers at Bulki conference were spurred on by the knowledge that within a radius of 15 miles there are 60,000 people. Many are black Shankalla (an Amharic term for Negroid people). Across two ranges we could see a peak marking the SIM's most southerly station, Bako. It is near the borders of Kenya and Sudan, surrounded by tens of thousands of pagan tribespeople. Muslims from Somalia were moving in, establishing Islam by intermarrying, but the governor of the area expelled them, saying he wanted Christians there, not Muslims. Missionaries nearly wrung their hands as they spoke of the need for missionary young men to trek all through that area and to teach.

The night before I left Bulki, I looked out over the ranges. As the earth turned away from the sun, the ridges became faceless black masses rising starkly against the twilight sky, like cardboard stage scenery, floodlit from behind. Already the valleys slumbered in the dusk, while the sun kissed ridge after ridge goodnight.

Singing started in the conference hall as I lingered outside. I praised God for those 1,300 happy, active believers. But I knew that what I saw on the mountain top did not mean the job down below was done. What were these among so many unreached? First fruits. Encouragement to do more, to press on. The need overpowered me as I looked toward the south. Muslims moving in; the governor wanting the Christian message; 100,000 pagans between Bulki and the Kenya border. Shadows filled the valleys between, and in the darkness of the shadows were people—families, clans, tribes, huddled in abysmal spiritual night.

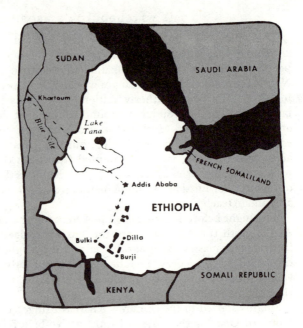

19. The Trail Blazers

The morning I was to leave Bulki, I listened in on the inter-station radio wavelength to check on arrangements. A Missionary Aviation Fellowship Cessna was to pick me up at the foot of the mountain and fly me to Burji. MAF headquarters at Jimma radioed our estimated time of arrival.

"Why is Mr. Fuller coming?" a lady's voice at Burji inquired.

"He wants to get information for a book," replied MAF.

"Does he know the men are all away?"

MAF said the flight was scheduled anyway, and the pilot and I would like to stop there for lunch.

All this increased my curiosity as to what I'd find at Burji, an isolated station on the eastern wall of the Rift Valley. A letter making arrangements had never reached the missionaries, and they didn't want me to have a wasted trip.

Bill Watson and I practically slid down the mountain side, on a trail which Bill said would cut the trip in half—if I didn't mind a rough ride. Ashamed to look like a softie, I agreed to the shortcut and clung suicidally to my mule. At times I was standing straight up in the stirrups with my body in line with the beast's back—its head down below somewhere and its tail up above. Ahead of me was space.

We reached the bottom, with relief on my part, just as the MAF plane flew in. Pilot Tom Frank flew me across the Rift Valley to Burji. To the south was Mount Kenya, barely visible on the equator. Eastward the desolate Ogaden plains sloped toward Somalia and the Indian Ocean.

Tom made a test run low over the crooked, sloping strip on the spine of a rocky hill. "The ladies reported on the radio that the wind was too gusty for a landing yesterday," he explained. "This is the first time in with our new Cessna. I'll be interested to see how it takes a cross wind on that short runway." We came in on the second try, bumping to a stop before the end of the strip. The three missionary ladies were out trying their utmost to hold back a great mass of curious humanity streaming over from the market.

No sooner had I shaken hands, than the ladies asked, "Why have you come?"

"Now, now!" I chided in fun. "Is that the way to receive a guest?"

"We don't mean you aren't welcome," they quickly assured me, "It's just that nobody ever comes to Burji. There's nothing spectacular here."

"That's why I've come," I said, with a catch in my throat at the thought of these people stuck out in the wilderness, embarrassed because they didn't think their work would interest a visitor. "I want to see a place that nobody ever comes to."

I saw it. In comparison to the burgeoning church areas, it

wasn't spectacular, but when I learned something about the place, I was ready to give three cheers for any missionary who had ever worked among these proud, difficult, scathingly blunt people. The 10,000-strong Burji tribe had resisted the Copts from the north and the Muslims from the east and south. The youth of one tribe in the area must still kill a man from another tribe to prove their manhood—a custom officially outlawed by the government.

When Alex Fellows opened the station, there were no believers, and he couldn't speak the language. He used to stand in front of his house for hours every day so the people would become accustomed to him. The Burjis are still largely unresponsive, but the gospel has reached the local Gujji people (8,000 in the area), and the Quara (20,000). There are 76 Quara churches, but no one knows how many Gujji Christians there are in their five churches, because the elders say, "This is the work of the Spirit. Why do you want to know how many believers there are?" They also proudly state, "We are born of the Spirit; *we* don't need to learn to read the Bible—the Spirit teaches us."

Over a meal of hot chicken and rolls, Frances Smith and her colleagues gave us more details about the whereabouts of her husband Ben and his colleague John Cumbers. They were away at a church conference 40 miles north. It was their second trip over a new trail they had opened by throwing logs across the Galana River.

Quara Christians helped to hack through the bush so the missionaries could visit them more frequently with Bible teaching. The trip would now take only four hours by Land-Rover instead of two days by mule. The Quara governor, police, and populace had received the missionaries with great fanfare when they drove the first car into their town.

The ladies were sure the men would have tried to be back if they had heard the MAF radio message about our coming. They had hoped to push the trail through another 20 miles to the Dilla road on the other side, and this might have delayed them. Both in their 30's, Ben Smith treks most of the time; John Cumbers teaches 14 men in a Bible school. John's wife looks after the clinic. I noticed the wild beauty of one Gujji woman who came for medicine. She wore a cow hide, 15 brass bangles on one arm, and a leopard's claw in the parting of her braided hair.

The little school is taught by Mary Gibson, who looked as if she had just come from a Parent-Teachers' Association meeting instead of from a 17-day evangelistic mule trek during the school holiday. She seats three pupils at each desk to accommodate the 108 children. There is only one girl, because the people say it is wrong to educate girls. Mary can't get Ethiopian teachers to stay. They consider Burji the end of the world, complaining that there isn't even a shop where they can buy kerosene for their lamps.

Until the new trail was put through, the missionaries had to bring in their supplies by mule. The last shipment of sugar fell into the Galana River on the way; the transport cost more than half the value of the sugar.

After lunch the local evangelist dropped in to sip cinnamon tea with us while he told me how he came to the Lord. His name, Bangay, meant "Servant of the Devil," and he had been officially that. Bangay did the bidding of an old woman who was demon possessed.

"There were no believers here 14 years ago," the 40-year-old Burji told us. "We thought that God and Satan were two equal gods; everyone feared and worshiped Satan. When the missionary came, it was just like turning on a battery light in a dark room."

Bangay heard the gospel from a man who had worked for Alex Fellows. He had never heard anything like it. He was dissatisfied with serving Satan, because his two children died in spite of many sacrifices. So he was delighted to hear that Jesus was stronger than Satan.

"But didn't you fear to leave Satan?" I asked.

"No," Bangay replied. "I was the one who had mediated

between Satan and my friends, and I knew he had failed me. Life couldn't be any worse."

Bangay gave up all his paraphernalia and renounced Satan. The people prophesied that he wouldn't live a year. They watched as he went through trials. His ox fell off a cliff, dragging him over the edge. The ox died but Bangay climbed back up. He bought another ox; it broke a leg. "Even if Satan takes all I have, I will still follow Jesus," Bangay told the people.

Then he began to learn Bible verses from the missionaries. "Go ye into all the world and preach the gospel" was one. Bangay couldn't stay at home after that. He studied at Burji Bible school, then went to the fierce Gujji people. They nearly killed him and his family before the missionaries rescued him. He now witnesses among his own people, without wages, living on food given him. It is a life of faith and spiritual warfare for him, often requiring prayer and fasting to cast demons out of pagans.

Tom Frank was looking anxiously at his watch—he had to get to Addis Ababa that night after dropping me off at Dilla and picking up another passenger at Jimma. So we climbed into the Cessna after checking that no souvenirs had been torn off by spectators.

As we flew off, I spotted a Land-Rover toiling up a rocky switch-back. It was Smith and Cumbers returning—they would be another half hour reaching the mission compound. Tom circled them before we headed northwards up the valley to Dilla. Unspectacular missionaries, I thought. Just blazing a 60-mile road through rugged terrain to open it up to the gospel! Nothing happened at Burji, the ladies had said.

Tom had to buzz the grass strip at Dilla three times before two herdsmen got the idea that we wanted to land and moved their cattle. I walked up to the neat mission compound and found that Ken and Shirley Craig, Australians in charge of the station, were attending the wedding of an Ethiopian school teacher. They later rode in on their mules. Ken was glad to hear we had sighted the Land-Rover pulling into Burji, because he had left Smith and Cumbers after helping them cut the remaining 20 miles of trail to the Dilla road.

The coming of the gospel to Dilla, on the edge of the Darassa area, is another story like that of Cornelius, the pagan Roman centurion who sought God. When people cannot read the Word, and when even believers are uninstructed, God seems to speak through visions and miracles.

Warrasa Wange, now a farmer of 45, had a vision when he was 20, before missionaries came to Dilla. Although a pagan, he had long sought the way to God. In his vision he saw white people pitch their tent under a sycamore tree in a clearing outside the town. A voice told him, "These are the people who will show you the way to me." He also saw many shiny roofs—inexplicable to him then, because all Darassa roofs were grass. In his dream he took up the center pole of his hut, symbol of a Darassa's family life, and set it up beside the white man's tent.

Eight years later SIM missionaries Glen Cain and Albert Brant pitched their tent under that sycamore tree. They were seeking to enter the Darassa tribe (500,000 population), a pagan people looked down on by people of other religions as not worth proselytizing. They had permission to stay at Dilla but not to enter Darassa country.

Warrasa joined Evelyn Brant's reading class. One day after she quoted Jesus' words, "I am the way, the truth, and the life," he told the Brants about the vision and the voice he had heard. He moved his hut down to the mission compound so his daughter could attend school. He later saw the shiny roofs not only on the mission compound but in the town as it developed.

Warrasa was one of the first Darassa converts, and the first to be imprisoned for his faith. Three of his children died. The missionaries sympathized, but he told them, "Don't feel sorry. Wherever I go I have children waiting for me—up in the mountains and down in the valleys there are spiritual children, and I have three in heaven!"

Now there are 100 churches among the Darassas. Their leader is 43-year-old Ato Daka Sairee, a former Copt who found Christ as Saviour the year after the Mission opened Dilla (1948). He believed through reading the Gospel of John in literacy classes.

The Dilla Bible School is training leaders. The course takes four years, but students go out on a year's practical assignment before the last year. One of the students didn't make it back last year. He received an unexpected "internship" in prison instead—for Christ's sake.

Beyena is his name. After he was converted in 1955 through the preaching of a Kambattan evangelist, he angered the local priest by his witnessing. In the course of persecution, he was singled out as the leader of the believers in 1958. Soldiers tried to force him to recant by stuffing cow dung up his nostrils. Even his uncle, fearing the people, witnessed against him when he was charged with reviling another religion. He was sentenced to prison for one year, after which he entered Bible school.

After his third year he went to a village 30 miles away where there were only four believers. In a few months their number had grown 10 times. One convert was the husband of a female witchdoctor. The furor resulting from his conversion resulted in Beyena's arrest for disturbing the peace.

When Beyena and two companions refused to give a bribe for their release, or to drink beer as a sign of recanting, they were chained down over a cold mountain spring for four days. In sun, rain, and the night's frosty air they lay naked in the oozing mud and horse manure, threatened with death if they would not deny their faith.

On the fourth morning the local people heard them singing hymns. Pricked with some commiseration, they appealed to the chief to put the men in prison instead. Bribed false witnesses avowed that the three had reviled the people's faith and told them not to pay taxes. When the trio were again called on to deny their faith, Beyena produced a "Heart of Man" poster (given him by another believer) and began preaching against sin. Angered, the guards beat the three and put them in jail for two years, where they continued to sing hymns and witness. The believers looked after his family and harvested his coffee for them.

Beyena and his friends have now been released (early, for good behavior), leaving behind them in jail 10 new converts. Too late to start school this year, he has asked for another pastorate until he can complete his studies next year.

A Darassa court judge once said, "Murderers we can handle, but we can't do anything with these believers."

I looked in at the Mission hospital at Dilla and found Dr. David Martin picking pieces of jagged metal out of what remained of the hand of a 12-year-old boy. I saw several cases like that while in Ethiopia. Children found "playthings": old Italian bombs, grenades, or land mines uncovered by erosion or ploughing. They often blew up, maiming or killing the children.

Day after day in a very inadequate operating room this red-haired Canadian doctor changed dressings and worked on that grisly stump to see how much he could save from amputation. Back home he might have had one such case in a year, and then would have been able to refer it to specialists to work on nerves, ligaments, bones, and skin grafting. At Dilla all that was just part of a day's work for one general practitioner.

Ken Craig introduced me to Ato Mahari Isaac, manager of the Dilla branch of the Commercial Bank of Ethiopia. Learning that I was interested in visiting Gidicho Island in nearby Lake Abaye, he said he too had often wanted to. So before dawn the next morning we set off in his Land-Rover.

Down at the lake's edge we installed Ken's outboard motor and headed for the "lost island," two miles from shore. The motor's roar seemed desecrating as it shattered the silence of this primeval world. Tiny birds flew up like blue, red, and yellow sparks out of the green reeds, in which hippos and crocodiles basked. As we slipped through a gap in the reeds, a large gray crane rose in alarm.

I was surprised to find that, unlike the mainland, the island was not fertile. The 2,000 inhabitants live there because it was the home of their fathers—a safe home cut off from slave raiders in bygone centuries, and still cut off from the changing world around them, thus preserving an ancient culture. A visiting ethnologist found that the language had a pattern similar to Somalia.

"We were created here," the priest-king told a missionary. "There are no wild animals, no enemies. The only thing that bothers us is death."

We walked toward the huts made of twigs and grass. Three women clothed in cow hides struggled along the path, with large water pots on their backs. An old man leaning on a spear greeted us.

"This is the man who built a little school room and gave it to the government so children could learn to read," Ken explained. "The government couldn't get a teacher to stay over here; so they have turned it over to us. We have a fine Christian teacher who has volunteered."

There are three villages on the island. The people of one village hunt hippos and don't mix with the others. The other villagers farm over on the mainland.

To get across the lake, the islanders use boats made of featherweight balsa-like wood. I easily lifted a 10-foot log with one hand. We saw several boats pulled up on the shore, their 10-foot-high sunbleached prows pointing upwards like Viking ships. Strangely, their sterns are not closed, and water can come in. They are in fact floating rafts with ornamental prows. People and their goods are piled in until the stern sinks under water; then men propel the sluggish craft with paddles. No nail or screw or wire is used in building the boats—only wooden pegs. The canoes become waterlogged and useless within six months. But they cost the people nothing to make, and new ones are constantly being built.

We sailed off from this island forgotten by the rest of the world, with the words ringing in my ears, *"The only thing that bothers us is death."* Only the gospel can remove the fear of death from Gidicho Island.

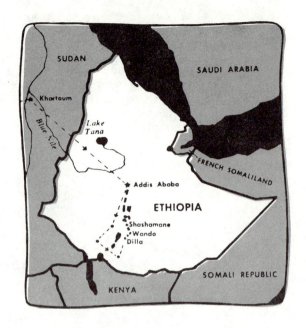

20. Snake Dancers and Backsliders

"Perhaps I should mention," my host thoughtfully said as I left his house late at night, "a black leopard has been prowling around the compound the last few nights. So don't be startled if you see it."

I was visiting Wando, 35 miles north along the wide Rift Valley. Peter Klassen's little announcement didn't help my peace of mind as I walked across the dark compound to my room on the edge of the clearing. My imagination was active enough after hearing one of Peter's Bible school students describe a weird snake dance.

The Klassens introduced me to Haile Yesus in their home. His name means "Power of Jesus," and it was thrilling to hear from this bright-eyed lad how the dynamic power of Jesus is at work today in his valley.

Haile (called Godato before his conversion) used to herd his father's cattle on the scrub-covered plains around Lake Abaye. Every compound had its fetish shrine, and his uncle was the feared leader of the Satan worshipers. During their annual festival Haile saw possessed devotees put live coals in their mouths, dance on fire, and lick red hot knives—without leaving any mark of burning. Then his uncle would invite leading community members into his sacred shrine for the snake dance orgy. Haile, a favorite nephew, would slip in too.

About 30 men crowded into the circular grass hut. As the drumming quickened, the men clapped and swayed their bodies, naked but for loincloths. The hut became fetid with the smell of beer-laden breath, sweating bodies, and dust stirred up by the dancers. At the crescendo of noise and movement all eyes turned toward the roof. A snake slowly descended from the rafters. Haile was convinced it was a real snake; he had often seen its brown back and white belly. The serpent would sway to the rhythm until the priest stopped the drumming—then it would quickly withdraw into the rafters. The devotees rejoiced; Satan was pleased with their sacrifices and worship.

I couldn't take my eyes off this handsome lad as he talked. It was hard to imagine that he would have been with the Satan worshipers right now, but for the power of Jesus. How many other benighted men and women could intelligently serve their Creator if they were freed from Satan by the gospel!

Haile's thirst for knowledge—awakened by a Wallamo evangelist who taught him the alphabet—led him to the Mission. He found Christ in school. God has used him to witness to his illiterate people and to deliver a brother from demon possession. While he was away from home preaching during Bible school vacation, his child died—because he had left following Satan, said the devil-worshipers. But Haile smiled happily as he told me that God had just given him and his wife another child.

Haile is one of 27 young men being taught the Bible by the Klassens. Peter Klassen was a Canadian prairie farmer with only grade school education until 20, then faced the challenge of preparing to be a missionary. With sheer grit and the SIM's advice, he went to high school, Bible school, and university, arriving in Ethiopia with a Science degree at the age of 32. A man who has that much perseverance at that age makes an effective missionary even if he starts six years later than the "ideal."

Illiteracy and indifference of the church are problems faced by Peter and his colleagues. As to illiteracy, it maintains its hold even on Christians because the people have to care for their farms; by the time their children can do the farming, the parents are too old to learn. In the Kambatta area farther north, Peter told me, church leaders require a new church to hold literacy classes for adults, as well as church schools for children.

As to indifference, it seems that the churches in this area have lost the glow of their first love for Christ. Most churches won't send young people to Bible school. The missionaries at Wando told me some of the heartaches in the church—heartaches which are seldom reported in prayer letters.

"The love of this present world" has caused one "Demas" to turn back. A prominent church leader, he became involved in a land court case against a thief. This consumed all his time and energy, and he started to slide. He began to drink, embezzled church money, and took another man's wife. Clan loyalty prevented the other elders from reporting these sins, and when "Demas" was finally disciplined, he became very anti-Mission and stalked off with all the churches in the area.

The heartbroken missionaries prayed. As "Demas" sank further into sin, the churches began to see the truth about him and one by one returned to the Evangelical Fellowship. Eventually he was convicted of cattle thieving and was imprisoned—in the same prison with believers who were shut up for their faith. In prison he made a false repentance, hoping to get food from relatives of the Christians. Missionaries despaired of his restoration but continued praying. Recently they dared hope as the man publicly confessed with tears and humbly returned to the local church as an ordinary member, not with the office and popularity which he had so loved before.

A number of pastors and elders are "out of fellowship" because of money matters. One church area has never been the same since the Christians won a court case. The governor made their enemies pay them for destroyed property and land. Believers who until then had suffered silently became covetous, demanding the last penny. In surprise the governor said, "I thought these Christians were spiritual, but they only want money. They are not showing love."

Corrupt elders who should be removed from office are not because of clan respect for their age, and because of reluctance to face problems. But God at times shows His hand of judgment. Fear came on one church when a disciplined elder, who had demanded back all the money he had ever given in offerings, was injured when his mule collapsed with no apparent cause. The mule died, and so did the man later. But before dying he repented and confessed his sin of covetousness.

The missionaries told me these incidents reluctantly, only after I plied them with questions. They naturally did not want to seem critical. But I knew that churches in Western lands face the same coldness and sin among believers. Church building in Ethiopia involves more than singing antiphonal hallelujahs on mountain tops.

*　　　*　　　*

When the missionaries returned to Wando in 1946, they found the scars of a crucial battle between the Italians and British, which led to the expulsion of the Italian invaders from Ethiopia in 1941. The grown-over trenches and bits of shells and cannon are still there, relics to remind the students at the SIM's Teacher Training College of their history.

The college principal, Harry Atkins, is a serious-minded young man with a forehead as high and hair as curly as an Amhara's.

Harry went to Ethiopia with an M.A. at the age of 20 to teach for the government. He also served in Eritrea, where he signed a life contract with a pretty missionary school teacher. Eventually he also signed up with the SIM.

An educator at heart, Harry had a desert experience when the Mission, needing someone who knew Eritrea, posted him in forsaken Nacfa in the far north—where hardly anyone reads or writes. He kept all his books nailed up in boxes.

"God knew it was good for me," Harry says now. "And my fellow missionaries can't say I don't understand the problems of the non-church areas."

Harry has a point there. It is naturally difficult for missionaries from an area where believers are in abundance, to understand the outlook and needs of missionaries where there isn't even one church—and vice versa. Harry has been a pioneer in pressing for higher training for Christian young men, to prepare them for leadership.

The situation is so different from Nigeria, for instance, where young people are tumbling over each other to get into schools, and where the government spends 40 percent of its budget financing education. Harry told me that in all of Sidamo Province, with a population of two million, only six students had reached grade 12. The government is trying to remedy this and is developing six secondary schools. Missions have as many students as the government in Sidamo Province (about 30,000 each). The SIM is responsible for half of all mission school enrolment in Ethiopia and for one tenth of all the country's education.

Unlike Nigeria, the Ethiopian Government provides no money for mission schools, and the SIM does not have adequate funds. So "community schools" are operated by the churches for the lower grades.

I stopped to see one and found a grade four boy aged 15 teaching grade one in a rustic grass shelter. (After completing four years' schooling, pupils must give a year to teaching in a church school.) The ages of the 15 pupils—in grade one— ranged between eight and 17, and they paid four cents fees per month. Although they had no textbooks, teacher Tadessa assured me he taught "Amharic grammar, arithmetic, hygiene, geography, local history, reading, and writing"!

That's a "grass roots" school. Of course many are better equipped and staffed. But these schools are doing a job which wouldn't be done otherwise, and the people feel they are doing something for themselves.

Community schools really started when the Mission found that their compound schools (then up to grade four—a relatively high level for their areas) were overcrowded, preventing expansion to higher grades. "You take over first grade, and we'll add fifth," the Mission told church leaders. For every lower grade taken over by the churches, the Mission adds an upper grade. Now the SIM has 30,000 pupils in 200 schools throughout its areas. Last year there was a 40 percent increase in teachers.

But there is a problem. The churches, also trying to send out evangelists, can't find enough money to pay its teachers. The Mission has difficulty finding funds to pay national staff in its institutions. From personal funds received, missionaries try to make up some of the $3,400 (U.S.) needed per month for the total program. It is hard to keep teachers if they aren't paid the government rate. This is one of the frustrations of working in a rapidly developing country.

Missionaries who have been occupied with rudimentary church growth among simple, New Testament-era believers in the mountains, are awake to the fact that winds of rapid change are blowing down the broad valleys from the capital city. They rejoice when a Spirit-filled illiterate marches off into the wilds to preach to unreached tribes. But they are realizing that, like it or not, the modern world with all its attitudes is moving in. The Mission's over-all strategy has to include a ministry to the educated elements at the other end of the national spectrum.

Mission leaders and men like Harry Atkins are doing something about it, but it is difficult. It needs the prayers and understanding not only of fellow missionaries but of people in the homelands. It needs the Lord's money, given by faithful stewards who want to strengthen Ethiopian church leadership for future days.

Harry's frustrations include finding textbooks for teaching. The government doesn't print enough textbooks—government schools even come to the Mission for theirs. Some of the official textbooks are very foreign; so SIM teachers are writing more relevant material—like the textbook on Maths by Ethel Shelton of Wando TTC. The only recognized history of Ethiopia, written by two Englishmen, ends with the Italian occupation (1936); so Harry has written an up-to-date one. In fact he has written 10 booklets on education subjects, as well as articles for the *Government Review*, and a travel book on Ethiopia. His Imperial Majesty's appreciative remarks to Harry whenever he visits Wando are rewarding. But more rewarding for him and his fellow teachers is the sight of 30 young men studying in a Christian teachers' college.

Before returning to Addis Ababa, I visited Shashamane Leprosarium. Hedley Waldock showed me around the extensive settlement, which includes a hospital, schools, church, workshops coffee plantation, and poultry farm. The staff treat about 3,000 patients. Of the 1,000 living in the settlement, only 300 can support themselves by farming.

The staff were rejoicing over recent answers to prayer. After resisting the Lord for 10 years, old Bocha raised his fingerless hands and shouted, "I renounce Satan and take Jesus Christ to be my Saviour!" Three schoolboys, all with ardently Muslim relatives, stood and testified they wanted to follow Christ.

At the nearby leprosy segregation village we met Dr. Mulatu Baffa, an Ethiopian who left a high-paying government post to become administrator of the 350-patient village. A born organizer, he is another encouraging result of the prayerful investment of time and money in the advanced training of dedicated Ethiopian believers.

From Shashamane to Addis Ababa I was to have the treat of a bus ride. Outside the leprosarium I boarded a modern Italian bus seating 75, counting the folding seats which completely blocked the aisle. I was fortunate to get a commanding view of all around me by being shoved toward the one remaining folding seat.

The passengers were of different shades: light Amharas, dark Shankallas. A sophisticated woman wearing a shawl and light-colored rayon stockings carried a transistor radio. A rough-looking tribesman peered from behind his dirty shawl, with which he covered his head and mouth to escape the evil eye along the highway. Unused to the movement of a bus, he obviously had been deathly sick out the window beside him. A young mother cuddled her infant son, watched approvingly by her husband. A Copt softly chanted canticles while a fat merchant hurled vituperations at the conductor for some slight.

The conductor wore a Scottish tartan scarf wound around his head like a turban; the bus driver wore an almost brimless Italian felt fedora. A white horse tail swayed from the rear-vision mirror. The driver made frequent and effective use of his airhorn, blasting opposition off the tarred road and heralding our approach to prospective passengers a mile ahead.

As we swept along like a carnival on wheels, I spotted the turnoff to Silti. I could never forget the night six years before, which I had spent with missionary Mel Donald in a Land-Rover on the Silti trail, bogged down past the axles in a stream. Now the Mission Council had decided to close Silti, at least temporarily, because of lack of staff.

Silti is a hard Muslim "pocket," but actually Islam is only a thin veneer over paganism. A Muslim priest is called the same as a witchdoctor. Muslims make sacrifices at "The Place of Satan" in a crater lake which changes color; the sacrificial animal must always be the same color as the lake at the time of sacrifice. The people haughtily tell missionaries, "The pagan Wallamos had no religion when the foreigner came. It is all right to preach to them, but don't come to us. We have our religion. We might become Copts, but we shall never become 'Jesus people.' "

The SIM opened work among these Gurages in 1947, but Silti has never had an established church. Several who made profession have gone back into Islam under great pressure. One man withstood all the persecution until his father took away his wife and threatened to give her to another man. It was too much.

What does a missionary do in a case like this? How long does he stay without seeing fruit? Some have persevered in such situations for a life time, feeling they must be faithful to witness even without seeing fruit. Others say, "Let down your nets on the other side" where there are fish ready to be drawn in. It is a difficult question which only the Spirit can answer in each situation.

Although it is scriptural to "shake the dust off your feet," it was not easy for the missionaries at Silti to lock up the mission compound and leave. They have asked friends to continue praying that God will yet break through in His own sovereign way. Meanwhile they have been re-deployed to fill other urgent staff needs where the Spirit is at work.

In contrast to Silti there was "abiding fruit" at the hospital at Leimo, and at Dugda, Hosanna, Durami, and Waka—all within 100 miles. I would not be able to see them this trip, but I remembered my visit to the Kambatta area six years before.

In no other place across Africa have I seen so many flies as I saw at Durami. Infants become so used to them that they do not brush them away. One boy stared straight at me with his eyes completely ringed by flies, like cattle drinking at a water hole. Tiny missionary children wear fly nets over their heads while outdoors, to avoid eye infection. When we walked along the trail to the thatched church, our backs were covered with flies; at the church door an usher whisked them off as we entered. I even found one in the communion glass of honey water passed to me during the service.

But the flies were not the thing uppermost in my memory. The warmth of Christian love among the believers was what impressed me. Perhaps it was typified by foot-washing. When we arrived at a local church conference after a tiring journey, the elders washed our feet in soothing warm water. They did it to all the incoming believers. Then I understood the significance of foot-washing among the early disciples. These believers are of the same spirit. They have no paid clergy. There are no written membership lists—the elders know every believer. They support their young men at Bible school, even building them huts as dormitories. Every Friday 150 farmers walk several miles to attend a day of Bible training at Durami, then return to their farms. There is also a girls' Bible school, which faces a peculiar problem. Non-Christian men try to steal the girls on their way to school—a literate girl has a high marriage premium. So now the elders escort them along the trails each weekend, to protect them.

My recollections were interrupted as our bus stopped at the junction of the highway with the French-operated railroad. Passengers bought oranges and tangerines from hawkers who swarmed around the windows. They also bought vines bearing soybeans, which they popped from the pods into their mouths as the bus proceeded. A dark elderly woman to whom I had given a banana from my lunch offered me a fistful of the vines. The bean looked and tasted like a raw pea.

As we sped toward Addis Ababa, the driver turned on a radio connected to loudspeakers concealed overhead. He turned the volume so high that the vibration of the speakers made almost unintelligible the Amharic disk jockey. There were occasional bursts of rock 'n roll, cathedral chimes, and an Arabic dirge. And thus we rode triumphantly into the empire's capital with blaring airhorn, vibrating radio loudspeakers, shouted exchanges between the conductor and passengers, and soybean pods all over us.

21. Of Missionaries and Demons

Back at SIM headquarters, Mrs. Ohman told me that her husband, whom I had left at Bulki, had not turned up yet. She had gone to meet the plane on which he was supposed to arrive. "You had better pray, Ma'am," an attendant told her. "That plane has disappeared somewhere between Jimma and here!" She eventually found that the plane had "disappeared" before her husband had boarded it.

The story pieced together was that a court-martialed airforce officer and two friends had hijacked the DC 3 at gunpoint just after it took off from Jimma with full fuel tanks. They flew east across the border into Somalia, where the hi-jackers asked for asylum.

The crew and nine passengers (who had expected to be home for supper in Addis) sat in Somalia for four months waiting to be repatriated. There was no hurry to return the plane, since a Somali flier had defected to Ethiopia some time before, and his plane had been impounded. Mr. Ohman turned up on a flight several days later, thankful he wasn't in Somalia.

Like the SIM headquarters in West Africa, life was busy around the offices in Addis Ababa. In the pharmacy I found a man who had *advertised* for a missionary post. Dr. Earl Siechert wanted to be more involved in Christian service but wasn't sure where his pharmaceutical training could be used. He placed an advertisement in the Christian Medical Society's *Journal*, asking about mission staff needs. He received letters from four people—one was an SIM doctor, who advised him to write to the SIM. He found that the Mission had been praying for another pharmacist. His wide experience was ideal for running the SIM's pharmacy supply laboratory in Ethiopia.

Jim Clark took me to the SIM printshop and explained some of the problems of setting type in a language which has 33 basic characters, each with seven variations, totaling 231, plus several diphthongs. The editors and printers somehow manage.

They put out an attractive 12-page magazine called *Kale Heywet* (Word of Life), which faces some of the toughest circulation problems in the world. Even if the magazine did reach a rural destination on time, there are no postmen, no box numbers, no street addresses. Therefore outside the cities most circulation is handled through missionaries or pastors, who know where the people live.

Besides *Kale Heywet*, the Addis Press turns out several million pages of Christian literature per year. Best sellers are ABC literacy primers (170,000 sold in three years) prepared by SIM missionaries Peter and Geraldine Cotterell. The government uses them too. With literacy extremely low, the main task in Ethiopia is to teach people to read.

Orthodox Church members who have learned to read in the past face another problem. They tend not to think about what they read, having been used to rote reading of religious passages. And Amharic has a built-in problem for modern journalism; it is a literary language, and sentences in newspapers tend to be lengthy and incoherent.

The ban on publishing anything in a tribal language other than Amharic makes learning very difficult for rural people, and millions will die before reading the Word of God for themselves. But the policy may eventually result in the spread of the gospel as everyone learns to read one language. Even now it enables national evangelists and missionaries to preach in many areas, although the message must still be interpreted for those who don't understand Amharic.

Peter Cotterell is preparing more material for the presses' rollers. As a member of the International Council of Ethiopian Studies, he has written several technical papers on the Amharic language. The Ministry of Education has asked him to prepare a series of eight readers and eight teachers' handbooks for learning Amharic, which will become the official textbooks for the nation. The government has agreed to the inclusion of Christian material. It is a thrilling opportunity for a servant of God who has put his learning into the Lord's hands.

Across the way from the Cotterells' house I found Gerry Nelson in charge of the Girls' Christian Academy, opened in 1957. Most of the 400 girls come from Orthodox Church families; by the eighth grade all of them so far have professed faith in Christ as Saviour. Each girl is a challenge to Gerry's faith, to see Christ formed in a life, and each girl has a story.

Bekelatch was one who started in second grade at the age of nine and came to love the Lord Jesus as her Saviour. Each day she walked four miles to school, her bundle of food slung over a shoulder. A crisis came in her life when she was in grade five. It was on the Feast of Adibar, the first day of the Ethiopian month Guenbot, the day when many families sacrifice a black sheep to Satan to protect them through the coming year. Bekelatch's father asked her to brew coffee.

"Is it for Satan?" asked the 12-year-old girl. In previous

years she had taken part in the feast, the only time a meal is taken outside the house (uninformed Ethiopians who see missionaries on an outdoor picnic sometimes think they have a similar religious custom).

Bekelatch had often thrown a chunk of the black sheep over her shoulder to signify her sins being removed and to insure that her prayers would be answered. With her family she had thrown grain on the fire and eaten the sheep with a special porridge, throwing over her shoulder any leftovers as a gift to Satan. Coffee was specially brewed for the feast.

"Of course it is for Satan," snapped her father, who recently had resented some of the Christian teaching Bekelatch had been bringing home.

The new little believer took a deep breath and lifted her face to meet her father's hard gaze. "Father," she said courageously, "I can't brew it. You see, I don't worship Satan any more. I belong to Jesus."

The father became furious, pushing her out of the house. He refused to let her stay with the family and stopped giving her food for school. Bekelatch didn't even tell her missionary teachers; she just prayed that the One she loved would care for her. Didn't the Bible say, "When my father and my mother forsake me, then the Lord will take me up."?

God used an old woman, to whom she had often shown kindness as she walked to school, to give her food and a mat to sleep on. Then a sympathetic sister let her live with her. The first the missionaries knew about her tribulation was when she stood in a testimony meeting to give God thanks for supplying her daily food. Gerry asked questions and got the whole story —and joined the girl in prayer for her father. Later he became seriously ill, and Bekelatch was able to show him kindness and witness quietly to him.

One day as Bekelatch was humming a hymn and sweeping out the house for him, he raised himself on an elbow and called her name. "My daughter," he said huskily, "surely God has looked after you, even when I would give you nothing. You are right to follow Jesus. You may come back to live with us."

Bekelatch has now finished eighth grade and is working as an office secretary, using every opportunity to tell others about her God who "took her up" when her parents forsook her.

Everywhere I went in Ethiopia I came across reports of demon activity—far more than I heard of in other countries. It may be more apparent because many of the people worship the devil himself, whereas most animistic religions try to appease spirits which, they hope, will protect them from Satan.

I talked with a European who was supposed to know a lot about local demon activity. He had heard of a house inhabited by ghosts or demons, who set the roof on fire. Stones appeared on the roof; pots exploded, and stones would inexplicably be found inside them. In discussing these phenomena, I found that the European was extremely vague and inclined to believe anything which was reported, perhaps enjoying the aura of mystery. A colleague said, "When one of our teachers had appendicitis, the villagers said it was the evil eye. I wonder . . . it is hard to know. . . ."

These Europeans believe that demons come from the north, especially from the notorious Danakil desert area by the Red Sea. They do not question the Danakil claim that every Danakil woman is demon possessed, and that the men chase the demons up trees with sticks.

On the other hand, I came across reports where the details have been carefully substantiated; no one would deny that Satan's power is very real in these instances. One was reported by Ato Moloro, a respected Kambattan pastor to whom God has given a ministry of delivering unbelievers from Satan. A believer appealed to him to pray for her daughter, who was possessed. The demon cried out through the girl, Tirungo, "Don't bring Ato Moloro to your home!" When Pastor Moloro came with the mother, the demon cried again amid uncontrollable sobs, "Why have you come to torment me? Please go; please go!" The pastor commanded the demon to come out in the name of Jesus Christ.

"Where will I go?" screamed the demon. "I have no place to rest. This girl belongs to me. She took part in the dance. She is my property!"

"No, by the power of Jesus' blood, I command you to depart," insisted Moloro. "Christ died for her. You must leave her."

"All right," agreed the demon after much insistence by the pastor. "But not today. I will come out on Sunday at your church. There are members there who are not genuine. I will tell you who these are on Sunday and then leave." As the pastor continued to insist that the demon leave immediately, it blurted out the name of an elder "who drinks beer every night before going to bed." The pastor was amazed to hear this, but the elder later confessed that it was so.

Ato Moloro resisted this further subterfuge; so the demon changed its tactics: "I'll go. Take a whip or a rod and beat the girl. Beat her without mercy and I'll go."

"I haven't the power of these grains of sand," said Moloro, picking up some dust off the dirt floor. "But Jesus lives in me, and I am trusting in the power of His blood. In Jesus' name depart."

Tirungo became strangely quiet—not normal, but dumb. Moloro knew the demon was trying to deceive him that it had left. It would not say another word. The pastor wrestled in prayer, putting away doubts, holding on in faith to God's promise of deliverance. After several hours Tirungo suddenly cried out in great torment, threshing around in distress and pain. It was the demon's last attack; it knew its defeat. Tirungo finally spoke in a normal voice as tears flowed down her face. She prayed, thanking God for delivering her and promising to give Him her heart.

The girl told the pastor she had taken part in an obscene demon dance, during which she knew the demon had entered her. She was helpless after that until her deliverance.

It was encouraging to hear of the conversion of a very powerful witchdoctor, or *tonquoy*. Known throughout the Janjero mountains, he served 33 demons who resided in a large hut with stalls, one for each demon—except for two who demanded separate huts. One of these was called The Black God, and a curse in his name always caused the victim to spit blood.

Each demon had a name; 15 were "leaders" who demanded separate pots and coffee cups for their rituals. The firstfruits of grain were offered to these 15, and the grain did not rot or mold all year, nor did rats touch it. The poles of the large hut were lined with the skulls of animal sacrifices brought by people seeking divination. For two months each year special feasting and sacrifice was performed, during which the 15 demon "leaders" were served by 15 specially chosen virgins.

One day the younger of the *tonquoy*'s two wives became ill. She was told by another witchdoctor that the senior wife had cursed her; she must bring three cows to have the curse removed. Not having three cows, she returned home with stiff limbs, cramps, and low fever—usual signs accompanying a curse.

Some of her relatives who were believers told her that Christ was the only One who could overcome demons. So one night she sent for the elders to pray for her. They hesitated because of the power of the *tonquoy*, but after a night of prayer they went the following morning and witnessed to the woman and her witchdoctor husband. For three hours the couple listened and asked questions. The Spirit convicted them, and at last they asked the elders to pray for their salvation. They stood up with raised hands and renounced Satan.

The local people were aghast as the *tonquoy* pulled down the spirit houses with all their stalls, skulls, and paraphernalia. "If you live a month, we shall all believe," they told the converted *tonquoy*. He slept in the main hut that night, as usual. Just before dawn three black snakes slithered down the poles of the hut. The *tonquoy* had often slept with snakes and even leopards without harm, but now he knew his life was changed. Calling on the name of Jesus he speared the snakes to the mud floor.

In the morning he took the money people had offered the demons and bought a new set of clothes to replace his filthy witchdoctor's garb. On Sunday he stood in the church and publicly confessed to be a follower of Christ. His wives and children also believed, and he gave a separate hut and allowance to the younger wife so she would not need to live with him. He recently took a short-term Bible course and is actively witnessing, especially to those to whom his demons said they were going. If he ever speaks about his past life, he always ends by saying, "Now I am free, praise the Lord!"

Stories of demon activity often raise questions, and missionaries don't pretend to have all the answers. But they told me they can be certain of two things:

(1) The power of the devil is great; they "wrestle not against flesh and blood, but against principalities, against powers, against rulers of the darkness of this world, against spiritual wickedness in high places." (2) The power of Christ is greater, and they hold on to His faithfulness to keep all who are His. They must stand on the assurance of the Scriptures, regardless of what an experience may indicate to the contrary.

Down country I had seen encouraging results. But a missionary's prayer letter I read at headquarters reminded me of difficult areas, such as I would see further north:

> "What if the road is rough, the visible fruit negligible? No children saved this year; funds insufficient to build classrooms; clinic patients uninterested in the gospel; division in the church; carnality; loved ones ill at home. The Lord's answer comes full and clear: 'Faithful is He that calleth you, who also *will* do it.' 'They that sow in tears *shall* reap in joy.' R. V. Bingham said, 'The normal life of the Christian is a triumphant life. The provision made for triumph is such that it is disloyal to consider defeat. We are *always* to triumph, to be more than conquerors.'"

It takes faith and courage to write like that in the face of discouragement. But discouragement is part of the missionary's battle, and folk at home need to realize it.

Ted Manzke asked me to speak at the SIM Youth Center down the street from Ethiopia's only university. In spite of a cold downpour, students were crowding into the old five-roomed bungalow as we arrived. Down in the basement boys played table tennis; upstairs boys and girls sat around reading old magazines and playing chess. When the film of the evening started, there were over 200 packed into and around the 100-seat "auditorium"—some leaning in the windows.

These were keen types: sharp-eyed young men, dusky girls with the latest bouffant hair styles. Some were undergraduates, some nurses, some clerks in various professions. After the service a self-declared Communist told Ted, "God won't guide my life; I'll guide my own." When Ted asked why he came to the service, he replied, "Because of the friendliness."

A third-year university student who had been expelled for arguing with his professor came up to ask me questions. His first was about the "unforgivable sin." "If Christ can forgive all our sins, how about this one?" Lakew had been attending the Youth Center for six weeks; he said he wanted to read the Scriptures before deciding to follow Christ. When I pointed out his immediate need of a Saviour, after which the Holy Spirit would further enlighten his mind, he agreed. Kneeling in the now empty room, he prayed:

"Oh God, You know I have sinned against You ever since I was born. Thank You for sending Christ to die for my sins. I now receive Jesus as my Saviour."

I later heard that Lakew planned to go on to Grace Bible College at Jimma, where the SIM gives a four-year course taught in English.

Ted Manzke told me about plans to build a Youth Center with more adequate space and facilities on a plot right across from the university, within sound of the Emperor's roaring lions.

Before leaving the capital I renewed acquaintance with the

President of Haile Selassie I University, Lij Kassa Wolde Mariam. When I first knew him he was a fellow Bible school student in Canada, where he had gone under SIM sponsorship. He went on to undergraduate and graduate studies in the United States, then returned to his homeland where he married one of the granddaughters of the Emperor.

I walked through two vast rooms in the university's administration building, the former palace. Ten-foot-high oak doors framed with maroon drapes opened, and Kassa stood with outstretched hand saying, "Welcome, Harold." He showed me to a seat by his spacious executive desk. No longer the slightly-built student, he was now the confident university president, gracious, composed—his large Amhara eyes quietly thoughtful as we discussed the work of the gospel.

In answer to my questions, Lij Kassa said he thought missions were keeping in step with the times. He specifically mentioned the SIM's Youth Center work at Jimma and Addis Ababa as one of the greatest contributions to the spiritual life of the students.

"Literature is one thing you should push," he said. "Our young people are reading anything they can find for sale. Secular education without a spiritual foundation can be harmful. If you get the Word of God into young people's hands, they will be awakened to their spiritual need and will turn to the Lord."

As I again shook that large, warm hand and walked through the maroon drapes, I thanked God that He has His Daniels in every age and in every nation.

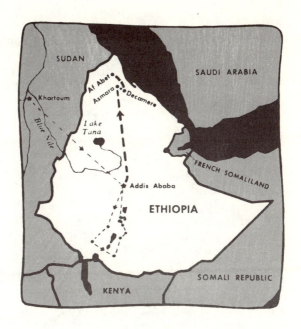

22. The Place No Doctor Would Live

The Borlases drove me north of Addis toward the Blue Nile through broad fertile valleys 10,000 feet above sea level. No wonder the Italians coveted these wheat fields studded with eucalyptus and cedar groves! It was a relaxed, 3-D picture world, far removed from the turmoil of city life.

Galla serfs herded their sheep, goats, and cattle among the red blossoms of aloes and blue-green leaves of gum tree seedlings. Women kept their babies covered from the evil eye; they also covered their earthen milk jugs so the evil eye would not harm the cattle which gave the milk. An aristocratic Amhara on a tassel-decked horse was followed by his servants on foot. They as well as other faithful Orthodox members were headed for their local churches on one of the Church's innumerable feast days; 33 alone are in honor of the Virgin Mary.

There have been no mission stations in this area, designated "closed" by the Orthodox church. It would be difficult for evangelists to reside here because there are no towns in which to rent a house; the people live in clusters of family huts. "It is a challenge to our faith," said Howard Borlase. "We are praying God will yet open up a way."

I asked Howard if it ever snowed at that altitude. "Not in memory," he replied. But 10 minutes later a raging hailstorm swept across the fields, turning them white. The ice pellets took over half an hour to melt. Then we suddenly came to the edge of the plateau, 11,000 feet above sea level. We looked down into a different world along a tributary of the Blue Nile. The cavernous chasm extended into the distance in gorge after gorge filled with ruddy vapor left by the passing hailstorm. Thunderous rumblings still echoed from the bastions of the granite precipices. Six thousand feet below, the river glistened like a silver thread in the late afternoon sun, its waters tumbling toward the Nile and the Sudan. We could have been looking on the antediluvian world, with giant dinosaurs roaming the river bed. Or was it a scene from Creation? The roll of thunder through the mists almost seemed like the voice of One pronouncing, "Let us make man in our image."

"You know," Howard Borlase said, "some tourists spend thousands of dollars to come out to see these things. Yet God lets us missionaries in on them along with our work. And the feeling I get when I take the Word to the people around here —you can't buy that."

I flew over even more spectacular escarpments and incredible gorges between Addis and Asmara, to the north. The Grand Canyon could be lost in them. Westward are Lake Tana, source of the Blue Nile, and the SIM stations at Debatie and Dangilla. Eastward the land slopes off to the Red Sea. Below me on the escarpment were the SIM leprosarium at Dessie and the stations at Alamatta and Mai Chau. A visiting

World Health Organization doctor said Dessie was the only leprosarium where he had seen every patient doing something useful—a major therapeutic objective in the treatment of leprosy patients. Every patient also attends literacy classes, where Bible lessons are taught. Released patients often return to enter Bible school at Dessie.

The northern scenic regions attract tourists, and missionaries never know who may be roaming the countryside. Graham and Mildred Hay once had a dusty couple stop at Dessie to freshen up. Mildred had experimented with homemade chocolates and brought them out as a treat. Learning that their name was Cadbury, Graham jokingly asked if they were related to the chocolate people. "We *are* the Cadburys," they replied, while Mildred wished she could whisk away the homemade candies.

Landing at Asmara airport 7,765 feet above sea level brought me into an entirely different world. I was still officially in Ethiopia, but it seemed more like Italy. Asmara is the capital of Eritrea, so named after the Roman name for the Red Sea, *Mare Erythraeum*, which it borders. An Italian colony from 1889 until the Second World War, it was administered by Britain for the U.N. until 1952, when it was federated with Ethiopia. In 1962 it became a province of Ethiopia.

Dr. and Mrs. Homer Wilson met me at the airport and drove me through palm-lined streets which might have been in southern Italy. There were Italian signs, like "Servizio Publico" on the back of horse-drawn taxis, but English signs were increasing.

We drove by the Coca-Cola bottling plant and the match factory, passing donkeys with canvas bags slung on each side for selling water. A farmer drove his oxen before him, carrying their yoke himself, while workers rode to the textile factory in a double-decker bus.

The three main religions vied for prestige in Asmara with imposing buildings all within sight of each other. The Muslims, nearly half of the population of Eritrea, have a three-tiered minaret. The Roman Catholics have built a new cathedral within a few blocks of their old one. Eritrea is their stronghold in Ethiopia. The Orthodox Church has an imposing twin-towered cathedral in modern design.

After seeing the SIM's guest house, and youth center work, I sat in on the Scripture classes held in a disused Italian candy factory. Then I drove to Decamere with the Wilsons. A session with Homer A. Wilson, M.A., M.Sc., Ph.D., is about the fastest way to sharpen one's thinking processes. The second of eight children raised on a farm, he kept earning degrees for the unusual reason that he couldn't get a job. It was during the Depression, and his chemistry professor kept finding scholarship assistance for him because of a personal interest in the young fellow who liked to analyze. Homer went on to become a research chemist. After he was converted, he attended Columbia Bible College and volunteered "to serve anywhere" with the SIM.

Building Christian character in the 172 boys at the Decamere Waifs' Home and Technical School means more to Homer Wilson than writing a dissertation for a degree. The boys study technical as well as academic subjects. So far not one boy has failed the government examinations, and Decamere boys usually have the top grades in Eritrea. Even the local governor sends his sons.

Most of the boys are orphans, several handicapped. Laura Steele showed me a well-tailored shirt sewn by a boy she had taught; then she showed me the boy. One hand and eye had been blown off by an old Italian grenade.

Like so many other schools in Africa, Decamere once had a strike. The students walked out because four boys had been expelled for stealing. A ringleader teacher, Teami Mogus, left. It happened to be a drought year, and to survive, Teami ate *sebero*, a narcotic grain which attacks the nervous system and cripples the limbs. He came back to ask for his job again. "God has judged me," he said. Teami hobbled up to greet me at the school, his limbs a pathetic sight.

Back at Asmara we prepared to set off for Af-Abet, a lonely outpost 100 miles north. Don and Muriel Stilwell from Nacfa, the SIM's most northerly station in Africa, had just driven down via Af-Abet. Although a pharmacist by profession, Don had built the mission house and clinic at Af-Abet. Now he was on a most unusual assignment—compiling a list of anything his pharmaceutical soul desired to equip a government hospital. To fulfill a federation promise, the government had built a spanking 38-bed hospital, complete with TB center, laundry, morgue, and two generating light plants. The only problem: no doctor, foreign or national, would agree to live in such a forsaken place as Af-Abet. In desperation the government turned to the Mission for a doctor.

"We already have hospitals without doctors," Dr. Wilson told them. "We'd like to help, but we can't."

"Well then," the government persisted, "if you can't supply a doctor, send a health supervisor."

The SIM finally agreed, on the condition that it would not take staff from other SIM medical work. The government told Don Stilwell to order anything he needed.

Dr. Wilson told me that the people at Nacfa look on the Stilwells with considerable awe; they couldn't be convinced that Don and Muriel aren't doctors, although the Stilwells always take care to stay within the limits of their training. However, in an emergency they may have to do anything. One occurred when the Senior District Officer's son lodged a pea in his windpipe. Don happened to have the right equipment on hand, fished out the pea. The grateful S.D.O. got the towns-people to donate an emergency operating table to the Nacfa clinic.

The people weren't always so sympathetic; at first they were suspicious. Then the Lord arranged an incident that broke resistance. Muriel was called to attend a woman having diffi-culty in labor. On arrival she found the baby apparently still-born, already wrapped for burial. Muriel gave artificial respiration and the baby spluttered into life. The marvel of that story opened the door of every hut in the area.

After all I had heard about the road, I would have felt more confident traveling to Af-Abet in the Stilwells' Land-Rover, but the Wilsons and I set out in a mini-sized Fiat.

For several miles we traveled on tarred surface, past small villages of stone huts. A Muslim priest sat by the roadside reading the Koran to two peasants. Small caravans of camels trudged back from market. An army outpost checked trucks loaded with cotton while sentinels kept a lookout from stone turrets, watching for *shiftas*, the notorious brigands of East Africa. A tr··k was parked incongruously by a water hole, surrounded by camels and cattle. It had brought in baled hay because of a drought parching the land.

Then the tarred road came to an end and we whined along serpentine dirt roads for the remainder of the six-hour trip. Range after range presented changing vistas, yet the land itself was depressingly unchanging: sand, shale, stones, rocks, thorns. Up the hillsides stones had been terraced to catch the sparse soil washed down by the scant annual rains. Ribs jutted through a rotting carcass—a cow which had grown too weak in the constant trek for bits of green thornbrush and brackish water. A jackal stared at us from a rocky point, then slunk off into the tangled briers. For 30 miles we saw no one as we snaked up one hill and down another until we topped a pass and looked down on the Af-Abet plain—a vast bed of sand and gravel spotted with thorntrees and sisal.

As we approached the town, Dr. Wilson asked his wife and me to keep a lookout for an armed guard at the army post. The last time he entered the town, he had not seen the guard until he heard the slap of the lock on a gun and a shouted warning to stop at once.

"There he is now!" Dr. Wilson pointed out. Lying at the foot of an acacia tree with a rifle trained on us was a guard. He raised his hand for us to stop; we did not argue. Another soldier approached us, his sub-machine gun at the ready. When he learned we were going to "the mission," he took our license number and raised the barrier for us. We drove across flat sand to the mission compound, where a Land-Rover was parked by the clinic. "Looks like the governor's," said Homer. It was. Nurse Elaine Douglas was treating his three-year-old son for bronchitis. She put the pills in a little envelope, cleverly folded from a magazine page. The governor greeted us in halting English.

In the burned-brick mission bungalow Geraldine Hinote was frying canned luncheon meat. Around the lunch table the girls explained why the soldiers were so jittery. Three weeks ago a party of bandits had attacked the garrison, only 300 feet from the mission house. The girls were just about to shut off their kerosene pressure lamp when they heard what sounded like fireworks. Then bullets whined by, followed by the boom of mortar fire. The two girls kept their heads down until the *shiftas* were routed. Now there are commandos at all key points and a curfew on all roads.

The clinic assistant, Ibrahim Mohammed, invited us to his home for tea. Like most houses in Af-Abet, where the sand won't make mud walls, Ibrahim's hut was a frame of poles covered with brier branches on the top and sides. The wind of course comes through—and so does the rain, accounting for the prevalence of TB.

Ibrahim was a Muslim—the missionaries were awaiting the arrival of a Christian lad still in training. Ibrahim's wife Sa'adiya wore no veil. Perhaps the lack of veils dates back to the era when these Tigrai people were Christian. They succumbed to Islam at the point of the saber.

Ibrahim and Sa'adiya made a charming host and hostess. Their fat little boy sat at his mother's feet as she tended the teapot boiling on a charcoal brazier. I learned that tea has to be boiled slightly to extract the flavor at this altitude, because water boils before it gets hot enough to infuse the tea properly. Sa'adiya wore a purple headscarf that partly concealed her long plaited tresses and solid gold ornaments: a three-inch-wide crescent hanging from each ear lobe, a gold plate on top of her head, gold coins in a necklace, and a two-inch gold "leaf" suspended from her nose—a hole is punctured in one nostril with a thorn at the time of engagement. These were all gifts of her husband as a kind of marriage security. Sa'adiya's eyes flashed happily as she poured the sweet tea spiced with cloves.

These Eritrean people are small-boned and more Arabian than Negroid. The town of Af-Abet is the center of 12 different tribes bonded together by the Tigri language and the Islamic religion. The smallest tribe has 300 members, the largest 17,000. Each is governed by its own sheik, who is also native "doctor" for some illnesses, such as TB and mental derangement.

The people are duskily attractive, and even the arid land is not without its rugged beauty: red-berried candelabra cactuses, splashes of orange and yellow blossoms against patches of twisted thornbrush. On the floor of the valley little thorny sprigs clung to the sand. As I took the trouble to bend down to look, I could see microscopic maroon blossoms—the handiwork of the Creator, lost under the feet of man and camel.

In spite of the stony land, the government gets a high per capita tax from the area because of the many cattle and camels. By keeping constantly on the move over a wide, sparsely populated area, the animals find enough foliage on thorn bushes and cactuses to feed on.

That evening the two ladies, the Wilsons, and I sat around the hissing pressure lamp for evening devotions. Dr. Wilson read from the Scriptures. Afterwards we sang, "Thou art coming to a King; large petitions with thee bring." We prayed. Not remote prayers for "missions," but the prayers of a little band in a gospel outpost in the Enemy's territory, armed with prayer and faith.

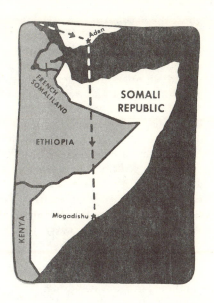

23. Cinnamon and Daggers

I moved my feet out of the way of juice oozing from raw fish on the floor of the plane. Howard Borlase and I were flying to Aden in South Arabia. We spent six rough hours on a vibrating DC 3 cargo flight, sitting sideways on canvas benches which ran the length of the bare fuselage. In the middle of the floor was a great pile of freight, including the fish. The juice made the floor slippery and added to the odors of the stifling cabin. A Russian passenger became nauseated and fainted several times.

We left the verdure of the Ethiopian highlands, and flew towards the Red Sea. Below us was the Danakil Desert, with yellow potash "flows," salt flats, and plains of sterile volcanic ash studded with extinct cones. At the Red Sea port of Assab, where the Russian disembarked, SIM missionaries live in temperatures which reach 120 degrees. This coast has the world's highest recorded annual day-and-night average temperature.

Flying across the Red Sea to the southern tip of Arabia, we landed at Aden just after its only rain of the year. Small puddles on the tarmac were quickly evaporating.

"No bombs went off," I said to Howard, as the plane stopped. People had warned us that the city was an armed camp, and that a grenade or bomb could go off any time.

The Yemeni Arabs, backed by Egypt, were seeking to take over the Federation of South Arabia. A Yemeni sitting on a doorstep might well have a grenade under his robe. The British, who have used Aden as a troop staging depot, want to withdraw. The local Arabs want them to stay to help the economy and thwart a Yemeni takeover.

In spite of the threat of violence, business carried on as usual in this intriguing city set in the craters of volcanoes. It is actually a city of bargain shops, where tourists can buy just about anything far below its normal retail price, because it is a duty-free port.

Tradition says two sons of Adam are buried in one of the craters, and that Noah built his ark across the bay. A series of monstrous reservoirs in an elongated crater were built for the Queen of Sheba, the people say, but archeologists date them anywhere from A.D. 100 to A.D. 1500. They could hold 100 million imperial gallons but would never be filled with Aden's current annual rainfall of one and one-half inches.

The thing which impressed me most was Arab hospitality. A merchant known to Howard lent us pocket money and told us not to worry about settling accounts until we were ready to leave. His brother sent his Mercedes Benz and driver to take us all around the suburbs, and wouldn't accept a penny payment. No time or trouble was too much for them.

Another brother, Zane, turned up and greeted Howard as if he were a brother, too. He had been the prime minister of Aden but refused to run again because he didn't want to be shot at. Zane and his brothers Mohammed and Aiderus invited us to their home for an Arabian night. "Home" turned out to be a three-story mansion built when Zane was national leader. Mosaics covered the walls. One room looked like a ballroom, with a scintillating chandelier imported from Czechoslovakia.

We sat on the rooftop under the tropical sky. The womenfolk were secluded down below. Mohammed had just returned from London, Zane from Washington. Aiderus was the congenial host and kept up a patter of conversation while a young boy kept bringing heaped dishes from the kitchen below: a spicy rice dish, great chunks of lamb, tossed vegetable salad, pickled limes, jellied fruit and cream. The Arabian coffee was syrupy sweet, with root ginger floating in it.

During our contacts with these brothers, Howard brought up spiritual matters. "I'm praying for the day of your conversion," he told them. "Ah, Meester Borrrlase!" they replied, "you keep praying for us. You have meant something to our lives. We want you missionaries to come back here. You are our friends."

Howard and I made our way to the SIM compound on Victory of God Street. The Mission moved there in 1945 with the idea of reaching the Somalis (now 20,000) who came to Aden for work. The missionaries prayed that God would open the door to Somalia. When tension arose over the Arabian Federation, missionaries were advised by their embassies to leave. The SIM also saw that its presence could bring added difficulties to the few Christians. So the missionaries moved out; a week later three buildings belonging to other missions were burned.

A Christian Somali was now living at the Mission compound, taking care of it while working and studying. We sat around a table and talked with him and three others and read the Scriptures together. We prayed for one another and especially for the believers in Somalia. We prayed that one day missionaries would be able to return to Aden. It was a strange little meeting, with such a sense of helplessness in the face of Islam. Yet the gospel was meant for this city too.

It was time to leave for Somalia, Africa's most easterly country. "Still no bombs," I said to Howard as we took off.

"We haven't landed yet," Howard dead-panned as we headed out over the Gulf of Aden to the Somali coastline. Several months later a plane *was* blown up, killing all on board.

Traveling with this lanky six-footer considerably brightened the trip for me, not only by his sense of humor as well as spiritual insight, but also by the fact that he has served in four countries where the Mission works and so could answer my many questions. I enjoyed learning how he came to Africa.

The prairie boy heard of the SIM when he went to see "lantern slides" shown by a missionary. Feeling like a man at 16, Howard fired off an application to the SIM in Toronto. The secretary tactfully suggested that he re-apply when 21. He did, and sailed for Nigeria at the ripe old age of 22. A young lady named Ruth Warn was on the same ship. Unfortunately so was Dr. Bingham, austere founder of the SIM. The first morning at sea, Howard was waiting in the cabin corridor when Dr. Bingham stepped out of his cabin.

"It is nice of you to wait for me to go to breakfast, young man," drawled the director.

"I'm not waiting for you, sir. I'm waiting for Miss Warn," Howard answered, and then realized he had made a bad start with the Mission director.

"Miss Warn doesn't need waiting for," replied Dr. Bingham, taking Howard by the arm. "You come to breakfast with *me*."

All ended well, though. A year after arriving in Nigeria, Howard and Ruth were married. Since then they have served in Sudan, Ethiopia, and Somalia. As we flew high over Somalia's wastes, Howard explained the background of the nation we would be visiting.

When Somalia came under United Nations' trusteeship in 1954, the U.N. insisted on including a religious liberty clause in the constitution. The whole land was opened to Protestant missions for the first time in history. The Eastern Mennonite

Board of Missions and Charities and the SIM, the only two Protestant missions, opened three boarding schools and two hospitals in one of the most zealous Islamic lands in the world.

The SIM received permission to open five more stations but could not do so before the new liberties were slowly choked off. First came a law forbidding students under 15 to receive any form of Bible teaching—a blow at the schools.

Then came the blow of June 5, 1963. The government newspaper headlined: "Constitution Article Reworded to Check Non-Islamic Faiths." Under the change, every person was guaranteed "the right to freedom of conscience and freely to profess his own religion," but "*it shall not be permissible to spread or propagandize any religions other than the True Religion of Islam.*"

This meant a whole new outlook on the part of missionaries. Now, no more Bible classes, no more distribution of Christian literature. Should they leave if they could not even witness? During the few years of liberty several young men had been saved. Under the amended constitution, it was possible to meet with them privately. The missionaries decided to stay to help strengthen the nucleus.

When the government insisted that the Koran must be taught in mission schools, but not the Bible, the SIM closed its schools. The Mennonite Mission did not. A local paper then charged that the SIM didn't want to help Africans, while the Mennonites did. Anxious to maintain democratic principles, however, the government did not expel the missionaries. After all, they couldn't do much harm now!

The missionaries had peace in themselves, but they were burdened for the struggling handful of believers and for the great mass of people around them. Possibly only 50,000 out of four million had heard the gospel.

It was difficult for Christian young men to find work or continue studies. One of their biggest problems was the lack of Christian girls. They couldn't marry Muslims; whom could they marry? It looked as if the nucleus church would die out because of lack of Christian homes. Was it possible to win a Somali girl to Christ? The very day after the amendment was announced, the Lord sent along an encouragement to the Borlases' front door, a modern Somali girl who eventually trusted Christ as Saviour. Today she is studying in a college overseas, living with a Christian family who have taken her in as one of their own daughters.

The "Fasten Seatbelts" sign went on in our aircraft. We were over Mogadishu, Somalia, on the Horn of Africa jutting into the Indian Ocean. We slid in between sand dunes and landed on an ex-military airstrip built by the Italians. Our passports were stamped with fair speed; then we passed through the most novel immigration formality I have seen.

A good natured Indian sat behind a cage clearing currency declarations. For a two-shilling fee he transformed a drab official form into a splendid work of contemporary art. When he finished with it, the form sparkled with 22 separate rubber stamp impressions in red, black, turquoise, and lurid purple.

My name was set up in half-inch-high capitals, stamped in black, with the four periods in "Mr. W. H. Fuller." individually inserted with a round red rubber stamp. There were date stamps and place stamps and "No" stamps and "Si" stamps, and arrow stamps to point to other stamps. Even the official seal stamp was over-stamped with the words, "Official Use Only." Habibbhoy earned every Somali cent of his fee.

We had arrived in the SIM's most southerly post, two degrees north of the equator.

Mogadishu is on a site with a millennium of recorded history. Fragments of Chinese pottery and Chinese coins dating from the Sung Dynasty (A.D. 960–1279) and the Ming Dynasty (1368–1644) have been found in the sandy soil. Somalia was the part of Africa nearest to the Far East, and with her flat scrub-covered plains the most accessible to traders in ivory and spices. Cinnamon was the chief spice.

In modern times the Italians made Mogadishu their administrative center until they were ousted during World War

II. The U.N. allowed them to return for 10 years after the war, until Somalia could draw up a constitution and become independent. Everywhere the Italian influence is still evident: the top of a wall painstakingly finished with Roman design, a gateway, a tower, and a road sign reading "Piano Prego" above the English and Arabic words for "Slow Please."

In the center of the capital of this fanatically Islamic nation I was surprised to see a massive twin-towered Roman Catholic cathedral, built, according to a Somali newspaper editor, "by slave labor and prisoners."

To placate the Muslims for the offensive cathedral, the Italians also built within 100 yards an equally imposing mosque with a neon-outlined crescent topping its minaret. There are 250 mosques in this city of 100,000 population.

Along the palm-lined avenues whizzed three-wheeled scooter taxis, with shawl-covered Arabs and Somalis crowded into the rear seats. Waiting for a traffic light to change was a Muslim woman covered from head to foot in shining black cloth, with a circle of bright red netting where her face should be. An Italian in shirt, gray flannel shorts, and knee-length stockings trudged solemnly to his office.

There are 20 foreign embassies in Mogadishu. We saw groups of men looking at photos outside the American and Russian embassies. "They are all lies anyway," one man stated emphatically.

Although Red China has given Somalia 21 million dollars in interest-free loans, some Somalis have seen that Communists are not their friends. During the Italian regime, when foreign control was resented, certain political parties leaned toward Communism. Russia built a large secondary school, radio station, press, and dairy.

Then Somali students began going to Russia and Eastern Europe on scholarships. Their intense nationalistic independence clashed with Marxism and they became disillusioned. Seven returned to Somalia and asked their government to protest before the United Nations. I read a 24-page booklet listing their grievances, ranging from forced political indoctrination to racial discrimination.

The Somali people are tall, thin, and cinnamon colored, with curly or wavy hair, not kinky. Their faces are V-shaped, with broad foreheads tapering down to pointed chins; their noses are long and high-bridged, and their lips thin. A British War Office report on the former British sector to the north stated: "These Muslims are a conservative, proud, fierce, and handsome people. Man and camel look with equal contempt at the white stranger."

Most men carry daggers or pistols. One of Howard Borlase's friends told him, with obvious relish, "We Somalis like to kill." Their current passion is to unite what they term "The Five Somalis": French Somaliland, ex-British Somaliland, ex-Italian Somaliland, the Ogaden in Ethiopia, and Kenya's Northern Frontier District. So far only the former British and Italian areas are united. The Somali flag bears a five-pointed star.

While killing may be considered enjoyable by some, work is not. Howard once introduced a white friend to a Somali friend. The white man asked, "How do you enjoy your work?"

"I don't understand your question, sir," the Somali replied. "How is it possible to work and also to enjoy oneself? We work because we have to, not because we enjoy it."

There are Somalis who enjoy working, though. We met one when we arrived at the SIM headquarters, located in an Italian walled "villa." Ahmed Osman was seated at a table surrounded by Bibles and reference books, assisting Warren and Dorothy Modricker in translating the Bible into the Somali language—a formidable task, considering that the nation does not agree on standard usage and orthography.

It is astonishing that in the past these proud, ancient people, prolific poets, have not written their own language; they have relied on Arabic or Italian. But their dislike of the Arabs keeps them from agreeing to an Arabic orthography for their own language, and a Roman script reminds them of imperialism.

So they have produced their own complicated orthography called Osmanian, but there is no literature in it.

Mrs. Modricker, an expert in the language, showed me some of the complexities. "What can wash away my sins?" becomes "What the sin my the and all me from to take able?" Of course there are the usual problems of using local idioms. The Somali believers solved the problem of saying "whiter than snow" in a snowless country by using "foam of camel's milk."

In spite of this staggering task, the Modrickers and their colleagues had translated and typed material on 888 stencils, ready to be mimeographed. They still had to complete the Old Testament.

Up on the top floor of the three-story main building I found missionaries teaching classes in typing and English. The instructors are very careful not to break the law by discussing the gospel, but the students see concern, love, and sincerity. They often drop in at other times for a cup of tea. Some ask questions privately.

Mohammed Nur is one who came back to ask more. During the day he studied at the Egyptian Secondary School, taught entirely in Arabic. His tutors knew he was attending the SIM night school to improve his English and offered him money if he would pass on to them information about the missionaries.

"How can I do that?" he asked them. "Those people are my friends." The Egyptians told him to think it over. He did and gave them his answer.

"You have your embassy staff," he told them. "This is their job. Send one of them to the night school as a spy." No, they wanted him to do the job. "If this is Islam, I don't want it," Mohammed thought to himself. He went to ask one of the missionaries the way of salvation, and gave his heart to Christ.

When Mohammed returned to his room, he realized there was no point in continuing the Islamic fast. The next day a student told his teacher he had seen Mohammed drinking tea during the hours of fasting. The teacher confronted Mohammed in the classroom, demanding to know why he had done so.

"Because I am now a follower of Jesus Christ," confessed Mohammed.

The teacher became livid. Pointing a finger at Mohammed, he ordered him to leave the school at once. To his surprise, three Muslim students jumped up and intervened.

"Our nation is a democracy," they declared. "You can't send a student out because he believes differently. He is entitled to believe what he wants."

The teacher backed down and Mohammed stayed.

Although the people say a man is no longer a true Somali if he is a Christian, their concept of the rights of individuals is strong. "Democracy" is the most precious word in their newly acquired English language—and they want to get the most out of it. Therefore relatives do not seem inclined to kill believers but rather ostracize them, making life unbearable.

In the evening a tall Somali came to keep an appointment with Warren Modricker. He had previously come to ask for Bible teaching, but had not been granted his request at once. A missionary has to be sure that each case is genuine and not an informer. At worship services held in homes, Somali believers closely question any stranger. One spy was so convicted by the love of Christ which he saw in the missionaries that he tore up his file of reports.

A missionary must use the unusual tactic of seeming offhanded when approached by inquirers. After cross-examining them he asks them to come back the next day. With an aching heart he watches them leave, praying fervently that they will return if they are serious. The wonderful thing is that they do. For two months after the constitution was amended, a Somali was converted every week at one SIM station.

There were five young men lined up that night in Mogadishu, each waiting his turn to sit for half an hour's Bible instruction. Because of the ban on holding religious classes for non-Christians, Warren took them one at a time. Each one had written a letter stating he wanted the missionary to teach him the Bible. This letter was kept on file in case of allegations of proselytizing. Warren gave each young man three Bible verses to copy out in his own hand (to avoid charges of distributing Christian literature). The inquirer went home to memorize the verses, returning to discuss their meaning week after week.

Before I left to visit SIM work inland, I went to see the grave of one who laid down his life for his Lord. The simple headstone lying in the sand reads: *Merlin R. Grove, Feb. 9, 1929— July 16, 1962. Jesus said . . . No one comes to God but by Me. John 14.6.*

As Mennonite missionary Merlin Grove was enrolling people in an English class, a fanatical priest brushed past the line and stabbed him 12 times. Merlin's wife, Dorothy, rushed out of a back room to find her husband dying on the floor. The assassin then turned on her and stabbed her in the abdomen before running off down the street.

Dorothy had often wondered if she could really love the Somali people. The answer came to her as she lay bleeding on the floor, she said later. A supernatural love, the love of Calvary, filled her heart. She knew she could love Somalis for Christ's sake.

On trial, the priest said that he could not have done the deed without God's help. Somali officials condemned his action and sentenced him to 25 years in solitary confinement, although later he was freed after a retrial. Dorothy Grove is praying for his salvation.

That night I heard the Back to the Bible Broadcast coming all the way across the continent over radio station ELWA. The choir was singing, "The Price of a Soul." The hymn took on new meaning for me as I thought of that simple grave in the Somali sand.

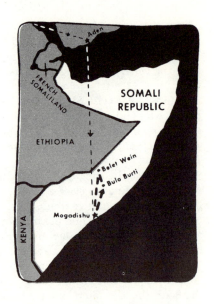

24. The Crime Worse Than Murder

Ahmed Osman, the translator, volunteered to accompany me
inland as far as Bulo Burti, so he could explain things along
the way. Even though every seat on the bus was filled, the
driver refused to make the trip that day because he couldn't
find an extra passenger to crowd on each row. So we had to
unload and contract with a taxi driver to make the 150-mile
trip, in order to catch up with Howard Borlase.

Howard had already left to see to Mission business at Bulo
Burti. In fact, he had left twice. The first time he set out, a
police road-block stopped the bus to examine baggage. The
police were particularly interested in a heavy box tied on top
of the bus. When they opened it, they found grapefruit inside

—and under the grapefruit 956 bullets. The police locked up most of the passengers, and Howard had to return to Mogadishu and start out the next day on another bus.

The ammunition apparently was meant to supply feuding clansmen, who had killed at least 300 in the last few days. With this encouraging information duly noted, Ahmed and I set off in the back seat of a medium-sized Fiat taxi. We traveled on the only highway inland, a tar-surfaced road built by the Italians 35 years before and scarcely repaired since. Our driver, a striking figure with two stainless steel teeth, tried his best to avoid the potholes that pocked the road.

Mileposts bearing the ancient Imperial Roman insignia marked our way straight as an arrow across flat plains. Whereas Ethiopia's scenery is vertical, Somalia's is horizontal. Hour after hour we drove through country with no visible change— just more flat land sparsely dotted with squat thorn brush. Fifty percent of the countryside is like this, used to graze bony cattle and camels. Forty percent is sandy desert, unusable for anything. Only 10 percent is considered arable land, and most of it is along the two main rivers.

Ahmed told me that most of the four million population in this land of 195,000 square miles is nomadic, herding their livestock from one precious grazing ground to another. This accounts for Somalia's keen interest in the greener grazing lands in Ethiopia and northern Kenya.

We saw 200 camels around one water hole. To a Somali a camel represents life itself. One missionary made a sad mistake in an English class. He was teaching the difference between *ugly* and *beautiful*. "A gazelle is beautiful, a camel is ugly," he said. A rumble went through the class and one student jumped to his feet to protest: "Sir, we object. The camel is the most beautiful thing in the world."

Ahmed and I struck up quite a friendship as we bumped along together in the back seat. He was one of the first SIM converts in Somalia. The son of Somali nomads in the Ogaden on the other side of the Ethiopian border, he attended a government school. The students had to recite the prayers of Ethiopia's Orthodox Church, and Ahmed attended some of their services in order to ridicule the Copts, whom he despised as hypocrites.

One day an unknown missionary drove through his village and handed out tracts in the market. Ahmed grabbed one. He hid it in his pocket when the village priest came to burn all the literature the missionary had left. The Somali lad read and re-read it to improve his English, and slowly the way of salvation began to penetrate his mind. When he later traveled to Mogadishu "to see the world," a friend told him about the SIM's meetings. This was before the amendment to the constitution. There he heard the way explained and gave his heart to the Lord.

I asked this spirited Somali what he felt were the main problems facing believers. He had them all thought out: (1) *Education.* Somali believers are very strong on the need for mission schools and hope the government will relax its rule that Islam must be taught. (2) *Marriage.* There are possibly 200 Protestant Christians among the four million population. Most are single young men; only a few are girls. Believers face a great problem in finding Christian wives. (3) *Employment.* Ahmed explained the difficulty believers have in finding jobs. He suggested industrial training for young men so they could start small local industries, like weaving.

About this time our driver decided the surface of the road was so bad he would do better on a dirt trail cut across the plains. It was smoother, but the tarred road at least had no dust. Buses and trucks plied the dirt track to save their springs, and at times the ruts were so deep that we became hung up on the ridges of loose sand. Passengers in the large vehicles could ride above the dust, but we ploughed through it like a schooner throwing up a bow wave. Red dust covered the side and back windows, which helped to shield us from the direct sun, but it also streamed in the front window, left open two inches for ventilation. I sat behind the driver and watched his black hair slowly turn red, then his shoulders—then I looked at my own arms and clothes and saw they were the same. Ahmed and I held hankies over our mouths to strain the dust.

Suddenly the taxi began to weave drunkenly. We had a flat. Alas, we had no good spare, and no matches to light the vulcanizing repair patch. But the driver produced an outsize tube and stuffed it in the tire. The next time we saw a truck approaching in a dust cloud, I suggested that the driver ask for matches. He did. A mile further we had another flat. This time we could light the hot patch and repair the puncture. When we got the tire back on, however, the car wouldn't start. Battery dead. No crank. Push. Push in the thick, clinging sand. Push back and forth on the flat trail. Push in the heat of noon two degrees from the equator.

At last the car started. Ten more miles we had another flat. A nail had made four holes in the tube. We patched them all. Again, the car wouldn't start. We pushed. We started off but got bogged in sand. The motor died. We pushed. That day I learned what Somali heat is like, all the while thinking of a missionary who died of a heart attack while pushing a car on furlough.

The mission compound at Bulo Burti was the fairest sight I had seen for a long time, for it marked the end of our taxi journey. A wash, lots of lime juice, a chair that stayed still, fresh air—what luxuries!

Dr. Jo Anne Ader was in the operating room of the SIM's hospital. She had jumped up from lunch to deliver a baby boy, and now, two hours later—her meal forgotten—she was still bending over the infant. "He's having a hard time," she explained. "He's the first baby of this young mother, and we do want to save him."

As a girl, Jo Anne had been a good church member who wanted to be a missionary. She took nurse's training, then worked her way through medical school by nursing. In her last year she was converted through Inter Varsity Christian Fellowship meetings. With a new outlook on the meaning of missionary service, she took Bible training and applied to the SIM for medical work among Muslims. She got it! I asked Dr. Jo Anne what she did when she needed medical consultation in an emergency.

"Pray," she said, pushing back a strand of her bobbed hair.

Dr. Ader wouldn't stay in Somalia if she couldn't witness. Because she is a doctor, patients don't object. But usually they ignore her spiritual advice. One TB patient, hemorrhaging in the lungs, yielded to the pressure of relatives to leave the hospital and try "bush medicine." Dr. Jo Anne pleaded with him to stay, knowing he would not last long otherwise. "Mohammed, God has sent you light," she told him. "Are you deliberately choosing darkness?"

Mohammed turned desperate eyes to her and said, "Yes, I choose darkness."

The staff flitted around with optimism in spite of towering obstacles—like waiting for 15 months for a shipment of medicines to come 1,000 miles from Addis Ababa. Doctors and nurses are traditionally forbearing, but what can you do when patients refuse to answer any of your questions about symptoms?

"After all," reasons a patient, "I am sick. The nurse should know what is wrong. It is none of her business what I ate or did or felt like yesterday."

Some patients are very fearful when they enter a hospital or clinic for the first time. One Arab's worst fears were confirmed at a dispensary when he read a large poster tacked to the wall by an unthinking person: "Without shedding of blood is no remission." He fled for his life as the nurse approached.

Before opening the Bulo Burti hospital in 1963, Dr. Jo Anne worked at the Mission's hospital at Kallafo, across the Ethiopian border. This five-foot-one-inch doctor told us about a hair-raising drive she and a nurse made from Bulo Burti to Kallafo. Ascending a knoll, she thought she saw something moving around the rocks on the crest. For some reason the 23rd Psalm started running through her mind.

Topping the crest, she saw at least 50 armed bandits. She couldn't gain speed on the washboard road; there was nothing to do but stop. Their leader poked his rifle in the doctor's face and ordered her out of the Land-Rover. He told the nurse to alight too. The other bandits ran towards them.

Then one tall brigand seemed to recognize Dr. Ader. Suddenly he pinned the leader's arms behind his back. "Get in and drive off—fast!" he barked at the two missionaries. They did, marveling that God had caused the tall bandit to oppose his leader and risk the wrath of the others for letting a valuable Land-Rover escape.

As they sped down the hill and along the isolated road, Jo Anne and her companion recited, "Yea, though I walk through the valley of the shadow of death, I will fear no evil; for thou art with me."

Bill Rogers was waiting to drive Howard and me a further 80 miles to Belet Wein. Off we set in Bill's red pickup. We were approaching a more wooded area. Tiny dikdik deer the size of toy terriers bounded across our path. Baboons scattered into the thorn brush. Bill said a roan antelope once charged his truck. Another missionary collided with the legs of a giraffe, which toppled on to the car and crushed the top.

We rounded a curve where bandits had fired at a bus only two weeks before. Then I blinked my eyes. In the dusk ahead I thought I saw electric lights, 230 miles inland on a desolate plain. "You're right," said Rogers. "For 50 years Belet Wein has been a military center, first for the Italians, then the British, and now the Somalis." This city of 12,000 is only 20 miles from the hotly-disputed Somali-Ethiopian border, and on the only highway between the coast and the railway in Ethiopia— 1,000 miles of lonely road through bandit-plagued wastes.

We drove through the dusty streets into the mission compound. Half a dozen believers were waiting to welcome us. We sat on folding canvas chairs in one of the mission cottages and talked about the Lord's goodness. When Howard told the believers how much I had to pay the taxi owner in order to be there, one said in halting English, "The money you spent to be with us has been replaced by the joy of our fellowship in Jesus."

They gave us a verse of Scripture they had specially chosen: "The Lord shall guide thee continually and satisfy thy soul in drought. . . ." (Isaiah 58.11). They knew what drought was—last year many cattle had died. After we prayed for one another and for the unsaved, they sang a hymn, written by Musa Sheikow, a Somali student whom I had met over in Ethiopia at the Grace Bible College.

So this was where Musa had made his bold stand for God. Some of these believers had heard the gospel from his lips. Nine years before, Musa had been a strong Muslim. He attended the SIM school across the Ethiopian border at Kallafo, where the Word of God entered his heart. He came to the missionaries at night to ask the way of salvation. When his parents found out, they told him never to return home. He trained under Dr. Dick Scheel at the SIM hospital in Kallafo, then returned to his homeland, Somalia, to work at the Mission's dispensary at Bulo Burti and then at Belet Wein.

Musa couldn't refrain from telling his own people the wondrous news he had found. As reports of his witnessing spread, the police watched him for five months, trying to catch him in the act of preaching. About a year ago a man who posed as a friend told the police that Musa had in his house a booklet, "How to Lead a Muslim to Christ." As he was treating patients one morning, police appeared at the dispensary door, ordered him to take them to his house. Inside they found the booklet and arrested him on a charge of trying to destroy the religion of the country.

Word of the arrest spread throughout the countryside, and 600 people crowded around the courthouse to hear the case.

"We have heard reports that you claim to be a Christian," began the judge. "What do you say to the charge?"

Musa stood alone in the dock while the crowd watched sullenly. He pulled himself up to his full six-foot height and spoke clearly: "It is true, Your Worship; I am following Jesus Christ, whether you imprison me or kill me!"

A shout ran through the crowd, "Jail him!" The entire crowd stamped out of the court, hissing in anger. The judge also retired and then returned to give his verdict.

"Because you have confessed yourself a Christian, and you have been found with this book, and you have been reported witnessing—you are given a sentence of six months' imprisonment or 500 shillings fine."

Musa lifted his face to heaven and prayed silently, "Thank you, Lord, that I can witness in this way." He had no money to pay the fine; so the guards put him in solitary confinement. In the main prison was a clan sheik, imprisoned for fighting another clan. A fanatical Muslim, he told the others, "Let's humiliate this infidel. We'll give him all the worst jobs." Amid jeers they made him clean the latrines the first day. But they were stunned the next day when Musa volunteered to clean the latrines again.

The amazing news that a Somali had declared in court that he was a Christian and was willing to go to jail for it spread through the nation. The provincial governor came to see the strange case.

"How can you, a Somali, stay in prison for being a Christian?" he asked. "Are you insane?" Musa witnessed to him, and when the governor came out he told the guards they must let him live with the other prisoners. He also ordered them to provide Musa with medicine to treat ill prisoners.

Musa's life won such respect that he was given the keys to all the prison rooms. What he could not do legally outside the prison, God now enabled him to do inside, bringing important visitors to ask him about his faith.

Somali society is divided into clans who help out their members with blood money. Musa's clan sent a delegation to apologize to him: "If you were in prison for killing someone, we could easily pay the fine and have you released. But we can't do it for your crime—it hasn't ever been done."

The sheik was enraged at the attention that Musa was getting, but Musa treated him courteously. Then he discovered that the sheik liked to hear the news from the newspaper but couldn't read Italian. Day after day Musa sat beside his persecutor and read the news to him. The old man softened.

"Musa," he said one day. "You are in prison for a good cause. If I get out first, I shall put down the money for your fine." And he did. Musa was freed before his sentence finished. He returned to work at the Mission dispensary and saved his wages to pay back the sheik, to whom he continued witnessing. The Word of God was more precious than ever to Musa, and he rejoiced when he was able to go to Ethiopia to study the Bible.

The missionaries at Belet Wein needed an encouragement like that. Because of the religious instruction law, they had to close their boarding school. They hoped to train Christian girls there; now the buildings stood vacant. Even the land seemed to mock them; they laid out a vegetable garden to help their diet, but the brackish well water made the soil sterile. A missionary couple lost their baby just two weeks before they were due to leave for furlough. Home seemed a planet away. The Rogers were still waiting for Christmas parcels posted six months before.

Even the Red Chinese staff at the government hospital were discouraged. Three American Peace Corps teachers wondered why the missionaries stayed on—they couldn't see any progress in their own teaching work. The only Somalis they thought showed prospects for learning were the believers—"but," they said, "they aren't Somalis any more."

A dismal picture? Not when you think of Musa Sheikow and other hand-picked fruit like him.

The Rogers' cook took me into the town the next morning. It was a peaceful community unspoiled by the turmoil of urban life. Children, like fat baked beans, laughed as they played. Women sold camel's milk in the market from large "jugs"— actually tightly woven baskets pitched with a red bark. Prospective buyers stuck out a hand to taste a sample. A bushy-haired nomad carried his little crescent-shaped wooden pedestal on which he rested his neck when sleeping, to avoid flattening his hair-do.

A handsome nomad loaded his kneeling camel. He had traveled two days with the milk, butter, and curds from his 10 camels and sold the lot for 110 shillings ($15). With part of this he bought a bolt of white cloth which he tied on top of his empty milk jugs. A nomad tried to sell me "a strong camel" for 250 shillings ($36). I declined but instead bought a pound of camel meat for a shilling. We ate it that night, thoroughly pounded; it tasted like dry beef.

I was surprised to see signs on several buildings reading "Bar". Islam forbids the use of alcohol. My guide explained that only cinnamon tea and camel's milk were sold inside.

We came on a crowd in the street. A Muslim priest was calling parents to pay him money so he could teach their children verses from the Koran. Boys and girls sat in the dust around him, responding with a chant each time he sang out a verse. Believing that the verses had talismanic value, parents crowded to press coins into the priest's palm. His eyes burned as he glowered at the white intruder. I moved on.

Beside the road we passed shacks of artisans sitting cross legged as they made leather goods, baskets, and knives. In a blacksmith's shop an old man squatted on the ground and hammered a big bolt into a narrow head, while another man made the coals glow with air pumped from two goatskin bags. Another blacksmith filed a sharp edge on the six-inch blade of a curved dagger. I felt its needle sharp point and remembered it was such a knife which a Muslim priest had plunged into Merlin Grove. Belet Wein had a peaceful atmosphere—a contented community living in its own world on the Somali plains —but at its heart was the Muslim teacher with his Koranic verses, and ready to defend the faith were curved daggers.

When Howard and I returned to Mogadishu, 12 of the believers gathered at the mission compound to commit us to the Lord before we left Somalia. Ahmed Osman, the translator, stepped forward and presented me with a six-foot-long wooden chain, with the links all carved from one piece of wood.

"We believers want to give this to you, to remind you and the Lord's people in other lands that we are one in Christ Jesus, and that we need to pray for one another."

As that little group of disciples left the compound to continue living in a hostile world, there rang in my ears the words of a Somali hymn written by Ahmed:

The Everlasting Father will never fail from His promise,
 And I will not deny my Saviour.
If I stay on the high mountains and ice fall over me,
 I will not deny my Saviour.
If I stay in the desert for one hundred years,
If I cannot have a farm or flocks or even a wife,
 I will not deny my Saviour.
If they beat me with a stick, slay me, and throw me in the sea,
 I will not deny my Saviour.
For I had a sin disease in my heart, and He is the One who healed me;
 So I will not deny my Saviour.

25. Epilog — from the Edge of Africa

Howard Borlase forced me to get up early to see the sun rise over the Indian Ocean and have a swim before flying from Somalia that morning. "An unforgettable experience," he assured me as I rubbed my eyes.

We stood on the very edge of Africa, with the warm surf swirling around our feet. Before us the restless ocean stretched all the way to Indonesia and Australia. We couldn't see the sun's sphere rising. Instead the heavy haze over the water glowed, then brightened, and finally blazed like a white-hot furnace. The dawn does come up like thunder, just as the old song says.

I turned away from the ocean and looked back at Africa

stretching westward. Many Africas really: desert Africa, rain-forest Africa, savannah Africa, mountainous Africa. Africa of both the camel driver and the truck driver. Africa of the Muslim, the animist, the Christian.

It was very quiet there on the edge of Africa—only the drumming of the eternal breakers rolling in. The vast kaleidoscope of all I had seen across Africa between the Atlantic and the Indian Ocean passed in colorful parade before my mind. Several significant facts came into focus, along with disturbing questions.

I had seen so much that it was impossible to pick out any one incident and say, "This is Africa." Actually I had just traveled through a microcosm of the centuries; there was something from every age. I had to keep this in mind in evaluating the needs of the continent. I was impressed by the diversity of ministries in the SIM, to meet this diversity of needs. It is not a literature mission, a medical mission, a pioneering mission; it is all these and more—using many channels as they are relevant to local needs.

I thought of the way Africa's needs have changed since R. V. Bingham's day—and are still changing. What Africa will become no one yet knows. Africans themselves don't know. They are now discovering themselves, and the present political upheavals are all part of the process. There are no comprehensive African-written histories to show me what the continent was really like before the colonial era, and the last two centuries couldn't give me an accurate picture, because Africa was then largely controlled by external powers. The much-discussed African Personality has yet to show its true self.

Through the sound of the surf I seemed to hear the antiphonal singing of a Wallamo church conference, and I wondered about the churches' outreach in evangelism. There is no single answer, I realized, because the churches differ so much in their development. There are the crowded churches of the Middle Belt in Nigeria and the south of Ethiopia. These are shouldering responsibility for church administration and evangelism. But there are also areas where there is no strong candle of church witness—only smoldering flax.

I found missionaries pondering over the question of how long to concentrate on unresponsive areas. How could greater use be made of fruitful areas to reach others? I could see that tribal animosity sometimes thwarts this strategy, and that in such areas a mission is still the essential channel.

It was relatively easy for me to look back from the edge of Africa and analyze the development of the gospel. The SIM pioneers who had landed on the opposite edge three-quarters of a century before, however, had faced an unwritten chapter. They didn't know what would eventuate. They had before them the primary task of winning men to Christ and turning over the work to them to carry on. Generally speaking, they faced simple animism, or Islam in a primitive context. But they did their job, and, by God's grace, they did it well.

Since then, however, the continent has not stood still. The population has doubled. During this period literacy, education, urbanization, ecumenism, nationalism, politics, and Communism have all been introduced.

The rapid pace of developing nations today produces pressures and problems which did not confront Christian growth in the more static Greco-Roman world, or in Medieval Europe, or North America's recent development. The number of forces competing for Africa has increased. Other religions will not sit back while the young church struggles alone to make an impact on the new Africa.

So today young evangelical churches may actually find themselves losing ground because of their lack of resources. I had heard some people at home say that when the primary task of introducing the gospel has been accomplished, the responsibility of Western churches is fulfilled. But I could see that the "sending churches" have an increasing duty to stand alongside their African brothers.

If the churches in Africa are going to evangelize their communities and reach the oncoming generation, they must not be saddled with heavy programs of hospitals and presses and radio stations. Their meager resources cannot undertake these. Yet these and other ministries *must* be carried on in order to reach the expanding frontiers of the new Africa. This is where the role of missions increasingly enters, providing these services to help the churches in their witness.

The contribution of churches in Western lands should not end at the elementary stage of evangelism but should develop an articulate, evangelical leadership for the body of Christ in Africa. The church leaders I met on this safari proved the strategic value of this. But their numbers are too few. I thanked God for the vision of leadership training that typifies so much SIM work.

I looked out across the ocean again and wondered about the future. What should be the relationship of a mission to its national churches? To preserve the principles of indigenous church growth, and yet help the church in its need, is it necessary to re-define the word "indigenous"? It was first defined in a colonial context. In those days African Christians were not aware of their sister-churches around the world. It seemed as though there were two worlds on this globe; in general, missionary strategy was to implant the gospel in the "other" world and let it develop on its own.

But today Christians in "mission lands" are conscious of the rest of the world. They ask if the Body of Christ is not one. If it is one Body, how can the work of the churches be separated from the work of the missions? To them it seems like a form of missionary apartheid. Can missions find ways of standing alongside the young churches, helping them without weakening them? The future of mission-church relations will require understanding on the part of both missionaries and their supporters.

I thought of Paul's words: *"Christ loved the church and gave himself for it."* I had seen churches with problems, and I wondered whether I was really ready to love and give as Christ had done. The task will never be completed until the church takes hold and does the work in the way in which the Holy Spirit leads it in its own context. What if that is not *our* way? What if the church makes mistakes? Would I still be ready to love the church and give myself for it?

The sea continued to roll in, as if to engulf Howard and me. Yet each breaker could only come so far before falling back, its fury broken. Then I remembered that the same sovereign God who set a bound to the seas is still in charge in Africa. How about the expulsion of missionaries from Ethiopia in 1937, the expulsion from southern Sudan in 1964, the tribal disturbances in Nigeria in 1966? I must believe in God's sovereignty. He could have restrained man's hand in each case, but He chose not to.

In Ethiopia, missionaries see the wisdom of His strategy. In Sudan they do not yet understand His purposes. But need we lose faith? Are we to faint in the face of militant Islam? In our thinking and praying, have we abandoned some areas? Or can we believe that the sovereign God who caused the Sudan to be evangelized 1,400 years ago can do it again?

Perhaps we are like the early disciples, more concerned about "the times and the seasons"—more worried about difficulties—than about fulfilling the Great Commission. Christ's answer to them was, "It is not for you to know the times or the seasons, which the father hath put in his power. But ye shall receive power: ye shall be witnesses unto the uttermost part of the earth."

It came to me that that was the answer: power. *God's* power. This accounted for what I had seen under the sun in Africa. God's power had been made available to His servants. This accounted for the existence of the church, for the victories that had been achieved in the face of humanly-insurmountable odds.

This explained why yesterday's pioneers had conquered, despite the loss of their lives. This explained why today's missionaries and African believers look to the future with such confidence. They have seen God's power unleashed. They know that this is *His* work, not theirs, and that His good purposes *will* be accomplished.

This explained why the SIM was pressing on, thankful for what has been accomplished, but looking ahead with even greater expectation to what God is going to do. My heart warmed within me as I thought in those terms: *God* at work, through human channels.

I thought of some who are holding back from the task, some who are faint-hearted in adversity, some young people who hesitate to commit their lives in this day of insecurity—because they are not convinced of the Lordship of the One who holds the times and seasons in His hands. They are not ready to utilize the power He has given to be His witnesses.

My heart burned for these as I came to the end of my safari across Africa. It seemed that the basic need of the church of Jesus Christ in Africa and in other lands is re-commitment to the will of God, a personal reviving by the Holy Spirit. I gave thanks for the healthy signs, after 75 years of fruitful ministry, of this renewal in the SIM, as well as among the new churches in Africa and the older "homeland" churches.

These thoughts drummed in my mind as the surf broke incessantly. Howard and I seemed so insignificant standing on the limitless stretch of sand. The continent with its nearly 300 millions was so vast. Yet the Creator, at whose command this shore rose out of the sea, was not without His plan for His fallen creatures. Christ commanded, "Go ye and preach and teach." He promised to empower His weak disciples through His Holy Spirit: "Lo, I am with you, even unto the end." And He also said, "I must work while it is day; the night cometh when no man can work."

It had never been an easy task. It was still one which would test every fiber in a disciple's body and mind and soul. It was a job which could be done effectively only by men and women empowered by God's Spirit.

The time was only 7 a.m., yet the sun was already a searing orb, magnified by the shimmering haze.

"Time to leave," Howard reminded me. "We've got things to do."

"Yes," I replied, "like our Ethiopian friend said, we must run while the sun is hot."

A Short Bibliography

Ajayi, J. F. A., *Christian Missions in Nigeria 1841–1891*, Longmans.

Anene & Brown, *Africa in the Nineteenth and Twentieth Centuries*, Ibadan University Press and Nelson.

Atkins, H. A., *A History of Ethiopia*, SIM.

Davis, R. J., *Swords in the Desert*, SIM.

Davis, R. J., *Fire on the Mountains*, Zondervan.

Forsberg, M. I., *Dry Season*, SIM.

Forsberg, M. I., *Last Days on the Nile*, Lippincott.

Gunther, John, *Inside Africa*, Hamish Hamilton.

Hailey, Lord, *An African Survey Revised, 1956*, Oxford.

Horn, L. W., *Hearth and Home in Ethiopia*, SIM.

Hunter, J. H., *A Flame of Fire*, SIM.

Lovering, K. E., *Root from Dry Ground*, SIM.

Meeker, O., *Report on Africa*, Scribners.

Moorehead, A., *The Blue Nile*, Dell.

Mosley, L., *Haile Selassie*, Weidenfeld & Nicolson.

Oduho and Deng, *The Problem of the Southern Sudan*, Oxford.

Price, W., *Incredible Africa*, Heinemann.

Shinnie, M., *A Short History of the Sudan*, Sudan Antiquities Service.

Somali Students, *The Communists Say; The Africans Reply*, Mogadishu.

Stamp, L. D., *Africa, a Study in Tropical Development*, John Wiley & Sons.

Trimingham, J. S., *The Christian Church in Post-War Sudan*, World Dominion Press.

Trimingham, J. S., *Islam in Ethiopia*, Frank Cass & Co.

Ullendorff, E., *The Ethiopians*, Oxford.

Willmott, H. M., *The Doors Were Opened*, SIM.

Other sources include *Africa Now* and *Sudan Witness*, published by the SIM; *Time*; *West African Review*; *West African Directory*; *Daily Times Year Book*; numerous African newspapers; SIM departmental reports; *Encyclopaedia Britannica*.

Index